WRITER'S GUIDE
TO 2014

Editor in Chief: Susan M. Tierney

Contributing Writers:

Katherine Ayres	Mark Haverstock
Devyani Borade	Veda Boyd Jones
Judy Bradbury	Marcia Amidon Lüsted
Michael Cooper	Mary Northrup
Chris Eboch	Mary Rosenblum
Sue Bradford Edwards	Katherine Swarts
Deborah Halverson	Catherine Welch
Christia Hamlett	Leslie J. Wyatt

Production Editor: Joanna Horvath
Assistant Editor: Sherri Keefe

Publisher: Prescott V. Kelly

Copy Editor: Mary Beth McMahon

Cover image supplied by Shutterstock.

International Standard Book Number: 978-1-889715-72-8

1-800-443-6078. www.writersbookstore.com
email: services@writersbookstore.com

Table of Contents

RESEARCH & IDEAS

CONTESTS & CONFERENCES

INDEX

MARKETS

GAINING MOMENTUM

The Year in Publishing

By Susan M. Tierney

Writers in 2014 need more than ever to be on top of the changes in publishing. It is an industry gaining momentum again after the economic struggles of a half-dozen years, and much of the activity is coming from changes in platforms for both writing and selling. Below is a look at the news of the past year, from book publishers to magazines, from social media developments to new ways of offering publications, and a look at the financial starts and stops. You will find a list of new ventures, of personnel changes, and of those who made a mark in the industry and have passed on.

January 2013

■ Crowd-sourced book tours—in which authors group together for appearances—have become more popular. New twists are making some stand out, and during one held in January 2013, readers were asked to vote where five YA authors should visit. The five authors make up Bringing YA to You (http://ya2u.blogspot.com/p/ the-authors.html): Beth Revis, Marissa Meyer, Marie Lu, Victoria Schwab, and Megan Shepherd, and their books were published by Razorbill, Feiwel and Friends, Putnam, Hyperion, and Balzer + Bray respectively. The "Win the Author" contest is being repeated in 2014.

■ *Understanding the Children's Book Consumer in the Digital Age,* a study from publications industry force R. R. Bowker, revealed that bookstores and libraries are becoming less influential in children's reading. More information is acquired, and more purchases are made, online. The study also found that most YA fiction consumers are adults purchasing the titles for themselves: 35 percent between ages 18 and 29, and ages 30 to 44 were the second largest consumers of YA. Growth in ebook reading by teens themselves was flat over the preceding year, according to Bowker.

■ The Newbery Medal was awarded to *The One and Only Ivan,* by Katherine Applegate (HarperCollins). The Caldecott Medal went to *This Is Not My Hat,* written and illustrated by Jon Klassen (Candlewick Press). The Michael L. Printz Award for YA fiction was won by Nick Lake's *In Darkness* (Bloomsbury).

■ The longtime vanity press Vantage Press closed its doors.

■ *Good Housekeeping* got a redesign in the January issue. Articles are shorter, graphics and sidebars are more frequent, and coverage of beauty has increased but parenting decreased.

■ New magazine launches: *Nintendo Force Magazine* (gaming). *Edible San Luis Obispo* (regional dining). *Craft Brewing Business* (trade). *Residential Building Products & Technology* (trade).

■ Magazine closings: *The Sporting News. Spin. Whole Living* (Martha Stewart Living). *Nintendo Power. Wisconsin Trails. More* and *Vita* (Canadian).

Financial Reporting:
■ Scholastic issued its biannual report on reading by kids and families, looking in particular at ebooks and digital devices. The study found that 46 percent of children ages 6 to 17 have read an ebook, which was up 21 percent higher than in the previous report two years earlier. Asked about whether they read for fun,

34 percent said yes, down 3 percent from the previous report. Smartphone use among kids was at 21 percent, up from 13 percent two years earlier. The Scholastic study indicated that parents are increasingly unhappy with kids' reading habits, with 49 percent of them saying their children do not read enough. Only 58 percent of kids planned to read books in print in the future, down from 66 percent.

February 2013

■ Bookish (www.bookish.com), a website co-sponsored by Hachette Book Group, Penguin Group, and Simon & Schuster, debuted on February 4. Oriented to consumers, the site promotes publishers' books and authors. Users can get recommendations based on their favorite or recent reads, hear what authors and editors have to say, look and they can purchase titles directly from the site. Sixteen other publishers eventually supported the launch. Bookish had some difficulties for a couple of years before launching, changing chief executives three times.

■ The nonprofit First Book has expanded its projects with OMG (Offering More Great) Books. The organization gives needy children new books.

■ Apple's iBooks added Breakout Books to include ebooks that are self-published through iBookstore.

■ HarperCollins earnings for the preceding quarter were helped along by its subsidiary, Christian publisher Thomas Nelson, and by the ongoing increase in the sale of ebooks internationally.

■ Canada's D & M Publishers, in bankruptcy protection, sold its Greystone Books imprint to Heritage House and its Douglas & McIntyre imprint to Harbour Publishing.

■ Scholarly journal publisher *PeerJ* launched. It is an open access journal for biomedicine and the life sciences.

■ Macmillan reached a settlement in a U.S. Department of

Justice ebook price-fixing case against several publishers, and Apple. Macmillan agreed to pay up to $20 million to settle with various states that brought action against it, and to a deeper discounting of its ebooks. The DOJ accused the publishers of collusion, with Apple, in using the *agency model* for pricing ebooks. Hachette, HarperCollins, and Simon & Schuster agreed to a $70 million settlement earlier, and Penguin had settled in 2012. Apple continued to contest the accusations, and did not come to an agreement with the DOJ until September 2013.

■ The Book Industry Study Group (BISG) released a report on college textbook publishing that found the industry is moving steadily toward digital libraries, though not at a rapid pace. Among the reasons is the high cost of print textbooks, and the ability to customize digital texts to specific classes.

■ Little, Brown Books for Young Readers debuted a website community for teens and fans of YA fiction, called NOVL (http://thenovl.com).

■ The imprints of Rowman & Littlefield were combined, and the company refocused as an academic, reference, professional, and textbook publisher. Scarecrow Press, Altamira Press, and Jason Aronson no longer exist. Newbridge and Sundance remain as separate educational publishers, for kindergarten to grade eight.

■ Plympton and Daily Lit merged, to provide a larger distribution platform for digital publishing in the form of serialized fiction (www.dailylit.com).

■ In what must have been the biggest publishing news of the year, Penguin and Random House received approval to merge from the U.S. Department of Justice. Other countries needed to sign off on the deal, between international parent companies Pearson and Bertelsmann.

■ Random House Children's Books and MeeGenius! joined

forces to produce and distribute digital versions of popular Random House titles.

■ Amazon and the Big Six publishers were hit with a class action suit filed by three independent bookstores. The file claims unreasonable restraints on trade and commerce for ebooks, which is a violation of the Sherman Act, because of contracts between Amazon and the publishers that limit digital content to use on Kindles.

■ The number of romance titles Grand Central Publishing will release under its Forever and Forever-Only imprints is increasing to 120, from 64 the previous year. About three-quarters will be from the digital Forever-Only line.

■ Len Riggio, Barnes & Noble Chairman, made an offer to buy the retail side of the company. In August he withdrew the offer, but said it remained a possibility at another time.

■ The National Book Critics Circle Awards were given to, for fiction *Billy Lynn's Long Halftime Walk,* by Ben Fountain; for non-fiction, *Far from the Tree,* by Andrew Solomon; for biography, *The Passage of Power,* the fourth volume in the biography of Lyndon Johnson, by Robert A. Caro; for autobiography, *Swimming Studies,* by Leanne Shapton; for criticism, *Stranger Magic,* by Marina Warner; and for poetry, *Useless Landscape, or A Guide for Boys,* by D. A. Powell.

■ I-5 Publishing, a newly formed company, acquired the assets of the failing BowTie, Inc., known best for its magazines *Dog Fancy, Cat Fancy,* and *Horse Illustrated.*

■ *Esquire,* a print monthly, launched *Esquire Weekly,* a complementary online site. At the same time NBCUniversal rebranded its cable television channel the *Esquire* Network.

■ New magazine launches: *GCaribbean* (men's lifestyle).

■ Magazine closings: *LA Youth.*

Financial Reporting:

■ The Reader's Digest Association filed for Chapter 11 Bankruptcy for the second time.

■ Reports on bookstore sales for the preceding year indicate that while they again experienced a drop, it was the smallest in quite some time, at 0.5 percent. December book sales, however, were up 2.9 percent.

■ Hachette reported an increase in publishing revenues of 1.9 percent worldwide in the preceding year, although in the U.S. revenues went down by 3.4 percent at Hachette Book Group. The reason for the decline was given as a shift to ebooks and audio from print.

■ Simon & Schuster reported an increase in profits over the preceding year—$790 million, up from $787 million—although overall sales were lower. Digital sales were up 35 percent. Children's books were up, but adult book sales were down.

■ Sales at Penguin internationally were reported to be up one percent over the year before, with an especially strong fourth quarter. Ebook sales in Britain were double and in the U.S., up the 30 percent.

■ Barnes & Noble revenue fell 8.8 percent for its third quarter, in good part because of poor response to the Nook. The e-reader sales fell 26 percent and Barnes & Noble decided to refocus, and decrease, the Nook business side. On the bookstore side, the company is opening three to five new stores in 2014, although others will close.

■ With numbers made available by the U.S. Census Bureau in March, bookstore sales increased 6.1 percent in January 2013 in comparison to the same period a year earlier.

March 2013

■ As reported in *Body Image* (March 2013, volume 10, issue 2, pages 255–258), a study by Virginia Tech found that so-called *chick lit* has a negative influence on women's self-esteem, both physically and mentally.

■ The PEN/Hemingway Award was given to debut novelist Kevin Powers for *The Yellow Birds* (Little, Brown).

■ Winners of the Society of Children's Book Writers and Illustrators (SCBWI) Golden Kite Awards were for fiction, *The Five Lives of Our Cat Zook,* by Joanne Rocklin (Abrams/Amulet); for nonfiction, *Noah Webster and His Words,* by Jeri Chase Ferris (Houghton Mifflin); for picture book illustration, *Lester's Dreadful Sweaters,* by K. G. Campbell (Kids Can Press); and for picture book text, *Me and Momma and Big John,* by Mara Rockliff, and illustrated by William Low (Candlewick). The Sid Fleischman Award for Humor went to *Goldilocks and the Three Dinosaurs,* by Mo Willems (Balzer + Bray).

■ Amplify, the educational division of News Corporation, debuted a tablet for use in elementary through high school classrooms.

■ Disney's book division Hyperion Books offered its older back-list titles for sale, as it changed its focus to publications based on Disney's ABC Television Group programming.

■ Australia and New Zealand approved the Penguin Random House merger.

■ Christian publisher Thomas Nelson, a subsidiary of Harper-Collins, has brought back two imprints: Nelson Books and W Publishing Group. Nelson Books will offer biography, history, memoir, culture, spirituality, inspiration, and practical living non-fiction. W Publishing will offer memoir and women's nonfiction, especially concerning spiritual growth and practical living. Zondervan is another imprint of HarperCollins Christian Publishing.

■ Amazon applied to use domain names that include .book,

.author, .read, and .app. The Association of American Publishers, Barnes & Noble, the Authors Guild, and others objected. Authors Guild President Scott Turow called the private use of generic domains anticompetitive, and rife for abuse.

■ Hachette Book Group announced it would begin handling sales, distribution, and collection internationally for Houghton Mifflin Harcourt in fall 2013.

■ Bank Street's Josette Frank Award for children's books went to *Wonder*, by R. J. Palacio (Knopf Books for Young Readers). The Claudia Lewis Award went to editor J. Patrick Lewis for the *National Geographic Book of Animal Poetry*. The Flora Sieglitz Straus Award was given to *Beyond Courage*, by Doreen Rappaport (Candlewick).

■ Random House announced changes to its contracts for its digital imprints, after author organizations such as the Science Fiction and Fantasy Writers of America (SFWA) and WriterBeware complained that across the industry, e-contracts were unfair to writers. Random House decided to offer authors two contract options, one the traditional advance and royalty, and the other a profit-sharing contract. Changes were also made to contract arrangements for rights acquisition and marketing, and other editorial and publishing services.

■ Britain's Literature Prize changed its name to the Folio Prize, under the sponsorship of the Folio Society.

■ Claire Vaye Watkins won the Story Prize for her story collection *Battleborn* (Riverhead Books).

■ Nonprofit First Book, which promotes literacy, awarded Lee & Low and HarperCollins $500,000 each to implement proposals for furthering their multicultural publishing programs.

■ The U.S. Supreme Court held that the first sale doctrine holds for books published internationally. The case involved Supap Kirtsaeng, a college student from Thailand studying at Cornell and USC. He imported textbooks from Thailand and sold them in the U.S. for income. John Wiley & Sons sued for violation of copyright laws and won in lower courts, but the Supreme Court ruled in Kirtsaeng's favor on the basis of the first sale doctrine, which allows the owner of a copy of a book to sell, lend, or give it away without the copyright owner's permission.

■ Amazon changed its author payment schedule from every three months to monthly, although on a 90-day cycle. For example, January royalties will be paid in March and February royalties in April, rather than January through March paid together.

■ To combat piracy, Simon & Schuster started providing infringement information to authors through its Author Portal, a website where authors can work on promotion, check on sales, get technology tips, and view anti-piracy activity.

■ NorthSouth Books, the American division of Switzerland's NordSüd Verlag, began acquiring original children's books by American authors and illustrators instead of translations of European titles. The company also planned to increase the number of U.S. books sold in the German market.

■ Houghton Mifflin Harcourt (HMH) announced it would start a major reorganization of its children's imprints, "to clarify our common purpose, define our space and capabilities, appeal to a broader audience, and signal a bold, confident future." In spring 2014 Houghton Mifflin Books for Children, Harcourt Children's Books, Sandpiper Paperback, Graphia, and HMH Books would all combine under Houghton Mifflin Harcourt Books for Young Readers. Clarion Books remained an independent imprint.

■ HarperCollins added hundreds of titles to Scholastic's digital sales platform, Storia.

■ Phillip Pullman succeeded P. D. James as President of the Society of Authors in the U.K.

■ Barnes & Noble and Simon & Schuster waged war over

whether the retailer or the publisher should absorb the cost of discounting ebooks, and the costs of promotions in brick-and-mortar stores. Barnes & Noble cut Simon & Schuster orders, author appearances, and store displays. The dispute would not be settled until August, but the terms remained largely unrevealed at that time.

■ McGraw-Hill completed the sale of its education division to Apollo Global Management. It had reported a loss of $406 million in the last quarter made public. The company continued to operate as McGraw-Hill Education.

■ The University of Nebraska Press acquired military history publisher Potomac Books, which the university press kept as a distinct imprint.

■ In March, HarperCollins and Open Road Media filed cross-motions for summary judgment in a HarperCollins-initiated lawsuit concerning Jean Graighead George's now classic *Julie of the Wolves*, published in 1972. George agreed to publish the ebook version with Open Road, but HarperCollins claimed that under contract it owned the right to license a digital edition. George died in May 2012.

■ Argentine picture book illustrator Marisol Misenta received the latest Astrid Lindgren Award for contributions to children's literature.

■ The *Wall Street Journal* spun off a quarterly personal finance magazine, *WSJ Money*.

■ *Glam Belleza Latina* is the Condé Nast spinoff from women's fashion and beauty magazine *Glamour*, targeting a Latina audience.

■ New magazine launches: *Edible Milwaukee* (regional dining). *Risk & Compliance Journal* (from the *Wall Street Journal*).

■ Magazine closings: *Garden Design. Boston Phoenix. Comic Buyer's Guide. Fiesta* (San Antonio). *Science Illustrated.*

Financial Reporting:

■ Harlequin parent company Torstar reported that sales declined 7.2 percent over the preceding year, and digital sales were down 11.6 percent. The company said it anticipated stabilizing numbers in the coming year in North America.

■ Lagardere, the French parent company of the American Hachette Book Group, said it had a revenue increase of 1.9 percent, although Hachette's sales fell 3.4 percent. The decrease was credited to an increase in sales of ebooks, which are priced lower than print. Lagardere's ebook sales internationally were up 8 percent.

■ In comparison to a year earlier when it had record sales because of the Hunger Games trilogy, Scholastic announced its revenue fell 18.5 percent. Company Chairman Dick Robinson also blamed delays in school and library purchases of a new line of Educational Technology products, including the Storia ebook app. He predicted the sales would improve later in 2013.

■ Annual Random House profits worldwide increased dramatically, according to parent company Bertelsmann, rising 22.5 percent. The megahit Fifty Shades of Grey trilogy was the main cause.

April 2013

■ The owners of Cadent Publishing acquired Maine-based Tilbury House, which publishes regional titles about Maine and New England; books about ships, boats, and canoes; and children's books. Cadent Publishing was founded in 2011 and publishes how-to, reference, and other nonfiction, as well as fiction.

■ Jan Greenburg and Sandra Jordan, who have collaborated for 20 years, were awarded the Children's Book Guild Nonfiction Award for their books.

■ Being given for the first time, the Bologna Children's Book Festival named Chronicle Books the Best Children's Publisher of the Year in North America.

■ With the support of Harvard and others, the Digital Public Library of America was launched to open up access to research libraries, archives, and museums online and for free.

■ The PEN/Malamud Award for a body of work demonstrating excellence in fiction was given to George Saunders. His most recent book is *Tenth of December: Stories* (Random House).

■ The European Union approved the merger of Penguin and Random House.

■ Canada approved the merger of Penguin and Random House.

■ The Christopher Awards, given by the ecumenical Catholic communications organization to honor quality in the media, were awarded in 2013 to *Carly's Voice,* by Arthur Fleischmann (Touchstone); *Fearless*, by Eric Blehm (Waterbrook Multnomah); *A Good Man*, by Mark Shriver (Henry Holt); *My Sisters the Saints,* by Colleen Carroll Campbell (Image Books); and *Road to Valor,* by Aili and Andres McConnon (Crown) for adult fiction. In the category of Books for Young People, the honorees were the picture book *Forever You: A Book About Your Soul and Body,* by Nicole Lataif (Pauline Media); *The Fantastic Flying Books of Mr. Morris Lessmore,* by William Joyce (Atheneum); *The House on Dirty-Third Street,* by Jo S. Kittinger (Peachtree); *The One and Only Ivan,* by Katherine Applegate (HarperCollins); *Wonder,* by R. J. Palacio (Knopf); and *Outcasts United,* by Warren St. John (Delacorte).

■ F + W Media licensed Germany-based *Burda Style* magazine and its website to expand the fashion and sewing brand into ecommerce, ebooks, books, and education. The arrangement also bolstered F + W's position in the craft and sewing market. Within weeks, F + W Media also announced it was acquiring the Sewing Studio and LoveSewing.com. The first BurdaStyle USA books were scheduled for spring 2014.

■ Adam Johnson was the recipient of the Pulitzer Prize for

fiction for *The Orphan Master's Son* (Random House). Other finalists were *The Snow Child,* by Eowyn Ivey (Reagan Arthur Books), and *What We Talk About When We Talk About Anne Frank,* by Nathan Englander (Knopf). The nonfiction award went to *Devil in the Grove: Thurgood Marshall, the Groveland Boys,* by Gilbert King (Harper). The winner for history was *Embers of War: The Fall of an Empire and the Making of America's Vietnam,* by Fredrik Logevall (Random House); for biography, *The Black Count: Glory, Revolution, Betrayal, and the Real Count of Monte Cristo,* by Tom Reiss (Crown); for poetry, *Stag's Leap,* by Sharon Olds (Knopf); and for drama, *Disgraced,* by Ayad Akhtar (Little, Brown).

■ Skyhorse Publishing and Start Publishing acquired science fiction and fantasy publisher Underland Press. Skyhorse is handling print production, and Start Publishing, ebooks.

■ The winner's of the American Booksellers Association (ABA) Indies Choice Book Award were, for adult fiction, *The Round House: A Novel,* by Louise Erdrich (Harper); for adult nonfiction, *Wild: From Lost to Found on the Pacific Crest Trail,* by Cheryl Strayed (Knopf); for adult debut book, *The Snow Child,* by Eowyn Ivey (Little, Brown); and for YA, *The Fault in Our Stars,* by John Green (Dutton). The ABA's E. B. White Read-Aloud Awards went to, for picture book, *Extra Yarn,* by Mac Barnett, illustrated by Jon Klassen (Balzer + Bray); for middle readers, *Wonder,* by R. J. Palacio (Knopf).

■ The more than 450 titles published by Maine regional small press Down East were acquired by Rowman & Littlefield Publishing Group, which will continue to publish under Down East Books and its other imprints, Shooting Sportsman Press, Fly Rod & Reel Books, and Countrysport Press. Down East retained its magazines, including *Down East: The Magazine of Maine; Shooting Sportsman;* and *Fly, Rod & Reel.*

■ Simon & Schuster set in place a one-year test program for

pricing ebook library lending with three major libraries in New York City. The publisher is allowing libraries to purchase all the ebooks in its catalogue for one year, with unlimited checkout, although only by one user at a time as with print copies. Books are also available to patrons for purchase on the library websites, with the libraries sharing in the sale. Books must then be bought again for a second year.

■ *Departures* started a spinoff magazine for premium credit card holders, called *Departures Home + Design*.

■ Bonnier sold three magazines, *Ski, Skiing,* and *Skiing Business* back to the original owner, Active Interest Media, after a decade.

■ New magazine launches: *Houstonia* (Houston regional). *Mindful* (lifestyle, inspiration). *Kayak Fishing. Walmart Live Better* (Canada, lifestyle). *Modern Farmer. Among Men* (lifestyle, online). *Nautilus* (science, culture, philosophy). *Paint-it Today* (crafts). *[wherever]* (quarterly, travel). *San Francisco Cottages & Gardens* (design).

Financial Reporting:

■ Amazon reported that in its first quarter of 2013, its sales were up 22 percent, but income was down 37 percent. Media sales, including books, were up 7 percent.

May 2013

■ The U.S. Senate approved the Marketplace Fairness Act, allowing states to collect taxes from remote retailers.

■ The gift book publisher with a growing children's line, Peter Pauper Press expanded into picture books. Most of its other children's titles have been activity books. The company publishes 100+ books, gifts, and other products annually. The plan is for two to four picture books a year.

■ The PEN/Faulkner Award was given to Benjamin Alire Saenz

for *Everything Begins and Ends at the Kentucky Club,* from Cinco Puntos Press. He was the first Latino to win the award.

■ Octopus Books, based in the U.K., acquired the children's nonfiction publisher Ticktock Entertainment.

■ After three years, the ebook catalogue of Hachette Book Group was again open to purchase by libraries. The publishing company developed a new pricing model. New ebooks are priced for libraries at three times the print retail amount for one year, and after that reduced to one-and-a-half times print price per year.

■ Self-publisher Author Solutions, acquired by Penguin about a year earlier, was sued by three authors seeking a class action. They claimed fraudulent practices and failure to pay royalties owed. In the same month, CEO Kevin Weiss left and Andrew Phillips filled the position. In June, Penguin and Author Solutions sought to have the suit dismissed.

■ Book manufacturer Courier Corp. acquired self-publishing platform FastPencil, which was already in a working arrangement with Barnes & Noble's Nook Press.

■ The Mystery Writers of America awarded its annual Edgars to *Live by Night,* by Dennis Lehane (Morrow), for best novel; *The Expats,* by Chris Pavone (Crown), for best first novel by an American author; *Midnight in Peking,* by Paul French (Penguin), for fact crime; *The Last Policeman: A Novel,* by Ben H. Winters (Quirk Books), for best original paperback; *Code Name Verity,* by Elizabeth Wein (Hyperion), for best YA fiction; and *The Quick Fix,* by Jack D. Ferraiolo, for best juvenile.

■ *Jesus Today*, by Sarah Young (Thomas Nelson) was named the Evangelical Christian Publishers Association's Christian Book of the Year. The best children's book of the year was *The Action Bible Devotional,* by Jeremy V. Jones (David C. Cook).

■ Open Road has partnered with Lerner's Kar-Ben Publishing to publish some of its titles as read-aloud ebooks.

■ The winners of the Children's Choice Book Awards, which are based on the votes of a million children across the country, were: for kindergarten to grade one, *Nighttime Ninja,* by Barbara DaCosta and illusrated by Ed Young (Little, Brown); for third to fourth grade, *Bad Kitty for President,* by Nick Bruel (Square Fish); for fifth to sixth grade, *Dork Diaries 4: Tales from a Not-So-Graceful Ice Princess,* by Rachel Renée Russell (Aladdin); and for YA, *The Fault in Our Stars,* by John Green (Dutton). The author of the year was Jeff Kinney for *Diary of a Wimpy Kid 7: The Third Wheel.* The illustrator of the year was Robin Preiss Glasser for *Fancy Nancy and the Mermaid Ballet,* by Jane O'Connor.

■ The American Academy of Arts and Letters awarded its gold medal for the arts to E. L. Doctorow.

■ The Chautauqua Prize was given to Timothy Egan for *Short Nights of the Shadow Catcher: The Epic Life and Immortal Photographs of Edward Curtis* (Houghton Mifflin Harcourt).

■ Kim Stanley Robinson's novel *2312* (Orbit Books) won the Science Ficton and Fantasy Writers Association Nebula Award.

■ The Association of American Publishers' (AAP) school division and the the Association of Educational Publishers (AEP) announced their agreement to merge.

■ Children's book publisher Barefoot Books stopped selling its books through Amazon, as it had done with Barnes & Noble in 2006. Barefoot has always sold directly through its bookstore in Cambridge, Massachusetts, and Oxford, England, and started selling through FAO Schwarz toy store in New York City as well. It also uses home-based sellers.

■ Pearson, the parent of Penguin, restructured as the Penguin merger with Bertelsmann-owned Random House approached. The new organization target date was January 1, 2014.

■ The U.K.-based Man Booker International Prize went to Lydia

Davis. She is a well-respected writer of short stories, novels, and is a translator. Her newest collection is *Can't and Won't: Stories* (Farrar, Straus and Giroux).

■ Bonnier Corporation made major motorcycle magazine purchases, acquiring nine publications from Source Interlink Media: *Motorcyclist, Sport Rider, Dirt Rider, Motorcycle Cruiser, Hot Bike, Baggers, Super Streetbike, Street Chopper* and *ATV Rider*.

■ Meredith acquired *Parenting* and *Babytalk* and their related websites from Bonnier Corporation, and closed them. Subscribers to the Bonnier magazines received Meredith's *Parents* and *American Baby* instead.

■ Twenty-two-year-old Gus Wenner was named by his father Jann Wenner to take over RollingStone.com.

■ New magazine launches: *Dare* (women sizes 12 and up, to go bimonthly). *In Play* (upscale golf lifestyle). *Remark* (women's style). *She* (Canadian women). *(585) Magazine* (regional, Rochester, NY).

Financial Reporting:

■ Book Stats, a statistics service provided by the Association of American Publishers and Book Industry Study Group, indicated that sales of trade books had risen 6.9 percent over the preceding year. Ebook sales rose 44.2 percent, and made up 20 percent of trade revenue. Down by a little under one percent was the educational, kindergarten to grade 12 market.

■ Profits in the first quarter were up 20 percent at Simon & Schuster, although sales decreased by 3 percent. The strongest segment was the children's publishing division.

■ Revenues dropped in the first quarter at Harlequin, after changing to a higher royalty rate policy. The expectation was that would not be a factor in the second quarter.

■ Cengage Learning negotiated with creditors to create a

restructuring plan, and possibly enter Chapter 11.

■ Hachette Book Group revenues increased by 14.9 percent in the first quarter in comparison to the previous year. Ebook sales in both the U.S. and U.K. were up 34 and 31 percent respectively.

■ Bloomsbury, based in the U.K., reported an annual revenue increase of one percent. Ebook market penetration remains highest in the U.S. arm of the company, at 27 percent of sales.

June 2013

■ Major magazine publisher Bauer Publishing announced the launch of three magazines in the coming year: *Girl's World*, a children's magazine for girls 6 to 10; *Closer*, a women's magazine for Generation X; and *Celebration*, a spinoff from the company's best-selling magazine *Woman's World*, that focuses on celebrations and holidays.

■ The Kerlan Award for children's literature was awarded by the University of Minnesota Libraries to Kate DiCamillo.

■ Random House began distributing titles for Archipelago Books, which publishes translations of international fiction and poetry.

■ The print editions of references such as *The Readers' Guide to Periodical Literature*, published since 1901 by H. W. Wilson, are now licensed for publication to Grey House Publishing. Other titles also licensed to Grey House include the *Children's Core Collection* and *Book Review Digest*.

■ Simon & Schuster began distributing titles for Good Books, a publisher of cooking, quilting, family, health, and other titles.

■ Britain's most recent Waterstones Children's Laureate was named: Marjorie Blackman, whose books and writing career champion diversity in authors, illustrators, genres, and forms.

■ The *Boston Globe-Horn Book* Awards were presented. They were, for picture book, *Building Our House*, by Jonathan Bean

(Farrar Straus and Giroux); for fiction, *Eleanor & Park,* by Rainbow Rowell (St. Martin's Griffin); for nonfiction, *Electric Ben: The Amazing Life and Times of Benjamin Franklin,* by Robert Byrd (Dial Books for Young Readers).

■ Rupert Murdoch's News Corp. divided into two companies. One comprised the original corporations newspapers, educational division, and HarperCollins. The second was Twenty-First Century Fox.

■ Rowman & Littlefield started selling 12,000 books on a new ebookstore, including trade, library, and professional titles.

■ The National Book Critics Circle added a new award, to be presented for the first time in the next year. The John Leonard Award, named after critic who wrote extensively for the *New York Times* but also for many other major publications, honors the best debut book.

■ Simon & Schuster was allowed, for the first time ever, to publish in Canada as a Canadian company. Until this point, it was permitted to distribute titles as a U.S. publisher, but not to publish its titles in Canada.

■ China approved the Penguin Random House merger.

■ Skyhorse Publishing and Start Publishing are partners in the acquisition of science fiction and fantasy publisher Night Shade Books, completing the deal in June. This was the second acquisition in months as Skyhorse shifted to a focus on this genre of fiction.

■ A. M. Homes won the U.K.'s Bailey's Women's Prize for Fiction for *May We Be Forgiven* (Viking).

■ Random House's Crown Publishing Group reorganized by moving two imprints, Watson-Guptill and Amphoto Books, to Ten Speed Press, and Potter Craft to Clarkson Potter. The editor of the three imprints, Victoria Craven, left the company. The focus of the three reassigned imprints is art, craft, and photography.

- Barnes & Noble's Nook Media expanded with Nook Snaps, short stories and narrative nonfiction.
- Toronto-based publisher McArthur & Company closed. Its books had been distributed by HarperCollins Canada.
- The Harry Frank Guggenheim Foundation created a new award for books about military history, the Guggenheim-Lehrman Prize in Military History, with a prize of $50,000.
- Kingfisher Books reduced its staff and number of titles published annually in the U.S. by about half. The U.K. publisher will continue publishing in the U.S. at least through 2015.
- The winner of the Amazon Breakthrough Novel Award was Rysa Walker for *Timebound* (Skyscape).
- The winners of the Bram Stoker Awards from the Horror Writers Association were, for a novel, *The Drowning Girl*, by Caitlín R. Kiernan (Roc); for a first novel, *Life Rage*, by L. L. Soares (Nightscape Press); for YA novel, *Flesh & Bone*, by Jonathan Maberry (Simon & Schuster); for a graphic novel, *Witch Hunts: A Graphic History of the Burning Times*, by Rocky Wood and Lisa Morton (McFarland); for long fiction, *The Blue Heron*, by Gene O'Neill (Dark Regions), for nonfiction, *Trick or Treat: A History of Halloween*, by Lisa Morton (Reaktion Books).
- The Walter Scott Prize for historical fiction went to Tan Twan Eng for *The Garden of Evening Mists* (Weinstein Books/Perseus).
- Fitness publishing company RKP closed after 40 years.
- To find an author for a prequel to *The Dark Crystal* movie, the Jim Henson Company joined with Grosset & Dunlap to hold a contest. Entrants were to write a story in the setting of the original movie, with the prize a $10,000 contract.
- Great Britain's children's book prizes, the CILIP Carnegie and the Kate Greenaway Medals went to *Maggot Moon*, by Sally Gardner (Hot Key Books) and *Black Dog*, by Levi Pinfold (Templar) respectively.

■ Graphic novel company Boom! Studios acquired Archaia Entertainment, which became an imprint.

■ The Pritzker Military Library Literature Award for Lifetime Achievement in Military Writing went to novelist Tim O'Brien. It was the first time the award was not given to a writer of nonfiction.

■ Hachette Book Group acquired Hyperion's adult titles. Disney Worldwide Publishing retained the Hyperion children's list.

■ *Road & Track* enjoyed a redesign, adding more lifestyle pieces and longer stories. It also became available for tablets.

■ The *Washington Examiner* shifted from a daily to a weekly.

■ New magazine launches: *New York SmartCEO* (business, entrepreneurship). *Click* (women photographers). *Huizache* (Hispanic literary magazine). *Modern Quilts Unlimited* (quarterly). *Radio Silence* (semiannual literary and rock-and-roll magazine). *Popular Hispanics* (quarterly, print issue based online edition). *Beach* (regional, the Hamptons). *CheerLiving* (cheerleading). *Verily* (women).

■ Magazine closings: *Maryland Life. VIVmag.*

Financial Reporting:

■ The AAP reported that children's book sales had fallen in the beginning of 2013 relative to the year before. Hardcover sales decreased 29.3 percent, and ebooks were down 36.2 percent. The reason: 2012's remarkable sales due to the Hunger Games trilogy.

■ John Wiley & Sons restructured over the year and closed or sold its consumer publishing divisions. The fiscal year saw revenue decrease by one percent.

■ Barnes & Noble's revenue was down 4.1 percent for the year, a decline blamed largely on the Nook. The company was attempting to reform its plans for the e-reader.

■ The Pew Research Center released a report on the reading habits of young people that indicated 75 percent of 16- to 29-

year-olds had read a book in the preceding year, in comparison to 64 percent of adults.

July 2013

■ The merger of Penguin and Random House was legally completed on July 1. The Chairman of Penguin Random House is John Makinson and the CEO is Markus Dohle. The President and COO in the U.S. is Madeline McIntosh.

■ Random House began distributing for U.S./U.K. publishing company Verso Books, whose titles had been distributed by W. W. Norton for 15 years. Verso publishes books on culture, anthropology, literature, philosophy, economics, politics, and more, from a radical leftist perspective.

■ Amazon completed its purchase of Goodreads, the social media website for lovers of books, with 16 million members. The proposed acquisition had been announced in March, when the reaction from users and others was negative, largely because of fear Goodreads would lose its open, independent, and noncommercial reputation. Some were pleased that Goodreads would be made available on the Kindle. The number of users of Goodreads, the online book-loving community, doubled to 20 million over the year.

■ The American Library Association awarded the Carnegie Medal to *Canada*, by Richard Ford (Ecco) for fiction, and to *Short Nights of the Shadow Catcher: The Epic Life and Immortal Photographs of Edward Curtis*, by Timothy Egan (Houghton Mifflin Harcourt) for nonfiction.

■ In the Authors Guild's fair use suit against Google for its scanning of books, the Guild lost in its attempt to gain class action status. The July ruling appeared to indicate Google had a strong argument for fair use. The case has been in the courts for eight years.

■ In May, Society of Children's Book Writers and Illustrators announced the Karen and Philip Cushman Late Bloomer Award, for authors over 50 years of age who have not published in the field of children's literature. Karen Cushman published her first book, Newbery Honor winner, *Catherine Called Birdy*, when she was 53. The first winner was announced in July: Edie Parson, author of the middle-grade fantasy *Mercury Sea*.

■ Textbook publisher Westview Press, part of the Avalon Group, restructured and created new policies for pricing, marketing, and sales.

■ Penguin's online writing community, Book Country, restructured and relaunched.

■ Scholastic partnered with Comixology to produce digital versions of its Graphix graphic novels imprint.

■ Amazon began deep-discounting titles between 50 and 65 percent, including such best-sellers as Dan Brown's *Inferno* and Sheryl Sandberg's *Lean In*. Typical discounts in the industry are usually 40 to 50 percent. In response, Overstock.com announced it would outdo Amazon by discounting 10 percent more than its competitor. The price war lasted two weeks, until August 8, when Overstock stopped discounting. In August Overstock announced a policy it would match Amazon prizes every day, and give 15 percent rebates on books to Overstock loyalty members.

■ Hearst Magazines announced it would be publishing a new magazine with medical personality Dr. Mehmet Oz in 2014. The Editor in Chief is Alison Brower. The name was not yet set, though speculaton later in the year was that it would be called *The Good Life*.

■ New magazine launches: *Bead-It Today* (crafts). *Hot Rods & Harleys*. *Maximum Drive* (Beckett Media, hot rods and classic cars). *Bon Voyage* (cruise travel). *Connote* (marketing). *Asia Eater* (international food magazine).

■ Magazine closings: *Pro Football Weekly* (published since 1967). *Go* (AirTran Airways).

Financial Reporting:

■ Cengage Learning filed for Chapter 11 bankruptcy to reduce its $5.8 million in debt.

■ Bloomsbury reported an increase of revenues of 19 percent in its first quarter. Digital sales were up 31 percent, and print revenue was up 16 percent.

■ The AAP reported that adult ebook sales were up 13.6 percent in the first quarter of the year. Adult trade was up 3.3 percent, while children's trade was down 24.6 percent. The lower numbers in children's continued to be based on a comparison to the extraordinary numbers in 2012 based on the Hunger Games trilogy.

■ The most specific downward trend in 2013 related to the Hunger Games juggernaut of 2012 was in its publisher's number: Scholastic's revenue fell 19.4 percent. The company's classroom and supplemental materials division was up 5 percent, while the educational technology side was down 11 percent.

■ Penguin's last numbers before the merger with Random House were a 16 percent increase in sales companywide, and up 10 percent in the U.S.

■ Harlequin's profits were down 7 percent in the second quarter, according to parent Torstar, although the company's newly expanded nonfiction publishing did well.

■ President Barack Obama visited an Amazon fulfillment center in connection with televised statements about economic recovery, and ignited a controversy in the publishing industry. The American Booksellers Association and regional bookseller associations and others directed remarks to the White House with complaints about Amazon's "predatory" practices, resistance to state sales taxes, and other issues that could hurt small businesses.

August 2013

■ Harlequin and *Cosmopolitan* magazine joined forces to launch an ebook program, Red Hot Reads. The first title appeared in August.

■ Canada's Dundurn Press purchased Thomas Allen Publishers.

■ Jeff Bezos, founder of Amazon, announced that he was acquiring the struggling *Washington Post*.

■ R. R. Bowker released figures on the number of print titles published the previous year: The total number of traditional and self-published print titles rose 3.3 percent. Fiction rose 10 percent; business books rose 38 percent; biographies fell 10 percent; religious books rose 2 percent; and children's books rose 6 percent.

■ Children's publisher Dalmatian Press, including its Piggy Toes Press and Intervisual Books divisions, were acquired by Bendon, Inc. These publishers specialize in activity and coloring books, as well as board and educational books.

■ The social networking site for writers and readers, Wattpad started offering users the possibility to raise funds for their projects, like Kickstarter.

■ The Dayton Literary Peace Prize's Richard C. Holbrooke Distinguished Achievement Award was awarded to Wendell Berry. The award honors literature that encourages social justice.

■ Random House's digital mystery and thriller imprint, Alibi, acquired six titles, appearing in late 2013 and through 2014.

■ With a poor showing by its Nook Media division and sales down overall at Barnes & Noble, the company outlined the strategy for improving business: a new management team with former President William Lynch leaving, partnering with manufacturers on the Nook, more integration of retail and the Nook, working with Microsoft and its investment in the company, and upgrades to the website.

■ Open Road Integrated Media and Peachtree Press partnered to produce ebooks for the Georgia-based children's publisher. The series to be digitalized is Fred Bowen Sports Story.

■ Human Kinetics acquired DSWFitness. Both publish titles on health, fitness, and sports.

■ Morgan James Publishing announced a new plan to bundle ebooks and print books, with the assistance of a smartphone app company, BitLit.

■ Sourcebooks acquired the motivational small press Simple Truths. Executive Editorial Director Mac Anderson of Simple Truths remains. This was the biggest acquisition Sourcebooks has made.

■ *PCWorld* went digital-only.

■ New magazine launches: *First American Art* (quarterly, Native Amerian art). *Our Wisconsin.*

Financial Reporting:

■ Second quarter Simon & Schuster sales numbers remained where they were in the first quarter. Ebook sales rose 39 percent, however.

■ Houghton Mifflin Harcourt revenues rose 5 percent for trade and educational divisions in the second quarter, in comparison to the year before. HMH attributed the increase to its acquisition of John Wiley's cookbook line in late 2012.

■ First quarter sales at Barnes & Noble were down 8.3 percent in comparison to the previous year.

■ Books-a-Million reported decreased sales of 8.6 percent in the second quarter.

■ Random House saw an increase in profits in the first half of 2013, the last period before its merger with Penguin. Parent company Bertelsmann reported a €3 million improvement.

■ Lagardere Publishing sales were up 1.4 percent in the first half of the year, and in the U.S. its Hachette Book Group's sales were up 7 percent.

September 2013

■ Start Publishing acquired Salvo Press, which publishes science fiction and fantasy. This follows on the Skyhorse/Start acquisitions earlier in the year of Underland Press and Night Shade Books.

■ The first Library of Congress Prize for American Fiction was awarded to Don DeLillo.

■ The Book Industry Study Group (BISG), gave several industry awards for the first time, including Friend of the Industry, Industry Innovation, and a Lifetime Achievement award.

■ Bloomsbury Children's Books USA undertook a major restructuring over several months. Publishing Director Cindy Loh heads the Bloomsbury imprint, and Walker Books for Young Readers. Senior Editor Mary Kate Castellani and Associate Editor Laura Whitaker moved to Bloomsbury in June, and Victoria Wells Arms left to begin a literary agency. In September, Catherine Onder joined the company as Editorial Director. Emily Easton is Publishing Director of Walker Books for Young Readers, which is now more of boutique publisher, offering 18 titles a year, including all new nonfiction for Bloomsbury Children's Books, and fiction. Bloomsbury will publish 100 to 125 books annually.

■ Christian self-publishing company Xulon Press began offering a free book publishing program, FreeChristianPublishing.com to help authors do ebook manuscript preparation.

■ Amazon began bundling digital and print boooks via its Kindle Matchbook program. Consumers of print titles are offered ebook versions for prices from free to $2.99.

■ The Hugo Awards were given to *Redshirts*, by John Scalzi (Tor), for novel; *The Emperor's Soul*, by Brandon Sanderson (Tachyon), for best novella; "The Girl-Thing Who Went Out for Sushi," by Pat Cadigan (*Edge of Infinity* anthology, Solaris Books), for novelette; and "Mono no Aware," by Liu (*The Future*), for best short story.

■ The bundling program of Angry Robot, which was tested in the U.K. in 2012, came to the U.S. Purchases of print titles at participating independent bookstores include a free ebook edition. The program is called Clonefiles.

■ Wattpad and the Sourcebooks Fire imprint joined to assist writers in their editing and publishing of YA fiction. Sourcebooks also committed to sponsoring the 2013 Watty Awards.

■ Bloomsbury acquired New Holland Publishers' natural history titles, amounting to more than 200 books. Bloomsbury was already strong in this nonfiction category.

■ Christian publishers Tyndale Press and NavPress joined forces, with the two maintaining their own acquisitions and content development but combining their manufacturing operations. NavPress was to lay off employees over the following months.

■ Also in September, Tyndale acquired the brands Happy Day children's books and Faith That Stirs from Standard Publishing. Standard plans on focusing on its curriculum and church program development instead of popular brands.

■ It was announced that the U.K.'s 45-year old Man Booker Prize, formerly limited to Britain, Ireland, and the Commonwealth, would open to all novels originally written in English for the first time next year.

■ The American Christian Fiction Writers gave its Carol Awards to *Heart Echoes*, by Sally John (Tyndale House), for contemporary fiction; *Where Lilacs Still Bloom*, by Jane Kirkpatrick (Waterbrook/Multnomah), for historical fiction; *Wildflowers from Winter*, by Katie Ganshert (WaterBrook), for debut novel; and *Like Moonlight at Low Tide*, by Nicole Quigley (Zondervan), for YA fiction; among others.

■ Penguin re-established its relationship with ebook distributor OverDrive Marketplace, which lends titles to public and college libraries.

■ The Carle Honors from the Eric Carle Museum of Picture Book Art were presented to author/illustrator Chris Van Allsburg in the *artist* category; editor Phyllis Fogelman Baker in the *mentor* category; to Lynda Johnson Robb and Carol Rasco in the *angel* category, for their literacy advocacy; and to Barbara Bader in the *bridge* category, for "inspired ways to bring the art of the picture book to larger audiences through work in other fields."

■ Digital distribution company and book platform Scribd started an ebook service to lend any number of books for $8.99 a month.

■ New magazine launches: *Wichita.*

■ Magazine closings: *American Medical News* (published for 55 years). *Mature Arkansas.*

Financial Reporting:

■ Second quarter Simon & Schuster sales numbers remained where they were in the first quarter. Ebook sales rose 39 percent, however.

■ John Wiley & Sons reported flat sales in their first quarter. Print sales dropped, and digital sales were up as the company moved more toward digital publishing—making up 52 percent of its revenue, up 7 percent over preceding year.

■ The sale of ebooks in the first half of 2013 increased by 4.8 percent over 2012.

■ Scholastic's first quarter report revealed sales down 5.8 percent. While trade books and book club were down, educational technology sales were up 19 percent, and classroom sales were flat.

■ The Society of Children's Book Writers and Illustrators announced a new award, the Spark Award, to be given to excellent books produced in a "nontraditional" way, as in self-publishing.

■ Random House and the social media platform Flipboard are

partnering to create custom digital magazines for its authors. The first were for Margaret Atwood and George R. R. Martin.

■ HarperCollins numbers continued to be strong, especially because of the Thomas Nelson acquisition. Annual revenue for HarperCollins grew by 15 percent.

October 2013

■ In June, HarperCollins challenged developers to be innovative and come up with new approaches to books, to "break the binding." The BookSmash Challenge lasted four months and offered a $15,000 prize. The winner was Qlovi, an educational startup company, that developed an app named Connections to help discover authors and books, and create a reading list.

■ Although Google had purchased Frommer's from John Wiley & Sons months before, Google announced in March 2013 that it would stop producing print editions of the travel guides. Travel book competitor Fodor's responded with a statement of commitment to print travel guides. In April, Arthur Frommer, reacquired the brand rights and intends to begin print, and ebook, publishing again. In October, the books were relaunched, including 10 updated guides as well as a new line of 20 EasyGuides. Frommer created the original company in 1957, and sold it to Simon & Schuster in 1971.

■ The PEN Literary Awards John Kenneth Galbraith Award for Nonfiction as given to Katherine Boo for *Behind the Beautiful Forevers: Life, Death, and Hope in a Mumbai Undercity* (Random House). The Robert W. Bingham Prize was given to Sergio De la Pava for *A Naked Singularity: A Novel* (University of Chicago Press), and Tom Reiss won the Jacqueline Bograd Weld Award for Biography for *The Black Count: Glory, Revolution, Betrayal, and the Real Count of Monte Cristo* (Crown).

■ Harlequin launched its first original digital lines for

Harlequin, Harlequin Teen, Harlequin Mira, and Harlequin HGN. It began offering a digital title bimonthly for the teen line on October 1. Mira and HQN titles started in January 2014. Harlequin-E is a new line that will produce mystery, romance, fantasy, science fiction, and YA. The company has another electronic imprint, Carina Press.

■ Atavist Books, new multimedia publishing company from Barry Diller, Scott Rudin, and former Picador Publisher Frances Coady revealed their new list at the Frankfurt Book Fair. In 2014, one title a month debuts.

■ Alice Munro, known for her extraordinary skill in writing short stories, won the Nobel Prize for Literature.

■ Razorbill, a Penguin YA imprint, and the magazine *Teen Vogue* joined to publish a serialized teen ebook, Jessa Holbrook's *While You're Away*, in weekly installments. The first appeared October 15.

■ The finalists for the National Book Award for Young People's Literature were *The True Blue Scouts of Sugar Man Swamp*, by Kathi Appelt (Atheneum); *The Thing About Luck*, by Cynthia Kadohata (Atheneum); *Far Far Away*, by Tom McNeal (Knopf); *Picture Me Gone*, by Meg Rosoff (Putnam); and *Boxers and Saints*, by Gene Luen Yang (FirstSecond).

■ Figment, an online writing community for teens, has been purchased by Random House.

■ Macmillan is making its full ebook backlist of 11,000+ available to libraries. Frontlist titles are not yet offered to libraries.

■ BelleBooks purchased Imajinn Books and is adding it as an imprint. Both specialize in romance.

■ TAN Books, an imprint of the Roman Catholic publisher St. Benedict Press, acquired Neumann Press, which had closed on the death of its owner in April. TAN gained children's titles and homeschooling books.

■ Source Interlink Media merged *Sound & Vision* and *Home*

Theater magazines, relaunching the single magazine in October as *Sound & Vision.*

■ Condé Nast relaunched *Domino.*

■ *Skateboarder* ended its print publications with the April/May edition and shifted to digital-only, with a print replica available bimonthly. It then ended regular publication in October.

■ New magazine launches: *Edible San Antonio* (regional dining). *Milieu* (home decor). *Natural Pet World. Punch* (online, wine and spirits).

Financial Reporting:

■ R. R. Bowker reported that last year the number of self-published books jumped by more than 59 percent. Eighty percent of those were produced by only eight companies, among them Smashwords and CreateSpace.

■ Graphic novel sales were up 6 percent in the third quarter of the year.

■ In the first half of the year, Bloomsbury's revenues increased by 13 percent. Print sales were up 13 percent, and ebooks up 22 percent.

November 2013

■ The National Book Foundation awarded E. L. Doctorow the Lifetime Achievement Medal for Distinguished Contribution to American Letters, and Maya Angelou the Literarian Award for Outstanding Service to the American Literary Community.

■ Literary fiction and poetry publisher Coffee House Press expanded into YA fiction. Its first title in the genre was *Angel de la Luna and the Fifth Glorious Mystery,* by E. Evelina Galang. The company has published crossover titles before.

■ November 30 was declared Small Business Saturday. In September, Sherman Alexie suggested to fellow authors that they handsell their books at local small bookstores on that Saturday after Thanksgiving. The American Booksellers Association supported the idea vigorously.

■ The Dayton Literary Peace Prize for Fiction was given to *The Orphan Master's Son,* by Adam Jonson (Random House). The nonfiction award went to *Far from the Tree: Parents, Children, and the Search for Identity,* by Andrew Solomon (Scribner).

■ Amazon is starting an early access program, Kindle First, to give owners of the ereader prepublication access to titles from its own Amazon Publishing division.

■ As the year neared its end, and after many back-and-forth moves on both sides in the case against Apple, Judge Denise Cote was determining the company's liability to each state among the plaintiffs. In July she had ruled that Apple, and major publishers, had indeed violated federal antitrust laws by conspiring to eliminate retail price competition for ebooks. The various states were to file their opening briefs by January 8, 2014. Apple had until February 10 to reply, and the states next reply by March 7. A two-day damages trial was scheduled for May.

■ The American Booksellers Association (ABA), the American Library Association (ALA), the Association of American Publishers (AAP), and PEN American Center formed the Campaign for Reader Privacy (CRP) in response to the privacy issues raised by the National Security Agency's information collection on American citizens. The Campaign issues a statement supporting the USA Freedom Act, saying the bill would reinstate privacy protections that the Patriot Act had eliminated

■ Jeter Publishing is the new publishing venture by Simon & Schuster and Derek Jeter, the New York Yankee shortshop. It will offer picture books, middle-grade fiction, and adult nonfiction. The children's books will be done with Simon & Schuster imprints Little Simon, Spotlight, and Paula Wiseman Books. The

Gallery Books imprint will its publish adult nonfiction.

■ New magazine launches: *Daily Herald Suburban Business* (Chicago). *Man of the World* (upscale lifestyle. *Nude* (surfing). *Rhapsody* (in-flight, United Airlines).

■ Magazine closings: *Space Quarterly.*

Financial Reporting:

■ Houghton Mifflin Harcourt announced it would make an initial public offering (IPO) as part of its reorganization plan. It is attempting to raise $292 million.

December 2013

■ Robin Desser was given the Maxwell E. Perkins Award for Distinguished Achievement in the Field of Fiction by the Center for Fiction. She is Editorial Director at Knopf.

■ Bloomsbury launched its new, first, ebook imprint, Bloomsbury Spark.

NEW BOOK PUBLISHING VENTURES

- *Publishers Weekly* reported an increase last year in publishers expanding into producing print-on-demand merchandise for their licensed brands, including t-shirts, electronic accessories, children's items, and more. Companies involved include Summit Entertainment and Penguin Young Readers Group, both of which work with CafePress.

- A new imprint at Simon & Schuster's Atria Publishing Group was named 37 Ink. It is led by Vice President and Publisher Dawn Davis. Its 10 titles a year will include literary fiction, narrative nonfiction, and memoir, and will also cover history and pop culture. Authors will come from different cultures and perspectives, and 37 Ink is also looking to support new talent.

- Atria Publishing also started a cooking imprint, Rachael Ray Books, which will produce two or three books a year by people selected by Ray.

- International publisher of crime novels, Europa Editions added a new imprint, World Noir.

- Children's publisher Candlewick Press began publication of titles from British company Templar Press. The new imprint, Big Picture Press, is producing eight hardcover and four paperback picture books a year.

- F + W Media released its first books after starting a teen imprint, Merit Press, under the editorial direction of best-selling author Jacquelyn Mitchard. Eight titles were published in 2013, and 10 will be published in 2014.

- Figure 1 Publishing is a new Canadian company that is concentrating on illustrated books. It was started by three former executives from D & M Publishing, which filed for bankruptcy. Figure 1 is using a hybrid model, doing editing, marketing, and distribution while authors and/or institutions or businesses pay for production. Chris Labonte is Publisher and Peter Cocking is Creative Director. Richard Nadeau is Director of Sales and Marketing. The company will publish books on art, architecture, history, and business.

- Start-up ebook retailer Zola Books began selling Macmillan titles. Zola aimed to create a different kind of "book paradise" by also offering blogs, book reviews, recommendations, and author interviews.

- A nonprofit publisher of literary fiction and poetry, Coffee House Press broadened its publishing plans, adding essay collections and creative nonfiction.

- Cavendish Square is a new educational publisher started by Roger Rosen.

It acquired the kindergarten to grade 12 library titles of Marshall Cavendish, which had already sold its trade children's list to Amazon Publishing.

■ Big Blue Marble Books, a children's book publisher concentrating on nature and the environment, was founded by Gabriella Francine with the help of Hooly Kondras, Editor in Chief. Books are targeted to ages 5 to seven, with two titles published in 2013 and five in 2014.

■ American West Books merged with Familius, which was founded in 2012 by former head of Gibbs Smith, Christopher Robbins. The company 's market is retail companies such as Costco and Whole Foods.

■ Google took its first steps into publishing ebooks and books, through its Niantic Labs division. The first title was a novella done in arrangement with author Thomas Greanias and his publishing company, @lantis Books. It is the first in a series called The Alignment.

■ Amazon began Little A, a literary fiction imprint that will also offer memoirs and story collections. Books are offered digitally and in print. Part of Little A is a digital line of short stories from new writers, Day One.

■ Hudson Booksellers, a company that focused on airport sales, began an online store.

■ Frederator Books is a new digital children's publisher from Fred Siebert, former head of Hanna-Barbara and an online media executive for MTV and Nickelodeon. It anticipated publishing 100 titles annually for kids of all ages, and parents. It launched with *LIEographies: The Totally Made Up, Absolutely Untrue, 100% Fake Life Stories of the World's Greatest Heroes,* by Alan Katz, and 60 ebooks by animator Joey Ahlbum targeting ages 2 to 4, which they called "the digital equivalent of board books." The Publisher is Davd Wilk.

■ In October 2013, Marvel Comics launched a new line of original graphic novels in conjunction with Italian publisher Panini. Marvel Editor in Chief Axel Alonso said it would be the first in a line of books still to be announced.

■ Ig Publishing started Lizzie Skurnick Books to bring back classic YA literature that is little-known today. Skurnick also plans to publish unpublished, new works by authors from the 1970s and 1980s.

■ Zondervan launched the YA imprint Blink, and is publishing general trade books for teens, although the company is a division of HarperCollins Christian Publlishing. Blink books have positive morals and ethics, and none are "dark" in the way of some YA fiction. Zondervan also continues to publish YA Christian fiction.

■ Random House launched a new imprint, Zink Ink, with David Zinczenko, formerly with Rodale's Health Living Group and Rodale Books. It will publish up to 12 lifestyle, health, nutrition, and other nonfiction titles annually. Zinczenko and Rodale colleague Stephen Perrine will also start another imprint, Galvanized Books, to package books with American Media Inc., and be distributed by Random House. America Media publishes *Shape* and *Men's Fitness* magazines.

■ Young Palmetto Books debuted, an imprint for children's and YA literature with a local tie, in a collaboration between the University of South Carolina Press and the South Carolina Center for Children's Books and Literacy. The Senior Editor is Kim Jeffcoat. Jonathan Haupt is Director of USC Press. Young Palmetto published two YA books in 2014, with four picture books planned for 2014.

■ Also at University of South Carolina Press, the new fiction imprint Story River Books will be mentored by Editor at Large, and best-selling author, Pat Conroy. It will publish three or four high-quality regional books annually, representing the many peoples and perspectives of South Carolina.

■ Despite disappointing Nook sales in the previous year, Barnes & Noble started Nook Press, a digital platform for self-publishing authors. Nook Press competes with Amazon's Kindle Direct Publishing, Apple's iBookstore, Smashwords.com, Bookbaby.com, and others. Barnes & Noble was looking to international expansion to improve the Nook ebooks numbers.

■ David Fickling, Publisher of Random House Children's Publishing UK for a dozen years, left to start his own company, David Fickling Books. Fickling has published such children's literature heavyweights as Philip Pullman, Jacqueline Wilson, and Mark Haddon, author of *The Curious Incident of the Dog in the Night-Time*.

■ William Morrow, an imprint of HarperCollins, announced a new digital line to focus on original mystery, suspense, and thrillers to be named Witness. The Executive Editor is Dan Mallory. At the announcement, a hundred titles had already signed, with the first 10 published in October.

■ Brooklyn, New York, small press PowerHouse Books has specialized in art, popular culture, and photography and runs two bookstores. It is now publishing children's books under the new Pow! imprint. Its titles will be very visual, like its adult titles, humorous, and offbeat. They will include board books, picture books, early readers, and middle-grade, with about a dozen published each year. The Publisher is Sharon Rosart. The first titles appeared in fall 2013.

■ At Akashic Books, also located in Brooklyn, New York, Publisher Johnny Temple launched new imprint for middle-grade and YA fiction called Black Sheep. The goal is to publish YA that appeals to all young readers, including reluctant reader teens, and that is somewhat unconventional. The first titles were scheduled for February 2014.

■ About two months after the purchase of Goodreads by Amazon was announced, a competitor to the book-based social media site launched: Riffle's goal is to connect readers, authors, and publishers.

■ The American Association of Retired Persons (AARP) joined with Rosetta Books for a new line of original ebooks on issues of interest to the AARP's over-50 audience. The Director of AARP's Book Division is Jodi Lipson.

■ A multiplatform book company called Atavist Books was backed by Barry Diller, movie producer Scott Rudin, and Frances Coady, the former publisher of Picador. It is publishing print, digital, and enhanced digital works. Its first release, in March 2014, is *Sleep Donation,* a novella by Pulitzer Prize finalist Karen Russell. The plan is for Atavist to release one title monthly, with digital versions preceding a paperback version with hardcover quality.

■ Political journal *The Nation* launched a digital book line to make its contributors available on ereaders and other digital platforms. The first title on eBook-Nation was *State of the Union, Nation Essays 1958-2005,* by Gore Vidal.

■ Sourcebooks and Discovery Communications partnered to start a new nonfiction ebook series based on Discovery's HowStuffWorks television show and website. The first ebooks were released in June.

■ MetaComet Systems started live beta testing of a new platform called Author Portal (www.authorportal.com) to help authors, agents, and publishers track and communicate and collaborate about manuscripts, contracts, rights, royalty statements. AuthorPortal officially launched in May.

■ The mainstay of publishing industry bibligraphic data, R. R. Bowker launched SelfPublishedAuthor.com, to provide self-publishing authors with resources and marketing guidance.

■ Moonbot Books is the new venture from author William Joyce's Moonbot Studios and Atheneum Books for Young Readers. The imprint is producing children's stories on a full range of platforms—books, apps, interactive media, and film. It started with picture books and middle-grade and will move into chapter and teen books at a later time. The first story to be published, in summer 2014, is Joyce's picture book, *The Numberlys,* which was originally released as an iPad app.

■ Amazon Started a fan fiction program that licenses the online works: Kindle Worlds. Fans are permitted to write stories based on copyrighted characters or established franchises, and earn royalties. License holders recive a royalty and the fan fiction author receives 35 percent of net revenue monthly. Kindle Worlds is also publishing short original fiction, 5,000 to 10,000 words, with a 20 percent royalty. Among those licensed are Alloy Entertainment (Warner Bros.), Valiant Entertainment, and several authors.

■ Macmillan announced it would start a new nonfiction publishing company under the direction of Bob Miller, who had been Group Publisher at Workman Publishing and had a long career at HarperCollins. The imprint's name was revealed in late July: Flatiron Books.

■ Ravenstone is the new children's imprint from U.K. publisher Rebellion. The company focuses on science fiction, fantasy, and horror. The Editor in Chief is Jon Oliver. Rebellion's books are distributed by Simon & Schuster in the U.S.

■ Small, Chicago-based press Curbside Splendor launched the Dark House Press imprint, to specialize in speculative fiction and neo-noir short stories and novels. The Editor in Chief is Richard Thomas. The first books were to be released spring 2014.

■ Candlewick Entertainment is the new imprint at Candlewick Press, created to bring together various media for its children's publishing, including movies and television.

■ Bloomsbury Children's Books USA not only restructured in 2013, but also announced two new imprints: Bloomsbury Activities, to launch in winter 2014, and Bloomsbury Spark, an ebook line that will publish original YA, crossover, and adult titles, in late 2013. Meredith Rich joined the company as the new

Digital Editor. The Publishing Director is Emily Easton.

- The U.K.- based Quercus Publishing debuted its first American children's list. The Associate Publisher based in New York is Nathaniel Marunas. The children's list will amount to about 10 titles a year, an grow to about 30 by 2016.

- Amazon started a graphic novels and comics imprint named Jet City Comics, with its first publications due by the end of the year. The Senior Editor is Alex Carr.

- Polis Books is the new digital company founded by Jason Pinter, an author and editor also known for his social media presence. Polis has a Vice imprint to publish crime fiction. The Elysium imprint publishes science fiction and fantasy. The Crave imprint publishes romance and women's fiction. YA and non-fiction imprints are also planned.

- Perfect Square is the new name of VizKids, which was relaunched as the children's imprint of Viz Media. Perfect Square offers manga, comics in book form, and other children's books. The Senior Editorial Director is Beth Kawasaki.

- Educational company Enslow Publishers lanuched two new trade imprints. Speeding Star targets boys ages middle-grade and young teens 9 to 14, and will publish 18 to 24 books a year. The Scarlet Voyage imprint is publishing about 12 YA fiction titles a year, in a variety of genres, including literary, contemporary, romance, and thrillers.

- American Girl Publishing started a picture book imprint, Bitty Baby Books, for ages three to six.

- Amazon Publishing began a new series of brief biographies, called Icon, the first appearing in December 2013.

- Random House's digital mystery and thriller imprint, Alibi, acquired six titles, appearing in late 2013 and through 2014.

- The publishing company that first offered choose-your-own adventure books for kids, ChooseCo, is relaunching the concept in digital books. It sought funds via Kickstarter.

- Harlequin lanched a new original ebook line, Harlequin-E, to publish mystery, romance, erotic romance, fantasy, science fiction, and YA stories, with word counts of 10,000+.

New Book Publishing Ventures

- Digital distribution company and book platform Scribd started an ebook service to lend any number of books for $8.99 a month.
- Four Christian publishing industry companies—Believers Press, Bethany Press, Anchor Distributors, and Jerry B. Jenkins Christiain Writers Guild—partnered to form a new company, 1Source. All will maintain separate identities but collaporate on bringing about 120 titles to publication by 2015.
- Xist Publishing is a new digital and print-on-demand (POD) children's book publisher founded by Calee M. Lee. The focus is "books for the touchscreen generation." Its Discover Series addresses babies and toddlers, and Xist also publishes picture books, and a multi-author chapter book series.
- Vital Shift is the new graphic novel program from Thomas Nelson, part of HarperCollins Christian Publishing. It will publish seven series over the next five years, targeting readers ages 18 to 34. Publisher Chip Brown said, "Graphic novels are the stained glass for this century."
- Mineditions, a picture book imprint, was relaunched by Michael Neugebauer Publishing. It had closed in 2009 in the U.S. It will publish a dozen books in the spring and another dozen each fall.
- Simon & Schuster will be launching a new science fiction and fantasy imprint for teens and adults, to be headed by Publisher Justin Chanda and Executive Editor Joe Monti. It will debut in late 2014 or 2015 and is yet unnamed, and publish 10 to 15 hardcovers a year.
- New Europe Books was started in fall 2012 to publish authors in eastern Europe and the region's expatriates living in the U.S., Australia, and elsewhere. Young Europe Books, for YA titles, has a February 2014 launch date.
- Bloomsbury launched Sigma, a new imprint to publish popular science books. Sigma will list about 15 titles annually.
- Skyhorse Publishing announced a new library imprint, Carrel Books, to publish its first print and digital titles in late 2014. Categories include health, medicine, hisotry, biography, memoir, and business.
- FunStitch Studio is a new imprint for children 8 to 14 interested in sewing and related crafts and hobbies, from C & T Publishing.
- Regnery Publishing started a new middle-grade imprint, Regnery Adventure.

Books

■ Kristen Reach joined Melville House as an editor. She was previously with Grand Central Publishing. Kelly Burdick became Associate Publisher.

■ Reagan Arthur became Publisher at Little, Brown, where she has an eponymous imprint her three-year-old imprint will close.

■ Rodale Books named Mary Ann Naples as Publisher of the books division.

■ Jim Hanas became HarperCollins's Director of Audience Development, to concentrate on growing imprint audiences through social media and other means.

■ Brandi Larsen became Director of Penguin's Book Country, with the task of increasing the community and promoting self-publishing through Penguin's ebook publishing services.

■ Putnam and Riverhead promoted Kate Stark to Associate Publisher.

■ Hannah Rahill was named Ten Speed Press Associate Publisher for nonfiction.

■ Dawn Davis became Vice President and Publisher at Atria Publishing, heading up a new imprint called 37 Ink. The imprint publishes literary literary fiction, narrative nonfiction, journalism, memoirs, and covers pop culture.

■ Valerie Gray retired from Harlequin. Tara Parsons became Executive Editor of Harlequin MIRA. In promotions, Tina James in Executive Editor of the Love Inspired imprint, Adrienne Macintosh is Series Editor, and Charles Griesman is Editor of Harlequin Desire.

■ Al Greco was named CEO of educational company Carson-Dellosa Publishing.

■ At Random House created a new position for Avideh Bashirrad, as Vice President and Associate Publisher of Dial Press fiction.

■ Hastings Entertainment promoted Alan Van Ongevalle to President and COO. Ongevalle started at the company as an intern in 1992.

■ Michele Martin became Vice President and Associate Publisher of Gallery Books Group. Previously, she had started MDM Management, launched the Doubleday Main Street Books imprint, and was Associate Publisher at Simon & Schuster in the 1990s.

■ After 44 years in the industry, Bob Campbell retired as John Wiley & Sons

Senior Publisher. John Kritzmacher was appointed Executive Vice President and CFO of John Wiley & Sons. He had been with Lucent Technologies and Global Crossing.

- Catherine Burke was named Publisher of Little, Brown's Sphere Fiction.
- Little, Brown Books for Young Readers Publisher Megan Tingley added the title of Executive Vice President.
- Houghton Mifflin Harcourt Books for Young Readers created a new position for Mary Wilcox, Vice President and Editor in Chief of the division.
- Changes at Houghton Mifflin Harcourt also included the naming of Ken Carpenter as Editorial Director of CliffsNotes, the same position he has at Mariner Books. Deanne Urmy was named Senior Executive Editor. Rux Martin becamse Editorial Director of the Rux Martin Books imprint. Colleen Murphy was promoted to Executive Director of mass market and specialty retail.
- Houghton Mifflin Harcourt promoted Mary Cullinane to Chief Content Officer for the K-12 education market and consumer market.
- At Katherine Tegen Books, an imprint of HarperCollins Children's Books, Jill Davis signed on as Executive Editor. She had been an editor at Farrar, Straus & Giroux, Bloomsbury, Viking, and Random House. Maria Barbo also was named Senior Editor at the imprint. She had worked at Scholastic and Feiwel and Friends.
- Also at HarperCollins Children's Books, Tara Weikum was promoted to Vice President, in addition to her existing title of Editorial Director. Nancy Inteli, who had been with the Disney Book Group, came on as Editorial Director of early childhood. Kristen Pettit was named Executive Editor, to acquire tween and teen fiction. She had been at Razorbill and Parachute Press. And Alexandra Cooper joined as Executive Editor, after working at Simon & Schuster.
- HarperCollins appointed Tracy Sherrod as Editorial Director of Amistad Press, replacing Publisher Dawn Davis, who moved to a new imprint at Atria. The company also promoted Cal Morgan to Senior Vice President and Executive Editor, while retaining his position as Editorial Director of Harper Perennial and Harper Paperbacks. Morgan was also responsible for the It

Books imprint for two years, but it will now be part of Morrow Books, where Lynn Grady became Senior Vice President and Publisher of It Books. Grady is also Deputy Publisher of Morrow/Voyager/Avon Books, reporting to Publisher Liate Stehlik. Erika Tsang was appointed Editorial Director at Morrow/Avon, and Amanda Bergeron was promoted to Editor.

■ Molly O'Neill left Katherine Tegen Books to become Editorial Director at Storybird, a visual storytelling platform.

■ Jennifer Lyell became trade book Publisher at B & H Publishing.

■ Anne Messitte was named promoted Executive Vice President of Knopf Doubleday Group, after heading up the company's Vintage Anchor division. She had acquired the *Fifty Shades of Grey* trilogy for Vintage. Messitte oversees editorial, publicity, and marketing. Beth Lamb joined Vintage Anchor as Vice President and Associate Publisher, reporting to Messitte. She had been at Rodale.

■ Also at Knopf, Robin Desser was appointed Editorial Director, a new position and part of what Chairman and Editor in Chief Sonny Mehta called the "core executive team" that would shape the Knopf list. Jordan Pavlin was promoted to Executive Editor.

■ University of North Carolina Press brought on Brandon Proia as Acquisitions Editor.

■ Christopher Sweet was named Editorial Director of trade books at Thames & Hudson. He had been with Artnet.com, Viking Studio, Abrams, Vendome Press, and the Metropolitan Museum of Art.

■ Dan Caton retired from McGraw-Hill School Education Group after 43 years in the industry. He was replaced by Peter Cohen as President. Cohen had been CEO of Pearson School. Mark Dorman was named President of McGraw-Hill Education International, after being President and CEO of Wolters Kluwer Law & Business.

■ Christina Amini was promoted to Editorial Director at Chronicle Books.

■ Bob Miller left as Publisher of Workman Publishing. Susan Bolotin served as acting publisher of the Workman imprint. The founder of the company, Peter Workman, had been ill and died without being able to return to the company. His wife Carolan and daughter Katie continued to work with the

PEOPLE

company. Vaughn Andrews came on as Creative Director. Raquel Jaramillo, who had been Acting Creative Director, returned to her position as Director of Children's Publishing but then moved to Editor at Large at the house, to focus on her writing. Under the name R. J. Palacio, she is the author of *Wonder*.

■ The President and Publisher of gardening, crafts, and country living company Storey Publishing Pamela Art retired. Storey is owned by Workman Publishing. Dan Reynolds became CEO and President and Deborah Balmuth became Publisher.

■ Random House Children's Books Editor at Large Jim Thomas left the company to freelance.

■ At Knopf Books for Young Readers, Michele Burke was promoted to Senior Editor and Allison Worchte to Editor.

■ Rolph Blythe became Publisher of Counterpoint, started a half-dozen years ago by Charlie Winton, who remains as Chairman, CEO, and Executive Editor at Large.

■ Graywolf Press welcomed back Ethan Nosowsky as Editorial Director. He had been Editor at Large but left to work for McSweeney's.

■ Peanuts Worldwide made some additions: Leigh Anne Brodsky became Managing Director and she hired Craig Herman as the Executive Director of Publishing. Herman had been at Running Press, which published Peanuts storybooks for about five years. Brodsky had been with Nickelodeon and Golden Books.

■ Holly Dolce became cookbooks Executive Editor at Stewart, Tabori & Chang. David Blatty was promoted to Director of Managing Editorial, Dervla Kelly to Senior Editor, and Laura Dozier to Editor.

■ Christian Trimmer joined Simon & Schuster Books for Young Readers as Senior Editor. He had been at the Disney Book Group.

■ Humanix Books, an imprint of Simon & Schuster that focuses on health, business, and current affairs, appointed Anthony Ziccardi Publisher.

■ Mary Colgan was named Senior Editor of Highlights Press, a newly created position.

■ Pamela Paul was named Editor of the *New York Times Book Review*. She had been the Children's Editor.

- Penguin Young Readers Group promoted Bonnie Bader to Frederick Warne Associate Publisher. She remains Editor in Chief of the Early Readers program.
- Deb Futter was appointed Publisher at the Twelve imprint of Grand Central Publishing. She remains as Editor in Chief, and is the company's third publisher in a three-year period. Sean Desmond filled the position of Editorial Director, after being Executive Editor at Crown.
- Bloomsbury Children's Books underwent a series of changes over the year, as it was reconfigured by Publishing Director Cindy Loh, who oversees Bloomsbury and Walker Books. Emily Easton is the Publishing Director of Walker Books. Bloomsbury ppointed Catherine Onder Editorial Director. She had been at Disney-Hyperion. Rachel Mannheimer was promoted to Editor. Caroline Abbey and Mary Kate Castellani were promoted to Senior Editor. Brett Wright and Laura Whitaker became Associate Editors. Whitaker and Castellani moved to Bloomsbury from Walker Books.
- Joan Strasbaugh joined Abbeville Press as named Senior Editor.
- John Simpson, Chief Editor of the *Oxford English Dictionary*, retired after 20 years and as only the seventh editor of the *OED* since its beginnings in 1879. Michael Proffitt became Chief Editor.
- Jessica Case became Associate Publisher of Pegasus Books.
- Angela Bole became Executive Director of the Independent Book Publishers Association (IBPA) on the retirement of Florrie Binford Kichler. Bole had been Deputy Executive Director of the Book Industry Study Group.
- Will Hinton is now Editor of Hachette Book Group's Orbit and Redhook imprints. He had been an editor with Harper U.K.'s science fiction Voyager imprint. Devi Pillai was also promoted to Orbit Editorial Director. Tim Holman, who had been Orbit's Senior Vice President and Publisher in the U.S. and of the Orbit imprint of Little, Brown in the U.K., returned to Britain but remains in charge of Orbit on both sides of the ocean, as well as Yen Press. U.K. Editorial Director Anne Clarke moved to New York to become Orbit and Redhook Deputy Publisher.
- Carina Press appointed Angela James Editorial Director.
- Brenda Knight is now Publisher of Cleis Press, which specializes in feminist

nonfiction and sexuality, and of New Age publisher Viva Editions, which she started.

■ Pete Beatty became Acquisitions Director of Open Road Media. He had been Senior Editor at Bloomsbury.

■ David Dilkes became Enslow Publishers' Editor in Chief, replacing Dorothy Goeller who continued as Editor at Large.

■ David Borgenicht is now the owner and CEO of Quirk Productions, focusing on film, television, and digital media. Brett Cohen was named President of Quirk Books and Jason Rekulak became Publisher. Rekulak had been Editor in Chief.

■ Best-selling author Pat Conroy has become Editor at Large for the University of South Carolina Press's new regional fiction series, Story River Books.

■ Jessica Sindler moved from Gotham Books to Spiegel & Grau as an editor of narrative nonfiction, self-help, humor, and style.

■ Andy Ward became Vice President and Editorial Director of nonfiction at Random House. David Ebershoff was named Vice President and Executive Editor.

■ Also at Random House, Suzanne O'Neill was promoted to Executive Editor of Crown Books. Jacob Lewis was named Vice President and Publishing Director of Crown, Hogarth, and Broadway Books. He had founded and headed Figment.com.

■ Dominick Anfuso moved to the Crown Archetype division as Vice President and Executive Editor, to acquire for Archetype, Harmony, Crown Business, and Crown Forum. He had been at Free Press. Matt Inman became Editor at Crown Archetype and Three Rivers Press. Heather Jackson was named Vice President and Executive Editor of Harmony.

■ At Random House Children's Books, Phoebe Yeh was given the newly created position of Vice President and Publisher of Crown Books for Young Readers. She had been HarperCollins Children's Books Editorial Director, and before that worked at Scholastic Press. Michelle Nagler became Associate Publishing Director of Random House's Golden Books. She had been Editorial Director of Bloomsbury Children's Books.

■ Ryan Doherty came on as Senior Editor at Random House's Ballantine

Bantam Dell.

■ Victoria Wells Arms left founding editor of Bloomsbury Children's Books USA, where she was the founding editor, to start Wells Arms Literary agency.

■ At Macmillan, Sean McDonald became Publisher of Farrar, Straus and Giroux's FSG Originals and Director of Digital and Paperback Publishing.

■ Farrar, Straus and Giroux's longtime editor Frances Foster, head of the eponymous children's imprint Frances Foster Books, retired after 55 years in publishing.

■ Palgrave Macmillan hired Elisabeth Dyssegaard as Executive Editor to acquire history books.

■ Rodale's trade books division is now headed by Editorial Director Jennifer Levesque. She left the same position at Abrams, and had also worked at Hyperion. Kristin Kiser moved to Rodale as Vice President and Deputy Publisher for trade books and Director of author programs. She had been at Hyperion.

■ The Poetry Foundation named Kenn Nesbitt the current U.S. Children's Poet Laureate.

■ Associate Publisher at Amazon Children's Publishing, Tim Ditlow left the company.

■ Sarah Jane Gunter became Publisher of Amazon Crossing, a foreign language translation imprint.

■ Owlkids Books's new Editorial Director is Karen Li, who had been at Kids Can Press.

■ William Lynch, resigned as CEO of Barnes & Noble in the aftermath of the poor showing by the Nook. Michael Huseby became CEO of Nook Media and President of Barnes & Noble.

■ Hachette Book Group brought on Martha Levin as Acting Publisher of Hyperion Books, after acquiring more than 1,000 Hyperion titles. Most recently publisher of Free Press, Levin had served as Hyperion's publisher.

■ The Feminist Press appointed Jennifer Baumgardner Publisher and Executive Director.

■ Colin Dickerman became Editorial Director of the new Macmillan nonfiction

PEOPLE

imprint Flatiron Books, headed up by Bob Miller. Miller had been Publisher of Workman Publishing. Dickerman had been Executive Editor of the Penguin Press.

■ Juliet Grames was promoted to Soho Press Associate Publisher. Mark Doten became Senior Editor.

■ Author James Frey's Full Fathom Five, a multimedia packaging business, hired Greg Ferguson as Editorial Director. He had been at Egmont USA.

■ Emma Boys Campion became Creative Director of Ten Speed Press. She had been with Weldon Owen Publishing. Patrick Barb and Emily Timberlake became editors at Ten Speed.

■ St. Martin's Press promoted Jennifer Enderlin to Senior Vice President of its Griffin and St. Martin's Paperbacks imprints.

■ The new multimedia imprints owned by Bloomsbury, Candlewick Entertainment and Walker Entertainment, named Joan Powers Group Editorial Director.

■ At Penguin Young Readers Group, Carmela Iaria is now Executive Director of Educational and Library Marketing. She had been with Scholastic's book clubs.

■ National Geographic Books promoted Melina Gerosa Bellows to Publisher, and she remains the Chief Creative Officer for Books, Kids, and Family.

Magazines
■ Stephen C. George became Editor in Chief of *Discover*.
■ Will Bourne became the new Editor in Chief of the *Village Voice*.
■ David Zinczenko left *Men's Health* and was replaced by Bill Phillips as Editor in Chief.
■ Scott Dadich is the new Editor in Chief of *Wired*.
■ Dennis Lewon became *Backpacker* Editor in Chief.
■ *Aviation Week & Space Technology* promoted Joe Anselmo to Editor in Chief.
■ Nicole Formosa became Managing Editor of *Bike*.
■ David Greenfield is the new Editor in Chief at *Automation World*.
■ *DC Magazine* named new Editor in Chief Michael McCarthy.

PEOPLE

- Constance White left as *Essence* Editor in Chief. Executive Editor Vanessa Karen Push became Interim Managing Editor.
- Irene Edwards became Editor in Chief of *Lonny*.
- Jessica Lyons Hardcastle became Editor of *Environmental Leader*.
- *Grid* added Jonathan McGoran as Editor in Chief.
- Pamela Paul became Editor of the *New York Times Book Review*. She had been Children's Book Editor, a position now filled by Sarah Harrison Smith.
- *Parents & Kids* named Rachel Perkins Managing Editor.
- Cindi Lash became Editor of *Pittsburgh*.
- *ReadWrite*'s Editor in Chief is Owen Thomas.
- Michael G. Riley became the new Editor in Chief of *The Chronicle of Higher Education*.
- The Editor in Chief of *Shape*, Tara Craft, was named Group Editorial Director and also named to oversee *Fit Pregnancy* and *Natural Health*.
- *Columbia Journalism Review* Editor in Chief Cyndi Stivers left to take the same position at AOL.com.
- Peggy Northrop became Editor in Chief of *Sunset*.
- *AARP the Magazine* named Robert Love Editor in Chief.
- Kris Frieswick became Editor in Chief of *On Wall Street*.
- Micah Abrams became Editor in Chief of *Digital Trends*.
- Erika Templeton is Editorial Director of *Interiors & Sources*.
- *Lucky* named Eva Chen the new Editor in Chief.
- Erika Taylor is Editor in Chief of *Aquatics International*.
- Marc Perton took the helm of *Engadget* when former Editor in Chief Tim Stevens left.
- *Gastroniomica: The Journal of Food and Culture* named Melissa Caldwell Editor.
- Tom Bergeron became Editor of *NJBIZ*.
- Elizabeth Ralls was named Editor in Chief of *Atlanta Homes & Lifestyle*.
- Jennifer Reynolds became Editor in Chief of *Canadian Living*.
- Pilar Guzman became Editor in Chief of *Condé Nast Traveler*.
- Mark B. Evans was named Editor of *Inside Tuscon Business*.
- Named as Editor in Chief of the teen celebrity *M Magazine* was Brittany Galla.

PEOPLE

- Eric Pike became Editor in Chief at *Martha Stewart Living*.
- Timi Grieve was named Editor in Chief of the print and online versions of *National Journal*.
- The latest Editor in Chief of *Newsweek* is Jim Impoco.
- *Boston Common* Editor in Chief is Lisa Pierpoint.
- *ForbesLife* named Michael Solomon Editor in Chief.
- Kelly Killian became Editor in Chief of *Restaurant Business*.
- Nancy Gibbs became Managing Editor of *Time*.
- *ForeWord Reviews* named Howard Lovy Executive Editor.
- Editor John Freeman left *Grānta* magazine after five years. The Acting Editor is Sigrid Rausing.
- Deanna Brown was appointed President of *Byliner*, a digital "short-content" producer that also publishes ebooks.
- *School Library Journal* Editor in Chief Rebecca Miller was named Editorial Director of *Library Journal* as well, replacing Michael Kelley.

Obituaries
- Children's author and folklorist Diane Wolkstein died at age 70.
- Cover Art Director James Plumeri, long with with Bantam Dell and New American Library, died at 79. Among his famous covers were the mass-market versions of Stephen King's *Salem's Lot* and *The Shining*.
- Author, intellectual, and longtime contributor to the *New York Review of Books,* Ronald Dworkin died yesterday at 81.
- James Herbert, the internationally best-selling British horror author, died at 69.
- The renowned Nigerian author Chinua Achebe, died at 82. He is probably best known for the novel *Things Fall Apart*.
- Two-time Pulitzer Prize winner, *New York Times* reporter, and book author Anthony Lewis died at 85.
- Ruth Prawer Jhabvala, the screenwriter behind many Merchant Ivory films and a novelist, died at 85.
- Children's author E. L. Konigsburg, who won the Newbery Medal for *From the Mixed-Up Files of Mrs. Basil E. Frankweiler* and The *View from Saturday,* died at age 83.

PEOPLE

- Children's author Fredrick L. McKissack, who wrote many books on the African-American experience with his wife Patricia, died at 73.
- The founder of MacAdam/Cage Publishing, 59-year-old David Poindexter died of cancer.
- Science fiction author of more than 50 books, Andrew J. Offutt, died at 78.
- Bernard Waber, author and illustrator of the Lyle the crocodile picture books, passed away at 91.
- Mary Ward Brown, winner of the Hemingway Foundation/PEN award for *Tongues of Flame*, died at 95.
- Scottish author Iain Banks died of gall bladder cancer at age 59. His last book, released mid-2-13, was *The Quarry*.
- Journalist Michael Hastings died in a car crash at age 33. He reported on politics and the military, including a *Rolling Stone* profile of General Stanley McChrystal that led to his being relieved of command in Afghanistan.
- Thriller author Vince Flynn died of prostate cancer at 47. His Mitch Rapp books were best sellers.
- Editor and Copublisher of Fantagraphics Books Kim Thompson died of lung cancer at 57.
- Richard Matheson, science fiction author of *I am Legend* and *What Dreams May Come*, among others books and screenplays, died at 87. He was a strong influence on Stephen King.
- Herbert Nagourney, first publisher of the company that became Times Books and a publishing veteran of 50 years, died at 87.
- Children's author Barbara Robinson, known for her books about the Herdman family, including *The Best Christmas Pageant Ever*, passed away at 85.
- Caldecott-winning illustrator Marc Simont, died at 97. Perhaps his most famous children's illustrations were for *A Tree Is Nice*, which won the Caldecott, and those James Thurber asked him to do for *The 13 Clocks*.
- The founder of Harper Colophon (now Harper Perennial) Cass Canfield, Jr., was an editor and publisher for around 45 years. He died at 90.
- Best-selling crime novelist Elmore Leonard, died at age 87, after writing more than 40 books, including *Get Shorty* and *3:10 to Yuma*.
- The poet John Hollander passed away at 83.

People

- St. Martin's Press Publisher Matthew Shear, 57, died from cancer. He was with the company since 1995.
- The Nobel-Prize-winning Irish poet and playwright Seamus Heaney died at 74.
- Science fiction author and editor Frederik Pohl passed away at 93.
- A. C. Crispin, a science fiction and fantasy author who specialized in novels with movie tie-ins died of cancer at 63. She cofounded the Writers Beware service of the Science Fiction and Fantasy Writers of America (SFWA).
- One of the founders of the self-help publisher Beyond Words, and its President and Editor in Chief Cynthia Black, passed away at 61.
- The basis of a character in Jack Kerouac's *On the Road*, writer Carolyn Cassady died at 90.
- Best-selling cookbook author Marcella Hazan died at 89.
- Among the best-sellling authors of all time, Tom Clancy died at 66. He was known for his thrillers, and spy and military novels, in particular his Jack Ryan books.
- Picture book author and illustrator Ann Jonas passed away at 81. Among them were *The Quilt* and *When You Were a Baby*.
- The founder of independent press Workman Publishing, Peter Workman, died at 74.
- Poet Daniel Hoffman, died at 89. He served a term as U.S. Poet Laureate in the 1970s.
- Pulitzer Prize-winning journalist and author Haynes Johnson died at 81. He won the Pulitzer for covering Civil Rights in Selma, Alabama, in 1966.
- Science fiction author Morris Renek, who wrote the Dying Earth Sequence, died at 88.
- Author and priest Andrew Greeley passed away at 85. He wrote more than 50 best-selling mysteries and thrillers, and nonfiction.
- Mystery and suspense author Barbara Mertz, who wrote under the pen names Elizabeth Peters and Barbara Michaels, died at 85.

Ebooks for All?

By Mary Rosenblum

Ebooks are everywhere! Everybody seems to have a Kindle or a Nook or is reading away on their iPad or phone. Pick up a newspaper or turn on the radio and you hear another story of the new author who sold a million copies of that first novel as an ebook. So shouldn't everybody rush right out to publish as an ebook?

Well, yes and no.

Ebooks can be a great way for a new author to break into the market. They are very inexpensive to publish. If you are willing to do the work of formatting the book yourself, it costs you nothing to publish it yourself. Many small publishers, new and established, are able to publish more authors as ebooks since their overhead is low. If the book sells well, the publisher may then bring it out as a print book.

But one size rarely fits all in the publishing world and ebook publication is no exception. So what *size* is your book? Does e-publishing suit it?

Marketing 101

Let's talk about your readers. Who are they? Are they reading ebooks or not? Whether your goal for your writing is to bring you eventually to a self-sustaining income or merely to put your memoir in front of readers, you still need to publish the book in a form that your readers want to read. If you have finished a hot romance, for example, then yes, the ebook is a good choice for you. Romance readers embraced ebooks immediately, and most romance publishers today begin with ebooks and bring out the print version only secondarily. Mystery is doing well with ebooks, but the readership is not as strong as for romance. Writing YA? You are good to go with ebook. The readers of that next Twilight saga are reading on tablets or smartphones right now. But if you are writing, say, a nonfiction book on biblical history or a nostalgic memoir about your stint in World War II, your readers might not be the ebook type.

Among those who do not own and use a Kindle or Nook or iPad already, few are willing to shell out money for new technology just to try your book. In general, the e-reader crowd includes young readers, romance readers, science fiction and fantasy fans, horror readers, and teens. Now, while that is a gross generalization to be sure, in terms of sales numbers ebooks sell to the *average* reader, not the atypical 85-year-old who loves her Kindle and is the exception who proves the rule.

Another ebook consideration is the nature of your content. Is this book all prose or does it include photographs or illustrations? The problem with the ebook format is that content is fluid. That means each reader will see a slightly different page. One of the benefits of an e-reader is that readers can size the font to suit their individual eyesight. People love not having to put on their reading glasses to read, but that means the page will look different for the reader who selects a 9-point font and the one who prefers 14 points. The variation in type size can make the placement of illustrations or photos awkward. They will *float* as the font is resized; the result may be blank pages or pictures that look very out of place.

Some children's book authors are getting around this issue by positioning their illustrations on one page and the text on the next page, with a hard page break between. Alas, you lose the direct connection between words and picture that way, since the reader can see only one page at a time. At the moment, ebook sales are not as strong for pre-reader books as they are for early readers through teens. That may be in part due to the issue with illustrations or it may be simply that the parents who buy prekindergarten books for their children want the print form for nostalgia's sake. But ebook sales climb significantly when you get into to tweens and teens, where kids buy or download their own books.

A big plus with ebooks is the price. Because the publisher does not have the overhead of printing and distributing a printed, paper product, an ebook can be priced much lower than the same book in print form. Generally, ebooks today run between $3.99 and $14.99. If you are a first-time author without an established fan base, this lower cover price works in your favor. (The $14.99 cover price is what best-selling authors with large New York publishers get for their new releases). Print books generally begin at about $7.99 for mass-market paperbacks and rise above $20 for trade paperback and hardcover editions. A low cover price may entice curious readers to give a book a try, even though they have never read anything by you before. And the low production cost of posting an ebook online means that you can offer the book at steep temporary discounts as a promotional tool. The high cost of producing a print book limits the discount you can apply for promotional purposes.

Many new authors are afraid of piracy if they publish an ebook. Actually, with today's high-quality scanners available at every office supply store, print books are just as easy to pirate. Piracy is not a huge issue for the new author, but modern digital technology does make it easier for book pirates to copy work and sell it without paying royalties. In today's digital world, it is still a very good idea to register the book with the U.S. Copyright Office. Their online copyright registration (www.copyright.gov/eco) costs $35, and makes it possible to upload the book directly to the Library of Congress. You then have the added protection of a registered copyright.

> The low production cost of posting an ebook online means that you can offer the book at steep temporary discounts as a promotional tool.

It's All in The Numbers!

Since around 2009, the growth in ebook sales has been called *explosive*—at more than 250 percent in 2010, and in 2012 still showed double-digit increases. In 2011, Amazon reported that ebooks were outselling print. Sales are leveling off now, with a growth of about 5 percent in the most recent numbers.

To hear the media tell it over recent years, you might think that publishing an ebook practically guarantees blockbusters and profits. Well, for a few folk, sure! Be realistic, however. Some high sales numbers come from well-established authors who published backlist titles as ebooks and immediately sold many thousands of copies. The numbers in ebook publishing are becoming similar to those in conventional publishing; a very few authors will see their books become best sellers, and most authors will see moderate sales. Publishing an ebook is no different than print publishing in that your book has to be well-written, well-edited, and engaging.

Those three elements are crucial to any book's success! The ebook form simply makes a title available more inexpensively to readers, and for some, provides a level of convenience. Another benefit to ebook publication is that the reader gets immediate gratification. A reader can purchase the book, download it, and be reading it within five minutes.

If you publish your ebook with a small publisher or on your own, and you are a new author without a fan base, your sales will be low early on—unless you promote your book vigorously through your website, a blog, and early price discounts. That is true for print formats as well.

How much do you earn? If you publish the ebook yourself through an *aggregator* like Smashwords (which distributes the ebook in the appropriate formats to Amazon, Barnes & Noble, iTunes, and Sony), or you publish directly through the Amazon or Barnes & Noble self-publishing portals, you can expect to earn about 35 percent of the cover price on each sale. For a $5.99 ebook, that means you earn $2.10. That is considerably more than the standard 6 percent of the cover price you might earn on the same book in print form, priced at $12.99—a whopping 78¢.

Now remember, that 35 percent figure holds if you publish the book yourself. Most ebook publishers will offer you 30 to 35 percent of net sales if they sell the book through Amazon or another online retailer. You will generally get a higher percentage if the book is sold directly from the publisher's website; this is, of course, because Amazon and other online retailers take their cut when the publisher uses them for sales. Be sure to send readers to the publisher's site to buy your book!

The Makings of a Good Ebook

Online bookstores unfortunately have many poorly published ebooks. The covers are terrible; text looks like raw manuscript

EBOOK PUBLISHERS

- Astraea Press: www.astraeapress.com. Romance.
- Bloomsbury Spark: www.bloomsburykids.com. A new kids' ebook line.
- Bondfire Books: www.bondfirebooks.com. Inspirational titles.
- Ebooksonthe.net: www.writewordsinc.com
- Familius: www.familius.com. Digital family and children's books.
- Frederator Books: http://frederatorbooks.frederator.com. Comics.
- Fire and Ice: www.fireandiceya.com.Young adult.
- Go Teach It: www.goteachit.com. Downloadable classroom materials.
- Guardian Angel Publishing: www.guardianangelpublishing.com. Children.
- Harlequin-E: www.harlequin.com. Romance.
- Imajin: www.imajinbooks.com. Genre fiction.
- Istoria Books: www.istoriabooks.com. Mystery, history, inspirational, YA.
- Learning A-Z: www.learninga-z.com. Digital learning materials.
- MeeGenius!: www.meegenius.com. Children's book app.
- Moonbot Books: http://moonbotstudios.com. William Joyce's Moonbot Studios partnered with Atheneum Books for multiple platforms.
- Musa Publishing: www.musapublishing.com. Romance, genre fiction, YA, middle-grade.
- MuseItUp Publishing: http://museituppublishing.com. Middle-grade, YA.
- *The Nation*: www.thenation.com/ebooks. Current affairs, politics.
- Open Road Integrated Media: www.openroadmedia.com. Digital formats.
- Rosetta Books: www.rosettabooks.com. Recently partnered with AARP to produce a new ebook line.
- Ruckus Media Group: www.ruckusmediagroup.com. Interactive, multimedia children's titles
- Sourcebooks: www.sourcebooks.com. Partnering with Discovery Communications for nonfiction ebook series, How Stuff Works.
- SynergEbooks: www.synergebooks.com. All genres and ages.
- Wild Child Publishing: www.wildchildpublishing.com. All genres and ages.
- Zola Books: Not a publisher, but a retailer and ebook-reading community.

when you open the book; they lack professionalism. That low level of quality will cost you dearly and must be avoided. Readers know an amateur project when they see one, and it is easy for them to infer that if a book is badly designed, it is likely poorly written too.

Make sure that your book, whether you publish it yourself or a publisher produces it, looks polished and professional. Remember that the cover sells the book, so spend some time in the online bookstores looking at covers. Is yours eye-catching? Are the title and author's name easy to read? Does the cover imply the type of story or information it contains? Does the book look professional inside, with a good font and, if possible, running heads or feet so that readers are reminded of the author's name and the title? Is it clean of typos, inappropriately skipped lines, or blank pages? A sloppy job of formatting sends a very negative message to potential readers. Today, you can 'look inside the book' on nearly every online bookstore. Realize that people do look inside the book, and they make buy or no-buy decisions based on what they see.

Be a discerning author. Because there is so little overhead required to publish ebooks, small press publishers are springing up like weeds after a summer rain. Many of them are good, many are well-intentioned but not very professional, and some are downright scams. Before you commit to publishing with any company, look at other books it has produced. Look inside their books online and do a survey of that publisher's work. Do its book covers look professional or do they have the look of a cheap template? Do the books' pages look good? If the publisher is charging you any money to publish that book, then you should expect not only high-quality work, but a better deal on your royalties than you might with a publisher who is picking up the entire cost of production—editing, formatting, cover design, and promotion.

Finally, read your contract thorougly. If you do not understand some aspect of it, find a professional who can translate it for you. Make sure that you know what you are giving up to that ebook publisher. Make sure you have a way to end the publishing agreement if you are not happy with the arrangement—that is critical. Usually, a publisher retains the right to publish your book for two years, but after that you should be able to terminate the agreement and take your book somewhere else. Make sure you are not signing away all rights or the copyright, because then the book is no longer yours. Never do that.

Ebook publishing, with its low overhead and the surging popularity of e-readers, has been a big part of opening up the publishing world to new options, even through a struggling economy. It makes it easier for you to publish your book but remember that one size does not fit all. You need to be an informed author before you commit to this brave new publishing world.

New Adult Fiction: Is It Real or Is It Hype?

By Deborah Halverson

The digital publishing revolution has led publishers and retailers to duke out details of new publishing models in both the marketplace and in federal court. But far from these noisy battlefields, the people's fiction revolution has quietly produced an important new category: New Adult fiction.

A Category Is Born

"I am born, therefore I am." In true grassroots fashion, readers and writers yearned for stories of young people navigating the post-high school, pre-adult experience, and when they found no such books in stores, they started writing them themselves and self-publishing electronically. Readers learned about these books through social media and book blogs and then bought them. They connected with the 18- to 26-year-old protagonists; they started interacting with the authors online. Soon blogs and countless fan groups solely dedicated to this New Adult fiction arose. Individual readers tagged New Adult titles in Goodreads and left voluminous comments at online retailer sites. Many readers even asked New Adult authors to pen follow-up stories, often from another character's point-of-view. The writers obliged. Eager readers downloaded the new books, and again asked for more. Series grew and authors made their marks.

Publishers, who for years had been turning down fiction centered on post-high school and college life as "too old for YA and too young for adult," entered this new dynamic only after self-published New Adult ebooks had ascended the bestseller lists. The new genre had not only emerged, but gained a notable foothold in the marketplace through an unprecedented communion between self-publishing authors and readers who bought directly from them.

And what a speedy revolution it has been. Barely three years passed from the day in 2009 when Publisher Dan Weiss settled on the term *New Adult* to categorize a kind of fiction he wanted to publish for St. Martin's Griffin imprint, to mid-2012 when blockbuster breakouts by self-published New Adult authors were scaling best-seller lists. While St. Martin's efforts yielded a name for the new category, the company had at that point failed to score its own breakout title and force acknowledgment of the new category by the publishing industry. It took a perfect storm of advancements in epublishing technology, self-publishing services, the maturation of social media, and plain old writer gumption to set the stage for the 2012 titles that trumpeted the arrival of NA fiction: Jamie McGuire's *Beautiful Disaster.* Tammara Webber's *Easy.* J. Lynn's *Wait for You.* Sylvia Day's *Bared to You.* Molly McAdams's *Taking Chances.* Cora Carmack's *Losing It.* Jessica Park's *Flat-Out Love.* All self-published and self-promoted, all were on multiple best-seller lists alongside traditionally published titles.

High-profile, high-figure contracts with traditional publishers followed, as did the roll-out in late 2012 and 2013 of New Adult imprints with small digital publishers such as Entangled Publishing, as well as big traditional houses like Random House (now Penguin Random House). New Adult fiction's growth has been a whirlwind without precedent in the notoriously snail-paced publishing industry.

Category Credibility

"I sell, therefore I am." With New Adult fiction's sudden emergence, its unprecedented initial distinction from traditional publishing, and the early disparagement that New Adult novels were nothing but "sexed-up YA," some people in the industry wondered if the category was more hype than substance. Articles like *Publishers Weekly*'s December 2012 "New Adult: Needless Marketing Speak or Valued Subgenre?" and *Today.com*'s January 2013 "Sex and the 'New Adult' Novel: Teen Fiction Gets Steamier" stoked the doubt. The *PW* article perspective was echoed to me in April 2013 by an editor questioning the long-term viability of the category: "My main question is whether the new adult category is more of an industry term for editors and publishers, and maybe sales reps and some booksellers," the editor asked, "rather than writers and readers?"

Waving off New Adult fiction as a marketing ploy devalues a fledgling category of fiction that has distinct features and the potential to include as many genres under its umbrella as YA or adult fiction. Mystery, thriller, dystopian: Any genre can explore the themes and sensibilities of young people in the early throes of adulthood. Penguin Random House's launch of their New Adult imprint Flirt draped much-needed in-house credibility over the new category. After all, a company does not create dedicated imprints for hype—imprints are costly long-term commitments. Imprints exist for substantial categories and genres.

Another validation was Amazon's recent decision to give New Adult its own listing under New Adult/College, although making it a subcategory of romance was more of a sidestep than a forward stride. That sub-ranking was a reflection of the nagging "sexed-up YA" sentiment that lumped New Adult titles like Tammara Webber's *Easy* into the *Fifty Shades of Grey* kinky phenomenon. Pointing to *Easy* and Jamie McGuire's sexually explicit *Beautiful*

- Atria Books: Simon & Schuster imprint. http://imprints.simonandschuster.biz/atria
- Avon Impulse: www.avonromance.com/impulse
- Belle Books: www.bellebooks.com/
- Berkley Publishing Group: www.us.penguingroup.com/static/pages/publishers/adult/berkley.html
- Carina Press: http://carinapress.com/ (Harlequin digital imprint)
- Entangled Publishing: www.entangledpublishing.com/
- Flirt: Random House imprint, www.randomhouse.com
- Grand Central Publishing: www.hachettebookgroup.com/publishers/grand-central-publishing
- Harlequin: www.harlequin.com
- Lyrical Press: http://lyricalpress.com
- William Morrow: www.harpercollins.com/imprints/index.aspx?imprintid=518003
- Noble Young Adult: www.nobleyoungadult.com/
- St. Martin's Press: http://us.macmillan.com/splash/publishers/st-martins-press.html
- Spencer Hill Press: http://www.spencerhillpress.com/

Disaster, some in the publishing industry wondered if this New Adult business was just a fad sparked by the success of *Fifty Shades*. That series, which dominated book retail two years ago, with 44 million copies sold, opened the wallets of the same readers who make up the 18- to 40-year-old YA crossover audience.

By this line of thinking, New Adult is a consumer-friendly alternative to the erotica label, useful for positioning the sex-heavy novels filling the post-*Fifty Shades* market. Yet, *Easy* does not have kinky sex. "I'd kept to the sexuality guidelines of the books written for the mature end of the YA spectrum," Webber explained in her blog (http://tammarawebber.blogspot.com/

2013_05_01_archive.html). "I didn't intend to write straight-up adult romance, or I'd have written more explicit sex scenes."

Even as it gained readers and sold in stunning numbers, New Adult fiction had baggage to shake off. Many authors crossed their fingers for the introduction of a BISAC (Book Industry Standards and Communications) code for the category, which would be a major step toward true legitimacy.

No More No Man's Land

"I fill a gap, therefore I am." Molly McAdams, author of *Taking Chances*, was 21 when she started writing. "I didn't make a conscious decision to write New Adult," she told me in a May 2013 interview. "I wrote about the kinds of experiences that happened to me or to people I knew in college. I like my books to be real so I put a lot of myself in my books. That's how they ended up being New Adult." Then she read Webber's *Easy* and McGuire's *Beautiful Disaster* and realized that other people wrote for the college age, too. "It wasn't until after I published *Taking Chances* that I first heard the words *New Adult*."

Many pioneering New Adult authors tell of experiences like McAdams's. They wrote about this stage of life even before there was a name for it. When they tried to shop these projects to YA publishers they were told that characters older than 18 did not sell to teens, while publishers for adult fiction deemed the stories still part of the YA experience. This new breed of fiction fell into a no man's land.

Yet the authors continued to write their stories, turning to self-publishing when that became a viable option. Often, they were shocked to find that not only were there readers, there were lots of them. Ignoring conventional wisdom and acting on their own creative impulses, the authors proved that college-aged people were eager for stories that spoke to their stage of life.

Let's be fair to publishers here: Prior to the phenomenon of the crossover readers who vaulted Harry Potter to stratospheric success and then took to the Twilight saga with hormonal fervor, perhaps there was not a large enough audience for post-teen, pre-adult themes. But the crossover phenomenon has stampeded into the second decade of the twenty-first century with The Hunger Games, and it looks to continue with the Divergent trilogy. We now know the crossover market exists and have empirical data confirming it: Bowker Market Research's 2012 study reported that 55 percent of the audience for YA fiction is 18 and older, with 30- to 40-year-olds making up more than half of that adult segment.

Authors, editors, agents, and bloggers generally agree that the New Adult audience is primarily that same older crossover audience, with college-aged readers coming in second. These claims have yet to be confirmed by researchers; for now, New Adult authors and editors are learning about the audience directly through that same author-reader online interaction that has fueled the category's growth.

Emergence

In the process of serving themselves as readers, these authors unwittingly filled a gap that St. Martin's Weiss recognized. "I got a great deal of data about the market," he told me regarding his publishing the Sweet Valley High series and working at the online study site SparkNotes, "and so knew the college crowd was still reading YA books. The only adult books they were reading were from the best-seller lists. I knew there was a gap in the market."

The publishing industry has middle-grade fiction for ages 9 to 12, and YA fiction for ages 12 to 18, and it has the adult fiction category. The gap comes with the immediate post-high school and college crowd, the 18- through 26-year-olds who are experiencing life no longer as teens but not yet as full adults, a group psychologists call *emerging adults*. Compared to teens, the stakes are higher for these young people, the consequences are longer-term, and the support group smaller now that mom and dad are not on hand to catch them when they fall. Not that they even want mom and dad's help. They are ready to deal with life on their own, taking their first steps in becoming the grown-ups they want to be. This perspective shows in the narrative sensibility of New Adult fiction, in the choices the characters make and in

> St. Martin's Publisher Dan Weiss, who coined the term *New Adult*, "knew the college crowd was still reading YA books. The only adult books they were reading were from the best-seller lists. I knew there was a gap in the market."

their situations. New Adult is not about the sex; it is about romantic relationships that can feel bigger, brasher, and more loaded those in teenhood. The characters are beyond the high school scene, with most living on their own. With their new free-doms come more responsibilities, greater consequences, more dangerous risks.

The stories most commonly take place in college, but not exclusively. Forty percent of Americans do not enter college immediately after high school, so the emerging adult experience includes entering the work force, joining the military, starting families early, or being stuck in limbo as the rest of the posse heads off to find their own path. This is all fascinating stuff to readers experiencing these situations themselves, and to the crossover readers who want to look back nostalgically on a life pre-kids and pre-marriage. They found those qualities in YA fiction and they are now finding them in New Adult, sometimes with more sex, and always with a more mature perspective.

Next?

"I can grow, therefore I am." The New Adult category remains defined by its original wave of titles, which were primarily contemporary romance. Readers and reviewers are starting to use their reviews and social media outlets to voice frustration with the *same ol', same ol'*. And so we come to NA's second test: Will it respond to readers again and extend beyond the story of hot love in the college dorms? YA fiction once faced a similar battle, with its challenges to be more than the issue books of the 1970s or stock boy-meets-girl romances; YA rose to the occasion with a series of exceptional novels over the course of several decades. New Adult fiction needs genre breakouts to expand the category and firmly establish it for the long haul.

Only as the genre matures will it gain heft, richness, and an expansive future. Brick-and-mortar stores have yet to clear the shelf space for New Adult beyond special sales promotions such as "Great Summer Reads." But maybe New Adult does not need a bookstore buy-in: Its publishing imprints are generally digital-only or digital-first, reflecting the readership's preference for ebooks and ordering print books through online retailers. These readers found their first New Adult titles online, and they will seek out more in the same way. The authors keep the grassroots spirit alive in their online engagement with readers, many of whom are constantly prowling the net for the next major discovery. Part of their enjoyment is then passing on the news to other book lovers.

The people's fiction revolution continues.

A DIFFERENT KIND OF CORPORATE JOB

The World of Freelance Business Writing

BY KATHERINE SWARTS

Consumers and publishers are not the only ones to buy writing —a manuscript, magazine, or book. Businesses do too. Many full-time writers create website text, product guides, and advertisements, and they are likely to be paid around $100 an hour.

Before you jettison your lower-paying article or fiction manuscript to try to bring in more bucks sooner, note that this is a not simple route to riches. "If you are a solid writer and have a solid business head," says business-writing trainer Paul Lima, "you can earn $50,000 to $150,000 per year. But you have to work at it. It can take two years to become established."

Getting Started

Peter Bowerman, among the best-known freelance commercial writers, started in 1993 and "actually took less than four months" to establish a healthy full-time income. But he would not say such quick success is typical. Of the latest edition of his book *The Well-Fed Writer*, Bowerman says he "really wrestled with" whether to keep the subtitle—*Financial Self-Sufficiency as a Commercial Freelancer in Six Months or Less*—lest it seem a guarantee. (The subtitle ultimately stayed, after blog readers voted in its favor.) He advises that "trying to find the best way is a waste of time," and that commercial writers should devote their energy to finding best *individual* approaches to making a business writing career.

Rarely should any approach immediately mean supporting your accustomed lifestyle through writing alone. "The first thing I did," says *authorpreneur* Dana Sitar, "was lower my standard of living. It took about six months to establish a steady income I could live simply on. It's been almost two years, and I am probably another year from a comfortable wage."

Many people work two jobs at first. "I advise clients to build a part-time business until it's oozing into full-time potential," says C. Hope Clark, author of the Carolina Slade Mystery series (Bell Bridge Books) and Editor of *FundsforWriters* (www.fundsforwriters. com). That is when "you have so much work you cannot meet the demands working part-time."

Former employers may become early freelance clients. Marilyn Anderson, a utility writer and church publications manager, notes, "When I left my full-time corporate communications job in 1993, the company approached me almost right away. My former corporate supervisor hired me as a freelancer when she moved to another company. Even my current large freelance account came from a contact I worked with during my corporate life."

"I had four full-time jobs over 15 years," says journalist Susan Kim. "I pulled clients from all those. When people ask me how to become a freelancer, I tell them to get a job, and then another job, and then a third job—and then think about freelancing. Establish expert status and professional relationships before becoming a freelancer."

Contrary to popular belief, freelance business writing has no education requirements. If anything has relevance to speed of success, says Bowerman, it's work experience—of all sorts. "If I had to pick the best bets to succeed fairly quickly," they would be "people who come from the corporate world, and are also good writers." For his own part, "I had no writing or corporate background, but I had been in sales for 15 years and wasn't afraid to pick up the phone and make cold calls. I must have made about a thousand in two months" to get started.

"My old corporate job was totally unrelated to writing," says content creator Jacquelyn Lynn, of Tuscawilla Creative Services. "It was in transportation sales and marketing."

Pounding the Pavement

Always commit yourself to marketing if you are going to create a writing career. Clark advises, "Create a portfolio and start knocking on doors. Join Chambers of Commerce and use the membership lists to generate business. Make the rounds to [conference expo] tables."

"Get in front of people," says Lynn. "Share expertise; be active on social media platforms. Treat yourself like a business, because you are."

Attitude counts for much. "I enjoy talking to people," says Bowerman. "I think 'I'm gonna make some new friends today,' rather than 'I have to close this deal.'"

Virtually every marketing plan includes an online element. "Lots of writers use job sites such as PeoplePerHour to get started. I got some long-term clients this way, although now we deal direct," says Dawn Copeman, Newsletter Editor of *Writing-World* (www.writing-world.com). "LinkedIn is a useful tool. Join groups where your clients could be hanging out and be there to offer solutions; join groups of professional writers and learn about opportunities."

"I've seen writers obtain gigs on Twitter several times," says Clark. "Many magazine editors comment on their needs, [however,] social networking needs to be focused. Show you are cutting-edge with current event links. Post testimonials as you receive them, aiding your client by linking back to his site."

Bowerman warns that the rumor of social media being the new quick route to success is "not accurate at all." Since most sites frown on obvious self-promotion, using them "is a longer-term strategy," best for building relationships that eventually provide regular referrals.

Personal business websites still matter. A few writers make do with social networking profiles, but relying on them is rarely advisable. It leaves too much at the mercy of outside administrators, and the extra step of logging in (or setting up accounts) can annoy potential clients. A separate website "doesn't have to be elaborate," says Lynn. It just "has to look good and be error-free."

Clark—whose FundsforWriters.com has been among the *Writer's Digest* 101 Best Websites for Writers since 2001—says an effective site needs a "welcoming page that is creatively eye-catching. So many draw yawns from the outset—and make potential clients wonder how creative this person really is." Keep bios to essential elements: "Nobody cares if you've written since you were nine."

Copeman adds these tips: "If you have a blog, update it regularly or it will act against you" by tagging you as not keeping up. Most experienced writers "agree your fees should not be on your site; each project is different and has to be priced accordingly." She also advises, when in doubt, to leave off the "why-you-need-a-copywriter" page because people looking for copywriters may may "feel insulted if you tell them what they already know."

"The essential elements are clarity and focus," for any website, says Lima. "What do you sell? Who do you sell to? That should be quickly apparent from your stellar copy. You are a writer, after all."

"Most important is strong samples," says Bowerman, at least a dozen relevant ones. Potential clients "want to see if you're the caliber of writer" they need, if you have "skills to mesh with what they're looking for."

As Time Goes By

As a business becomes established, the amount of time necessary for marketing decreases. Do not, however, expect to reach the point of setting aside marketing forever. Bowerman still does cold calling after 20 years of successful freelancing. Anderson notes that "corporate accounts can come and go as the wind blows." More than one writer who became dependent on a single client has had to resume marketing from scratch when that relationship suddenly ended. "Even when up to your eyeballs in work," says Copeman, "keep marketing or one day you'll [end up] with no work to do."

Developing a business writing career "does get a lot easier once you get established; it's not a constant battle year after year. Always be prepared to market on an ongoing basis, but if you build a strong business, you won't have to market as much," agrees Bowerman.

As your career progresses, you will likely also move into a niche. Even in the beginning, says Sitar, "just because you love writing doesn't mean you will love any kind of writing work. Don't take every offer. Be completely in love with [each project], and clients will love you for the fabulous work you do."

"If you try to sell everything to everybody," says Lima, "you end up selling nothing to nobody. I don't know if that is grammatically correct, but it's true. If you know nothing about health, why target health care organizations? Focus your marketing based on your work experience, education, and interests."

Eventually finding a niche often just happens. Clark says, "I've seen writers start writing what they know, then branch into areas they don't know. I've also seen writers write anything for anybody

CONTENT MILLS: STARTING POINT OR DEAD END?

Surfing for writing jobs online invariably turns up potential gigs at sites like the *Examiner,* the *Huffington Post,* and others like them. They are marked by wanting copy on a plethora of nonfiction topics; payment of less than $20 per article; encouragement to submit in quantity rather than quality; and promotional pitches that imply you can build a successful career there. Can you?

Unless you are writing merely for a hobby and coffee money, successful writers almost unanimously say *no.* These news aggregation sites are largely a "waste of time," says successful business writer Peter Bowerman, and tend to "create victims [who] think that's all freelance writing is." Even at its best, writing for these sites is not likely to give you "the kinds of samples" that impress those "who understand writing is a skill worth paying for." Nor does it encourage further skill development. Content managers are satisfied with merely adequate work that many people are capable of throwing together. These "content mills [are] a different world from that which anyone truly interested in being a good writer operates in," says Bowerman. "I wouldn't even think of them in the same breath."

C. Hope Clark, who publishes *Funds for Writers,* says, "When I see a writer listing those sites as experience, I have doubts about his abilities to write a catchy, snappy, personality-filled piece. A writer [who lets] these sites dominate his career strategy is greatly limiting himself."

"I would never write for these content mills," says Dawn Copeman, of *Writing-World.com.* "Pay is low, work is hard and long and totally unrewarding. You're better off spending your time working on your own site and prospecting for clients, rather than slaving away for such sites. It might sound like easy money, but it isn't."

until they grabbed some good clips in one particular area; then they focused on that. Repeat-work happens more often with specialists—the industry recognizes them—but they have to be generalists until they see enough income from the specialty side."

"I write for business newspapers, faith-based organizations, and nonprofits," says Kim. "While my clients are diverse, I become a

CONTENT MILLS: STARTING POINT OR DEAD END?

Carol Tice's *Make a Living Writing* includes articles with excellent information on most aspects of professional freelance writing. Here are some of her remarks on content mills:

■ "If you write for content mills or bid sites . . . it's easy to get discouraged [and] think there is no good-paying writing work left in the world." (From "7 Move-Up Markets for Freelance Writers Looking to Earn More.")

■ "Most of their articles are low quality, so they have to flog the Internet to drive traffic in the door." (From "5 Reasons Demand Studios Only Pays Writers Peanuts—and Won't Change.")

■ "Trying to make a living off $15 articles (or $5 ones) both starves your wallet and impoverishes your soul." (From "Are You Addicted to the Heroin of Freelancing?")

If you still want to try —say you blog on a topic few obvious markets pay for, and figure it can't hurt to make a few dollars in the bargain by selling your pieces—go in with eyes your open. "I've written for a comedy news aggregation website," says writer Dana Sitar. "If you're going to do it, look for a site that allows you to cover something you're passionate about; a position that pays, at least a little; and opportunities to write original content in addition to news aggregation—if there's not a single original piece [on the site], don't take the position!" In addition, read contracts carefully, figure maximum time you can give, and determine how this writing serves your long-term goals. If you are still sure you can live with it—and are doing it for love, not money—go ahead. But when in doubt, stay out!

specialist for each. The learning curve is high at first, but this approach gets more long-term assignments."

When All Is Said and Done

Never pick a focus because you think that is where the money is. Sitar notes the importance of being your authentic self. "On my website, I make my *passion projects* prominent rather than my résumé and testimonials. People read my book—which has nothing to do with my freelance work—and hire me because they love my style and skill. It's about honestly engaging and offering value."

As important as authenticity is excellence, which "I put as the first quality," says Bowerman. Such obvious traits as reliability, punctuality, and detail orientation "are actually fairly rare in the business world. So you can really stand out, with absolutely no experience, by using that secret weapon. And those are the qualities sought by clients for whom money is second priority, for whom the most important thing is the predictable superior outcome." It pays to "take pride in what you do."

"Keep it professional," says Clark. "Never argue. Never gripe about negative impressions or experiences. That's sabotaging your career."

A business-writing career, like any career, is genuine work. But for those who love what they do, work is no drudgery. It is pure delight.

Small Presses: Teamwork & Trust

By Mark Haverstock

For many authors, publishing with a big-name house is the ultimate dream, with visions of book tours, media interviews, and movie deals. But the fact is, with rare exceptions, getting to that level is an uphill climb, even if you have credentials or exceptional writing skills. An author has to make it through a maze of gatekeepers, more often from the sales and marketing departments than editorial, before their books see the light of day.

If you are fortunate enough to sign with one of the major houses, congratulations. But big houses are often less concerned with long-term potential than with how well a book or author performs out of the gate. If you fail to get the major reviews or find your audience the first time around, the likelihood of a second printing or a second book deal decreases.

Unlike the big publishers, small presses are not betting so much on your immediate sales, or how great you will be when Oprah interviews you. They are more likely to bet on you—your voice, your expertise, what you have to say. Small presses tend to think about author relationships long-term, as both an investment and a labor of love.

Teamwork

Small presses have a reputation for being hands-on, and will work with authors and their books, not simply acquire them. "We have a lot of personal contact with our authors and have a little more time to work closely with them," says Nicole Carriere, Publisher of Blue Bike Books. "We're also more willing to give beginning authors a chance—those who want to get a foot in the door."

"Our size creates a culture that allows for more interaction and engagement with the authors throughout the process," says Peggy Schaefer, Publisher of Ideals Publications, a division of Guideposts. "We have editorial, design, production, marketing, and sales resources in one office, so we are able to bounce ideas off of each other at any time. And we can include our authors in that process when it makes sense."

Liz Van Doren, Editorial Director of Boyds Mills Press, points out that authors have immediate access to the people working on their books at small presses. "We are able to get out contracts quickly, we are able to respond to authors, and our designers have a very hands-on relationship with our illustrators."

That process may begin even before the submission. Boyds Mills is connected to the Highlights Foundation, which sponsors workshops to give writers and illustrators the opportunity to come together with editors and writing professionals to work on their craft, whether they are beginners or well-published. "The existence of the Highlights Foundation reflects the corporation's commitment to people who are creating good stories and art for children," says Van Doren.

Newbies and Seasoned Authors Need Apply

Small presses are not for beginners only. "I work with a number of authors who also work with big houses, and we continue to work together because there is an affinity between what we want to accomplish and we've been successful in marketing their works," Schaefer says. "I do agree that first-time authors can find it difficult to break into a big house, but that has as much to do with the need to find an agent as with the house itself."

Eileen Robinson, Publisher of Move Books, says, "There's more opportunity here for newer writers because small presses are more willing to discover someone in the slush pile, their doors tend to be open more than larger publishers, and most don't require you have an agent. The mistake that some authors make is that they don't realize that many of the same guidelines apply, regardless of where you submit your work. You still need to do the same things you'd do if you were submitting to Penguin, Simon & Schuster, or any other big publisher."

The ratio of established to debut authors on the Creston Books list is about 50/50, and Editor in Chief Marissa Moss, also a successful author, is excited about finding more debut authors in the future. "It's really important to me to include debut authors," she says. "One of my authors sent me two manuscripts, and they were both just so heart-wrenchingly beautiful, so poetic and touching, that I bought them both. And one is in the process of being illustrated by a debut illustrator. Normally, the paradigm is to pair seasoned authors with debut illustrators, and vice versa. But this debut illustrator—the work just fits."

Making It Work

Small publishers generally have more room to maneuver and do not have the same financial pressures as the big guys. "I can do this because I don't have huge overhead," says Moss. "Basically, all the money goes to the authors, the illustrators, the printing, and the promotion. I'm hoping that means we can take chances on books that wouldn't get published by New York. Not that New

Sales and marketing used to be primarily the job of the publisher, but today it is imperative that authors partner with their publishers in marketing their books, no matter what the size of the company. "No publisher has the resources to shoulder the entire burden of marketing and promotion," says Boyds Mills Press Editorial Director Liz Van Doren. "There are things that an author can do through his or her own contacts that are even more effective. We take very seriously a partnership with our authors."

Move Books Publisher Eileen Robinson observes that many authors come to publishing with the idea they are going to write and the publisher will do everything else. "That's just not the case these days–they have to get out there and market their own book," she says. "That doesn't necessarily mean spending money. There are so many ways that a book can be marketed these days that they can get the word out–through social media, author websites, and other avenues. Whatever you do should align with what the publisher is trying to do, focusing on options that give books the most quality exposure."

York is terrible; I have great relationships with my New York publishers and I love working with them, but they really can't afford to take those risks because they're just too big. But I think those books, the ones that are at risk, often end up being the books that stick with kids the most. It's a passion for me. I really want children's books to survive."

In a small operation, the majority of the process is overseen by the editorial staff. "We spend a lot of time on books—editing, layout, everything is done in-house," says Doris Replogle Wenzel, Publisher of Mayhaven Publishing. "This also includes sales and marketing. The only thing done outside is the printing and the binding." She notes that Mayhaven also does audio books and some electronic books.

No one knows for sure how long a book will stay in print, but small presses are likely to nurture the growth of their books over the long term. "When we acquire a book, we try, as with any publisher, to have some clarity about who the audience is and how we're going to reach them," says Van Doren. "As the book evolves, we support that with our author promotion plans and attend all the major conferences. But we don't have to know that a book is going to sell a certain amount of copies out of the gate to acquire it. We have a higher tolerance for a slower build."

Blue Bike has a philosophy called the *long tail*. "We don't print books that are necessarily best sellers," says Carriere. "The books we produce are generally midrange titles and so the sales philosophy is selling smaller numbers over a longer period of time. We don't drop a title after a year; we will keep it out there as long as there are modest sales."

The numbers support this. "We've been publishing children's books since the 1960s, and we have titles that have been in print in some form since then. We sometimes reformat or re-illustrate to keep a great story current in the market," says Ideals's Schaefer. "If I had to guess, I would think that most books remain on the list a minimum of three to five years. The majority of our backlist have probably been on the list 5 to 10 years, and the top performers remain indefinitely."

Niche, or Not

Blue Bike works a little differently than the larger publishing houses. "We come up with a list of book ideas and then we look for authors to write them for us. We work in reverse," says Carriere. "Authors are welcome to send a résumé and samples of their writing, but remember we are very genre-specific. We work within a fairly narrow niche."

The company publishes only trivia and quirky science books for readers ages 10 and up, and it is looking to do more titles with a fun science emphasis in the kids' market. "We have a book titled *Gross and Disgusting Things About the Human Body*—with burps, farts and crazy illustrations—and it really sells well," she says. "We also did a book called *Bugs vs. Humans,* written by Peter Heule, etymologist at the Royal Alberta Museum, which looks at bugs and their relationship with people."

As for Move Books, it is looking for middle-grade books of interest to boys. "We want boys to be compelled and inspired to read on their own because the stories and experiences mean something to them," says Robinson. "We hope to excite them with adventure, fantasy, mystery, and humor and give them the confidence to read more."

Because they have a small list of about 25 books a year, the editors at Boyds Mills are extremely selective about what they accept. "Our focus is on stories that are clearly for kids: fiction, nonfiction and poetry," says Van Doren. "We're just looking for great stories." Boyds Mills includes Wordsong, the only poetry-only imprint in the children's publishing world, as well as Calkins Creek, which publishes books on American history topics.

What makes Van Doren's day at Boyds Mills is a genuine fresh exciting voice. "Voice is one of the things that speaks to me as an editor, whether they be chapter books or middle-grade," she says. "For picture books, I don't want to see things that I've seen before, things that are derivative, or ones that are obviously trying to teach a lesson."

Creston's 2013 launch list featured only picture books, but future lists will include middle-grade novels. "I have an upcoming debut middle-grade novel I'm very pleased with," says Moss. "I love the main character's voice; it's what hooked me right away. And with middle-grade, the voice has got to be compelling. Give me a great voice, and we'll work everything else out." She notes that her list is set already through 2014.

■ Blue Bike Books: 11919-125 Street, Edmonton, Alberta T5L0S3 Canada. www.bluebikebooks.com. Guidelines available on website. Since most ideas are developed in-house, query with résumé and list of hobbies/interests, and three writing samples (preferably humorous). Accepts email submission to info@bluebikebooks.com and electronic format for manuscripts.

■ Boyds Mills Press: 815 Church Street, Honesdale, PA 18431. www.boydsmillspress.com. Guidelines available at website. For middle-grade and YA fiction, query with first three chapters and plot summary. Send complete manuscript for poetry books and picture books only. For nonfiction, send the manuscript, a detailed bibliography, an expert's review of the manuscript, and a detailed explanation of competitive titles. Accepts hard copy. SASE. Responds in 3 months.

■ Creston Books: P.O. Box 9369, Berkeley, CA 94709. www.crestonbooks. com. Please submit digitally to submissions@crestonbooks.co. Multiple submissions are fine, but no more than one project per month from the same author. Do your homework–know the market. For example, if your submitting an alphabet book, know that your work will be compared to *Chicka Chicka Boom Boom*.

■ Ideals Publications: 2630 Elm Hill Pike, Suite 100, Nashville, TN 37214. www.idealsbooks.com. Guidelines available at website. Learn about the books we publish (board books, picture books) and submit manuscripts that are appropriate for us in terms of age group and subject. Send complete manuscript. Accepts hard copy only. SASE. Responds in 2 months.

■ Mayhaven Publishing: P.O. Box 557, Mahomet, IL 61853. www.mayhavenpublishing.com. Mayhaven does both traditional publishing as well as co-op publishing. Query or send complete manuscript. Accepts hard copy or electronic submissions to mayhavenpublishing@mchsi.com

■ Move Books: P.O. Box 183, Beacon Falls, CT06403. www.move-books. com. Guidelines available at website. Open to single titles or series geared to boys, 8 to 12. Send query with synopsis and first 25 pages of manuscript. Accepts hard copy. SASE. Responds in 3 to 7 months.

Mayhaven is open to a variety of topics and formats in the children's arena. Wenzel receives 2,500 to 3,000 manuscripts every year, all over-the-transom, and commits to printing about a dozen. " We're not a niche publisher, and we will look at the individual project and take chances," she says. "We offer a variety of children's books. Authors don't have to worry about what we want this month."

Size Does Matter

Perhaps one of the most common reasons small presses see submissions, especially from authors early in their careers, is accessibility. "Ideals doesn't require an agent as some of the larger houses do," says Schaefer. "And we review every submission that comes in—not always as quickly as an author might like, but we do review every one. For me, a better reason is that you know our books and love what we publish and have something you think can be a part of that. I think that more than the size of the house, the most important thing to consider in submitting your work is the fit between what you are submitting and what the publisher is seeking."

THE CORE OF WRITING FOR EDUCATORS

BY JUDY BRADBURY

American education is humming with change. Across the country, educators are exploring fresh perspectives and approaches to instruction as they endeavor to meet the demands—and commands—of the Common Core State Standards, the national initiative setting forth academic expectations. The transition has been challenging, and in many ways enlivening, as educators strive to interpret and integrate mandated goals for preparing children to be college- and career-ready. Writers for educators must be cognizant of the state of education today and connect with educators at this epic juncture, providing them with something they can put to use on Monday morning.

Tap Into Needs

Virginia Dooley is Editor in Chief of Teaching Resources at Scholastic. She encourages those interested in writing for Scholastic Professional Books to study the guidelines for submitting proposals set forth on the website. Not surprisingly, prospective authors will find the first suggestion is to review Scholastic's line of professional books thoroughly. Does your idea complement Scholastic's published titles? "Our books provide in-depth discussion of current research, theory, and teaching practices, in a voice that engages classroom teachers."

Dooley points to *The Next Step in Guided Reading*, by Jan Richardson, and *Traits of Writing: The Complete Guide Grades 3 and up*, by Ruth Culham, as among their most successful titles. "Guided reading and traits writing are two important areas of practice that teachers struggle with. That is the key to a successful book: tapping into a strong need for teachers,which may be different from an administrator's need," says Dooley. Scholastic welcomes submissions from educators with "helpful, insightful, and inspiring ideas." Proposals concerning Common Core, the topic occupying just about every educator's mind, are also in demand. "The Common Core State Standards are a huge focus for teachers. It's the usual suspects: close reading, complex texts, academic vocabulary, evidence-based writing." Acceptance of proposals is based on "originality, potential usefulness to educators, and compatibility with the direction and goals of Scholastic Professional Books."

Consider Challenges

Darcie Johnston, is the former editor of *LibrarySparks* magazine and Upstart Books. "What I know about the audience for *LibrarySparks* and Upstart Books is this: School librarians and media specialists are squeezed in every way. They have no time, their budgets are slashed, and their numbers are being cut as districts struggle to cope with economic challenges."

Johnston continues, "Of course I look for material that is well-written—engaging, lively, well-constructed, skilled in terms of mechanics, and thoughtful. I also seek material that is not necessarily on the cutting edge but on the crest of a wave: up-to-date and knowledgeable about educational systems, requirements, standards, philosophy, and practice. I want materials that implicitly understand the librarian's time constraints: succinctly written and designed for at-a-glance usefulness. For example, in planning the 2013-14 volume of *LibrarySparks*, we added a column that features nonfiction books on STEM topics, with lesson plans and Common Core correlations. We also changed an article about professional resources for librarians from a narrative format to one that resembles a bulletin board."

Johnston encourages writers to take into account current educational challenges. "Generate materials that save time and money. Offer librarians ways to demonstrate their value to faculty and students. Of equal worth are materials that advance the librarian's skills and unique role with technology, information literacy, and research. Also of high interest are resources that help librarians collaborate with and support teachers, who are equally strapped for time and funding now more than ever with Common Core's emphasis on reading."

Prepare Proposals Well

Craig Thomas is Senior Editor, Education, at Guilford Publications. He offers a checklist for creating a successful book proposal. "Convey a solid grounding in research and the important literature on the topic; indicate the intended audience(s); and suggest how the book is likely to be used. Will individual teachers buy it? Is it more appropriate for professional development or as a text for teacher preparation?"

Also essential, says Thomas, is an ability to communicate effectively with readers. "Avoid academic-speak or an artificial voice. The best proposals are concise, show attention to a structure that makes sense to the reader, and above all, are practical in a way that hasn't been seen a thousand times before. Chapter topics and the writing itself should indicate a strong knowledge of classroom practice and the issues educators face. These days, making Common Core connections is a welcome feature in most proposals."

Thomas points writers to successful Guilford titles, such as *Close Reading of Informational Texts,* by Sunday Cummins. "The book addresses two topics that are highlighted in Common Core: close reading and teaching with informational texts. The timing of the publication helped get the book noticed, but really it's the writing that makes it work for teachers. Feedback has been extremely positive about the book's clarity and practicality. The core of the book is concerned with showing readers what close reading looks like through numerous analyses of text passages and features, vignettes of real classrooms, student writing samples, and descriptions of specific instructional and assessment practices."

Bringing Words to Life, by Isabel L. Beck, Margaret G. McKeown, and Linda Kucan, is another successful title for Guilford. "At first it might not seem clear why this short, uncomplicated book has become so hugely successful. I think the reasons are exactly those I mentioned in regard to the best book proposals. *Bringing Words to Life* is informed by decades of top-notch research, but it reads like a one-to-one conversation between educators. A how-to and why book, it focuses on practical instructional issues, but it's fueled by the authors' passionate concern for helping students learn—and love—vocabulary. I suggest it as an excellent model for all educational writers, especially in its newly updated second edition," says Thomas.

Go Above and Beyond

David V. Loertscher is a Professor in the School of Library and Information Science at San Jose State University. He is past president of the American Association of School Librarians, and the author of several books for educators. He is also owner and publisher of Hi Willow Research & Publishing and Syba Signs, and Co-editor of the bimonthly *Teacher Librarian.* At the journal, Loertscher says, "We look for ideas and practices that utilize the

A Word of Common Caution

"While it's important to stay on top of recent developments in education, I would emphasize the need to think beyond current trends," says Craig Thomas, Senior Editor, Education, at Guilford Publications. "Nothing is hotter in education today than the Common Core State Standards, but this has led to a glut of publications on the topic—some very good, some not so good. Eventually I expect to see a backlash as the demands of Common Core square off against tried-and-true instructional methods teachers have used successfully for years. There's no need for conflict, however. The standards aren't dictating instruction or a fixed curriculum; there remains an essential role for flexible, individualized teaching.

"As an author, if you feel passionately about a particular aspect of classroom practice, whether it's word study or writer's workshop, or choosing quality texts, this passion will be a much better compass for solid educational writing than trying to hitch to the latest bandwagon. Educational initiatives come and go, but dedicated, knowledgeable instruction always remains useful and interesting.

"In short, writing on a hot topic such as Common Core can help to get a *hearing* for a book proposal but also puts it in competition with a flood of new titles. Focusing on the basics—a research grounding; an individual voice; a structure attuned to the audience; and direct, practical examples—still makes the difference in creating a book with lasting appeal."

many magnificent Web 2.0 tools that actually boost deep understanding of the topics being taught, as well as increasing the skills of the user. So, it is not only about efficiency, but also the learning that takes place. We are also looking for ideas that engage learners far beyond just the passing of tests: creativity, inquiry, global communication, problem-solving, and collaborative teaching among classroom teachers, librarians, and other specialists."

Loertscher is clear: "I think those interested in writing for educators need to be aware not only of the *party line* of Common

EDUCATIONAL SUBMISSIONS

- Guilford Press: www.guilford.com/authors
- Hi Willow Research & Publishing: http://lmcsource.com/ Contact Loertscher at reader.david@gmail.com.
- *LibrarySparks*: http://www.librarysparks.com/librarysparks/pages/contact-us
- Pearson: http://www.allynbaconmerrill.com/about/write_for_us.aspx
- Scholastic Professional Books: http://teacher.scholastic.com/products/ scholasticprofessional/about/proposal.htm.
- *Teacher Librarian*: www.teacherlibrarian.com/submissions/and http://www.teacherlibrarian.com/submissions/author-guidelines/.
- Upstart Books: www.upstartbooks.com. Books program has been under review. Query first. Upstart Editor, 4810 Forest Run Rd., Madison, WI 53704.

More Selected Markets
- ABC-CLIO: www.abc-clio.com
- Academic Therapy: www.academictherapy.com
- Cavendish Square: www.cavendishsq.com
- Corwin Press: www.corwin.com
- Didax: www.didax.com
- Edupress: www.edupressinc.com
- Heinemann: www.heinemann.com
- Incentive Publications: www.incentivepublications.com
- Jossey-Bass: www.josseybass.com/WileyCDA/
- Key Education Publishing: www.keyeducationpublishing.com
- Maupin House: www.maupinhouse.com
- Mondo Publishing: www.mondopub.com
- Prufrock Press: www.prufrock.com
- Red Line Editorial: http://reditorial.com
- Smith and Kraus: www.smithandkraus.com
- Teacher Created Resources: www.teachercreated.com
- Charles C. Thomas, Publisher: www.ccthomas.com

Core and all the proposed testing to start next year, but also of major reform movements going on that are disruptive to the cookie cutter approach being pursued by large corporate interests that are in education to make huge profits."

Teacher Librarian is dedicated to fostering "collaborative partnerships for improved student learning through thought-provoking and challenging feature articles, strategies for effective advocacy, regular review columns, and critical analysis of management and programming issues." The editors welcome "original manuscripts on any aspect of library services for children and young adults that will contribute to excellence in programs and improved support for their delivery."

At Hi Willow Research & Publishing and Syba Signs, Loertscher is seeking "significant manuscripts related to the creation and sustainability of the Learning Commons concepts, including both the physical Learning Commons and the Virtual Learning Commons."

Offer Tools

Aurora Martinez, Vice President and Editor in Chief of Higher Education & School Achievement Services at Pearson, has been with the company for 13 years. Previously, she edited in the K-12 programs at McGraw-Hill and Scholastic. At Pearson, the world's largest educational publisher, Martinez specializes in editing books for higher education and teacher preparation, and practical materials for practicing teachers.

"Although it may sound cliché," says Martinez, "the essential factor that sometimes gets lost in a proposal is the theory-to-practice piece. When writing a book for teachers, it's important to offer the tools they need to be effective in the classroom. The writer must have a good grasp of the challenges teachers face today." Martinez has edited *Literature for Today's Young Adults,* by

Aileen Pace Nilsen, James Blasingame, Kenneth L. Donelson, and Don L. F. Nilsen, and *Essentials of Children's Literature,* by Carol Lynch-Brown, Carl M. Tomlinson, and Kathy G. Short. "These books are valuable because they identify what makes a children's book worthwhile. They help teachers identify reading levels, interest levels, and key elements of genre in order to best match trade books to students."

Martinez identifies the elements that make for a solid professional book proposal. "First and foremost, I look to see if the writing is acceptable for the audience. Then I ask, has the author narrowed the focus? Is it inherent in the style of writing who the book is for—whether it is undergraduates, graduate students, or practicing professionals? Finally, I consider if the proposal is what I call a *me, too* book. How is this book different? What is it contributing to the field? What is the author bringing to readers that hasn't already been done?" In books that offer practical application advice, Martinez favors accessibility, such as clearly laid out activities teachers can implement, book lists, and top-ten picks. "Make your book come alive for teachers," advises Martinez. Wise counsel for writers across the country who hope to aid educators striving to meet the demands of the twenty-first century.

The Future of Picture Books

Book, Ebook, App?

By Chris Eboch

Picture book writers and illustrators have faced extra challenges for the last decade. At last, however, sales in all formats have begun to increase again, and electronic formats are showing especially strong growth thanks to technology advances and a greater willingness by adults to share ebooks and apps with kids. According to a Scholastic reading study, the percentage of children who had read an ebook by about a year ago was 46 percent, nearly double the 25 percent in 2010. In a separate study question, about 72 percent of parents also indicated they were *interested in* having their children read ebooks. These numbers will grow.

It is in the interest of children's writers who want to keep their writing careers growing over the next years to consider how ebooks and apps may change the market, and what opportunities they may bring.

Nils von Heijne, founder of uTales.com, a digital platform for children's ebooks, says, "The ebook market for children's picture books is lagging behind compared to the general ebook market, but it is growing. The increasing use of tablets is driving both industries, but for children the growth has been stronger in games and educational apps, rather than ebooks. As that market develops, however, ebooks will follow. I think accessibility and platforms that focus on attracting kids to start reading, as opposed to replacing reading with games, will dominate the next few years of market development."

The first step is understanding the terminology. At the most basic level, an ebook is an electronic version of a linear print book, while an app is interactive.

Apps that are more like books than games encourage reading and learning, and they offer writers the chance to experiment with new methods of storytelling. Karen Robertson, author of the Treasure Kai book app series, says, "When it comes to true innovation in storytelling, and delivering an interactive, multi-sensory reading experience, book apps far surpass ebooks."

Alternate Opportunities

The reality has been that, so far, most books being released as picture ebooks and apps were first best-sellers in print, or involve well-known licensed properties. That is changing, and alternatives for writers of all levels of success are increasing.

Some companies now provide opportunities for new writers or writers with lesser-known or backlist titles—not just the big-name best-sellers—to create apps for kids. These include platforms such as uTales, Storybird, MeeGenius!, and KiteReaders. The way they create the apps differs, however. Some accept submissions of text-only manuscripts, illustrated manuscripts, or published books and create the apps. Other sites need authors to bring completed apps, and allow them to market the apps.

"Ebooks are easier to adapt and format from print than apps," says Roxie Munro, author and illustrator of 35 children's books and 13 interactive apps. "Not as many publishers are doing inter-active apps; apps are more expensive to make, sell for less, and can be tough to market. [However,] the school and library market is growing, particularly for apps, I think. Many schools are getting iPads, and they need good content for them."

The differences between print and electronic formats, even apps, are not always as vast as they first seem. "I write and illustrate mainly nonfiction and concept children's picture books," Munro says. "They are considered interactive, and include guessing games, mazes, search-and-find, counting games, lift-the-flap paper engineering, hidden objects, and so forth. The books already use a form of *gamification* to engage children in reading, using the books, and learning. So evolving into making interactive apps felt like the next step."

What Works

Authors and illustrators considering the ebook and app markets must determine which manuscripts will translate well. "I don't see many big differences in terms of page count, etc.," von Heijne says, "but on digital platforms, there is no room for lots of text on each page. To some extent, the visual aspects of the book become even more crucial."

According to Emma D. Dryden, founder of Drydenbks, "If an author/illustrator is thinking about publishing their picture books directly into digital, they need to decide whether they are going to be offering enhancements and some sort of basic interactivity, or if the ebook is going to be more static—a digital experience that essentially mimics the bound book experience: art and text that's immovable on spreads, with a method of page turning that mimics the page turns of print books."

Dryden continues, "Ebooks are far easier to produce and think about than apps, since picture book ebooks are basically digital picture books. Apps are far more interactive and complex than traditional books; the app experience is a more layered, varied experience than a book experience, and so any picture book authors and illustrators thinking about creating story apps for

App ABCs for Kid Books

- Printed books and ebooks are linear, while in an app the reader may be able to choose what happens next, or the story may change randomly.
- Apps have additional features, such as narration, animated elements, sound effects, and games.
- A print picture book usually has 32 pages. The number of pages is flexible with ebooks and apps.
- A printed picture book can have double page spreads, while ebooks and apps have single pages. Because different electronic devices have different screen sizes, ebooks and apps must be readable/usable at every size.

young readers need to think visually about their story from the very beginning."

"For an app, you want more interactive books, with maybe some gamification, and elements that work well for animation," Munro says. "Apps don't have to be linear, like a classic print picture book."

Good apps take advantage of all that the format offers. "Within the book app category, very few book apps currently integrate interactivity and gameplay within the narrative itself," Robertson says. "That type of integration is what makes this medium so unique, and I'd like to see more book apps doing this."

Simply taking a manuscript and adding random interactive elements is not enough. Munro warns, "There are some books, wonderful though they may be in print, that do not adapt well to an interactive app; studies have shown that adding all the bells and whistles, unless relevant to the idea, actually detracts from reading and comprehension."

More Than a Book

"It's not a simple transformation from book to app," Dryden says. "It's a highly complex process whereby the app becomes its own experience separate from, and more varied than, the experience of reading a book. Apps rely on a certain kind of physical interaction with a story that's different from interaction with a book—apps employ a multitude of sensory experiences, such as audio, finger-swiping or tapping, shaking, voice recognition and recording, visual choices, global positioning (GPS), and more."

"To convert a published picture book into an ebook or book app, you're really talking about bringing more of the senses into the story," Robertson says. "You look at sound—by adding high-quality narration and possibly music, background sounds, and sound effects. You bring the eyes into the story by adding movement like animations and possibly text highlighting. And you bring touch into the story by adding touch-triggered animations, sounds, and discoveries. I believe the best book apps bring interactivity and touch into the narrative itself."

A good app also allows readers options, such as turning the narration, sound effects, or music on and off. This allows younger children to hear the story read aloud, while older children can read the story themselves. Some apps allow users to record their own voices reading the story or to create new stories by filling in blanks.

Doing all this well can be expensive and time-consuming. Munro's *Roxie's a-MAZE-ing Vacation Adventure* includes sounds, original commissioned music, hidden objects, and more. Munro spent four months creating a detailed maze and 400 spot illustrations. Two app developers spent an additional three months making the app. Munro also says there is another consideration: "There are so many devices and platforms around. Developers have to build differently for each one."

RESOURCES

■ For picture book ebooks, platforms such as uTales (http://utales.com), Storybird (http://storybird.com), MeeGenius! (www.meegenius.com/faqauthor) and KiteReaders (http://kitereaders.com) provide submission guidelines and instructions on how to upload materials. In some cases you must have illustrations.

■ Book apps are sold via app stores: the Apple iTunes App Store for iPad/iPhone (https://itunes.apple.com/us/genre/ios/id36?mt=8) and Android App Stores for Android (www.android.com/apps).

■ iBooks Author: www.apple.com/ibooks-author. A Mac app that allows you to create interactive books for the iPad.

■ Book Creator: www.redjumper.net. Create books on an iPad.

■ AerBook Maker: http://aerbook.com. Create graphic books in your browser without knowing code.

■ Graphicly: http://graphicly.com. Convert and distribute visual stories across all major digital platforms.

■ Twitter #storyappchat: Sunday chat about apps at 9:00 pm. For more information, go to http://storyappchat.wordpress.com.

■ Digital Storytime: http://digital-storytime.com. Reviews of children's book apps, information on reviewers, and blog posts on digital topics.

■ "What Makes a Good Picture Book App?" A helpful article by Katie Bircher in *The Horn Book,* www.hbook.com/2012/02/using-books/what-makes-a-good-picturebook-app.

■ Roxie Munro: www.roxiemunro.com/makingtheapps.html. Information about making apps.

■ Digital Kid's Author: The website of Karen Robertson, www.digitalkids-author.com, offers free training, articles, and how-to books for sale.

■ Julie Hedlund: www.juliehedlund.com/products. Offers a template for Storybook App Proposals for sale.

■ *Digital Book World:* www.digitalbookworld.com. Reports on digital publishing, including new companies and programs.

■ Drydenbks: www.drydenbks.com. The children's book editorial and publishing consultancy company of Emma D. Dryden.

Digital picture books have advantages, first and foremost among them the greater simplicity. It can be difficult to sell book manuscripts as apps. "Developers are hesitant right now about taking on projects by most authors and illustrators, unless they are a big brand," Munro says. "Most major developers make apps from licensed properties, fairy tales, or out-of-copyright works."

Dryden adds, "Any publishers offering picture book apps are having a much harder time finding an audience than publishers offering picture book ebooks, though the audience for picture book ebooks is not significant yet by any means."

"The trend is that book apps are priced the same as ebooks, and sometimes lower, but cost more to create," says Robertson. New programs are simplifying the app development process, however, and some authors are producing their own apps. The complex options may intimidate all but the most tech-savvy authors and illustrators, but it is not as bad as it sounds, according to Robertson. "This might seem daunting, but it's a step-by-step process that starts with assessing and planning the book app. And finding resources to narrate, create sound effects, etc., is also quite straightforward."

Despite the many challenges, going the app route has advantages. "I recently surveyed my colleagues who have published the same story in multiple formats," Robertson says. "Without exception, every single one of them said they sell far more book apps than ebooks. While the price point is low, digital does give authors access to a global market with no back-end fulfillment or inventory costs."

This could provide opportunities for writers and illustrators who struggle to break into the tight print market, or whose books have gone out of print. As with all forms of content creation, the most important consideration is to start with a fabulous manuscript. Dryden says, "My test for a great story app is to determine whether the story holds up when you strip away the interactivity —turn off the audio, turn off the recording, turn off the sounds, etc. If you're left with a satisfying reading experience, that's the sign of a smart children's book app that can serve as something more than just a one-time game or momentary distraction. The most successful picture book apps will be the ones that keep a richly realized story front and center."

Getting the Sales

Choosing the right story and producing an app, even a great one, is only the start. "Marketing apps is challenging," Munro says. "There are a lot of review websites—Moms with Apps, Digital Storytime, Common Sense Media, etc.—that are helpful."

Some companies are experimenting with different models to address discoverability and pricing concerns. For example, a subscription model allows kids to choose what they want to read, without requiring a parent to buy individual books. Follow a blog like *Digital Book World* and you will see new companies promising innovative opportunities almost weekly. So far, proven success stories are few, but many experts predict a golden digital future.

"Compared with traditional publishing, picture book app and picture book ebook publishing is really still in its infancy," Dryden says. "This is all going to change, because children are *digital natives* and expect interactivity in the entertainment they consume, including stories."

Authors and illustrators who are willing to learn the technology and take some chances could position themselves to take advantage of the growing market. Digital formats—both ebooks and apps—will be a staple of the picture book future.

Poetic Possibilities

In his poem, "Request," Lawrence Raab writes:

understand what a poem—or perhaps only
the making of a poem, just that moment
when it starts, when so much
is still possible—

has allowed me to feel.
Happy to be there. Carried away.
        From *Visible Signs* (Penguin)

A poet who seeks to publish must continually strive to achieve that deep, certain, and satisfying sense of being carried away, and to write what award-winning poet and anthologist Lee Bennett Hopkins describes as "serious, heartfelt works."

Poetry should cause an editor to "utter 'Oooh!' and truly sit up and take notice," says Hopkins, who in July 2011 was recognized by Guinness World Records as the world's most prolific anthologist of poetry for children. He has "118 anthologies and counting" to his credit; include his personal collections, and his total number of published works tops 200. Hopkins might review as many as a

One Poet's Journey to a Debut Collection

Amy Ludwig VanDerwater's debut collection of poetry, *Forest Has a Song*, was published by Clarion Books in 2013. Clarion Vice President and Publisher, Dinah Stevenson, who acquired the manuscript, lists VanDerwater as one of her favorite contemporary poets. "I find her work original and charming and accessible."

It was a long journey from creating the poems found in *Forest Has a Song* to seeing them in print on bookshelves and in reader's hands. VanDerwater recounts, "In 2000, I had the opportunity to meet award-winning and award-giving poet Lee Bennett Hopkins. I took down his address and sent him a few poems. Soon after, he invited me to submit to his children's anthologies, and I did so right away. This was life-changing; Lee's mentorship deepened my mental toughness and sense of humor as well as my craft. It is Lee who first read the manuscript of my first book of poems, and it is Lee to whom I often send new poems.

"Once Clarion purchased *Forest Has a Song* (illustrated by Robbin Gourley), I spent a very excited six years waiting for the book to be published. I began *The Poem Farm* blog (www.poemfarm.amylv.com) as a place to reach out to readers, blogging a new children's poem and lesson each day from April 2010 to April 2011. The Kidlitosphere community (www.kidlitosphere.org/), particularly my dear Poetry Friday friends, welcomed me warmly, and I made faraway writing friends.

"Since then, I have co-written a book about teaching poetry (*Poetry: Big Thoughts in Small Packages,* with Lucy Calkins and Stephanie Parsons, from Heinemann), and have two new poetry collections (*Reading Time,* from Word-Song and *With My Hands,* from Clarion) on the way.

"I cling to Samuel Beckett's words, "Ever tried. Ever failed. No matter. Try again. Fail again. Try harder. Fail better." I have learned to appreciate the struggle. Through it all—revisions, rejections, insecurities, fear—I work. And I try to give back. If you love the work, the uncertainty and mystery of it all, then each success is a sweet surprise. I love the act of writing, and I am grateful to the people who have taught me what I know and who have believed that my words might be worth a read."

thousand submissions for a collection containing 16 to 18 poems. He then gets to work crafting the anthology so it has a beginning, a middle, and an end. "My anthologies read like novels," says Hopkins, whose latest publication targeting young adults explores what Shakespeare called the seven ages of man. *All the World's a Stage*, illustrated by Guy Billout and published by Creative Editions, was released in August 2013.

The Power of Poetry

Dinah Stevenson, Vice President and Publisher at Clarion Books, an imprint of Houghton Mifflin Harcourt, lists her must-have qualities: "poetry that is actually poetry, not just text forced into rhyme; skillful use of language; and verse that has a natural flow, with no feet added just to serve the form and no words added solely for the sake of rhyme." She seeks "poetry in which the form enhances or reflects the content."

Wendy Lesser is Editor of *The Threepenny Review*, a quarterly review of the arts and society that features poetry, fiction, nonfiction essays, and reviews. For its audience, which Lesser characterizes as "general but intelligent readers, not specialists in any particular field, but well-educated and/or interested in literature and the arts," Lesser chooses poetry "with a distinctive voice, not straining for experimentalism or effects, but nonetheless unique in approach." Poems can be "rhymed or unrhymed, formal or free verse."

Rebecca Davis is Senior Editor at Wordsong, an imprint of Highlights for Children, Inc., dedicated to children's poetry—and, Davis points out, the only imprint in the United States exclusively devoted to publishing poetry for children. "Mostly I'm looking for fresh perspectives and language, and playful use of language. Poetry is powerful partly because it helps us see things in new ways and make unusual connections. It can capture

The sources for this article suggested the following resources.

■ Rebecca Davis, Senior Editor, Wordsong: "The ones I'm familiar with are written by children's poets. I recommend *Poem-Making: Ways to Begin Writing Poetry,* by Myra Cohn Livingston; *Knock at a Star: A Children's Introduction to Poetry,* X. J. Kennedy and Dorothy M. Kennedy; *Poetry Matters: Writing a Poem from the Inside Out,* by Ralph Fletcher; and *Poetry from A to Z: A Guide for Young Writers,* by Paul Janeczko."

■ Lee Bennett Hopkins: "Rather than a handbook, have a good rhyming dictionary and thesaurus on hand."

■ Wendy Lesser, Editor, *The Threepenny Review*: "Rather than poetry handbooks, read outstanding poetry. One of my favorite contemporary poets is Louise Gluck, for the strength of her voice and the precision of her language."

■ Amy Ludwig VanDerwater: *The Poetry Home Repair Manual: Practical Advice for Beginning Poets,* by Ted Kooser, and *Writing the Life Poetic: An Invitation to Read and Write Poetry,* by Sage Cohen.

the wonder in a moment and the wonder in the world around us, whether the subject is something small like an ant or something huge like reading or science," reflects Davis. "For a collection of poetry, it helps if the manuscript has a strong theme because readers may be drawn to the subject matter, even if they wouldn't normally be looking for a poetry book. And because school and library sales are still an important part of children's poetry sales, if the theme is one that teachers and librarians appreciate (something that might be useful in a classroom or that lends itself to multidisciplinary learning), that can be helpful too."

Like Hopkins, Davis requires the *oooh* factor. "Just as I appreciate fresh perspectives and language in the poems themselves, I also appreciate a fresh perspective on a well-trod subject. For example, many collections of school poems have been published, so the competition for a book of school poems is great. But if the perspective for the collection were unusual, that would make me sit up and take notice. What would be unusual? Lee Bennett Hopkins created an anthology of school poems called *School Supplies: A Book of Poems,* in which all of the poems focus on the supplies you need for school. Betsy Franco wrote a book of school poems in two voices called *Messing Around on the Monkey Bars, and Other School Poems for Two Voices.* There are always new ways of looking at specific subjects."

"There are so many wonderful contemporary children's poets whose work I love for so many different reasons," says Davis. "If I may, I'll let our audience speak for a moment. My son, who is 10, would say his favorite poet is Lee Bennett Hopkins, partly because Lee's "Wisconsin in Feb-b-rr-uary" in *My America* made him laugh so hard he got the hiccups, had to get out of bed to drink water to try to banish them, came back and couldn't stop laughing again. He remembers that experience and that poem—and periodically mentions it—to this day, although this happened several years ago. My daughter, who is 8, would say her favorite poet is Rebecca Kai Dotlich and though my daughter wouldn't put it in these terms, it's because of Rebecca's use of rhythm, rhyme, and playful word combinations. My daughter can recognize a Rebecca Kai Dotlich poem unfailingly if I'm reading from an anthology and not telling her the names of the poets. A few weeks ago, when I asked her what her favorite book was, my daughter said, 'Anything by Rebecca Kai Dotlich.' Children love poetry of all kinds—if they're exposed to it. And it doesn't have to be funny!"

Open Submissions

"It's probably obvious, but the writer should be aware of which houses are currently publishing poetry and which are not," says Stevenson. "Once a submission is made, the writer is swimming in the same pool as Joyce Sidman and other contemporary poets of stature and should be confident that his or her work is on that level."

Hopkins has a number of anthologies and a personal collection scheduled to be published through 2016. Yet, he laments, "Poetry is at its lowest ebb ever. Only two anthologies were released in 2013—mine and *Poems to Learn by Heart*, by Caroline Kennedy— and only one is scheduled for 2014." Still, he regularly receives queries from those hoping to be included in his themed anthologies. "It's hard to get published, but when I find a good poet, I go to them for work." One soon-to-be-published anthology Hopkins is editing features 30 poems, many of them by previously unpublished poets. Despite the steep odds, Hopkins advises, "Be persistent. Keep sending your work out. A manuscript is better in the mail than sitting on your desk." He cautions, however, "There is far too much light verse and *slight verse* around. Craft your work to the fullest."

Davis echoes this. "Do everything you can to become a better poet. Focus on your craft. Take classes; go to workshops; read many, many children's poetry books and lots of children's literature; and, most important, write, write, write, and then revise and revise and revise again. Read your work aloud. Have others read your poems to you, because they may read them differently. Listening to someone else read your poem can help you see where the rhythm might be off, where a fresh reader might stumble."

For *The Threepenny Review*, Lesser encourages poets to, "Take a look at poetry we've published in the past, either by going to our online Reading Room (www.threepennyreview.com/readingroom. html) or ordering a copy of the magazine." For those who wish

IT'S POETICAL

Poetry Friday (www.kidlitosphere.org/poetry-friday) is a forum for poets sponsored by Kidlitosphere Central, which is a "society of bloggers in children's and young adult literature." Each week, one blogger rounds up links to posts on a chosen subject, and a link on Kidlitosphere brings visitors to the the blogger's site, where they can conveniently read a wide range of posts on the topic. A schedule of the Poetry Friday Round-Up hosts and an archive dating back to 2008 is available.

The features that are included may be targeted at kids or adults, and include "original poems, reviews of poetry books, reviews of poetic picture books, links to poems at copyright protected sites, thoughts about poetry, and more. Song lyrics have even been featured."

to submit, Lesser advises, "Look at the guidelines on the submissions page of our website and then follow the instructions. Send five or fewer poems at once." Lesser notes, "From January to June, we will be looking for poetry that fits the criteria I've mentioned. But please be aware that we get many submissions and we only accept about one out of every thousand or so. Also, we don't read submissions from July to December."

Poetry magazine, published by the Poetry Foundation, is a long-standing, highly respected magazine touted as "the oldest monthly devoted to verse in the English-speaking world." According to the mission statement set forth by founder Harriet Monroe in the inaugural volume, *Poetry* aims "to print the best poetry written today, in whatever style, genre, or approach." In the first year of publication, *Poetry* featured such august poets as William Carlos Williams, William Butler Yeats, Joyce Kilmer, and Ezra Pound, and the monthly lays claim to being the original publisher of T. S. Eliot's "The Love Song of J. Alfred Prufrock." *Poetry* currently is open to online submissions exclusively. A

Poetic Justice

Poetry awards are bestowed by a host of organizations, including the American Academy of Arts and Letters, Poetry Society of America, and the Academy of American Poets.

The Library of Congress annually designates a Poet Laureate who serves as a consultant to promote poetry. The position is currently held by Natasha Trethewey.

The Poetry Foundation offers a number of awards, including the annual Pegasus Awards, which celebrate "under-recognized poets and types of poetry." The Foundation names a Children's Poet Laureate who serves for two years as a consultant to the foundation. The latest, named in June 2013, is Kenn Nesbitt.

The National Council of Teachers of English (NCTE) presents the Award for Excellence in Poetry for Children.

Lee Bennett Hopkins has founded two poetry awards. The Lee Bennett Hopkins Poetry Award, established in 1993, is presented annually to an American poet or anthologist for the most outstanding new book of children's poetry. It is co-sponsored by Hopkins, the Pennsylvania State University Libraries, the Pennsylvania Center for the Book, and the Pennsylvania School Librarians Association. The Lee Bennett Hopkins/IRA Promising Poet Award is granted every three years to a promising new poet of poetry for children and young adults who has published no more than two books of children's poetry.

maximum of four poems, and up to 10 pages, will be reviewed. Simultaneous submissions are not considered. Those interested in submitting are encouraged to become familiar with the publication prior to opening an online submission account. Back issues dating to the magazine's inception in 1912 can be accessed on the website (www.poetryfoundation.org/poetrymagazine/archive).

For concise advise that will have you musing and laughing, do not miss the blog entry titled "My Own Ten Rules for Writing Children's Poetry," by J. Patrick Lewis, former United States Children's Poet Laureate and winner of the 2011 National

Council of Teachers of English (NCTE) Award for Excellence in Children's Poetry. The entry, dated February 3, 2013, can be found on "Poetry at Play" (http://poetryatplay.org). Other blog entries, including interviews of award-winning poets and a discussion of poetry and Common Core, offer valuable insights for aspiring and working poets.

"Writers often ask me about what subject matter I'm looking for, what they should put in their cover letter, and how many poems they should include, but mostly they are asking about window dressing," says Davis. "What's important are the poems themselves. I will be drawn to a fresh, powerful poem, even if it's about a subject I wouldn't normally think of, regardless of what the cover letter says. It's all in the writing."

Article Sources
- Lee Bennett Hopkins: www.leebennetthopkins.com
- Houghton Mifflin Harcourt: www.hmhco.com/popular-reading/authors/manuscript-submissions
- *Poetry*: www.poetryfoundation.org/poetrymagazine/submissions
- *The Threepenny Review*: www.threepennyreview.com/submissions.html
- Wordsong: www.boydsmillspress.com/writers-and-illustrators-guidelines

Children's Poetry Markets
- *Anansesem*: www.anansesem.com
- *Babybug*: www.babybugmagkids.com
- Bayard Magazines: www.bayard-magazines.co.uk
- *Black Fox Literary Magazine*: www.blackfoxlitmag.com
- *Bumples*: www.bumples.com
- *Click*: www.clickmagkids.com
- *Cobblestone*: www.cobblestonepub.com
- *Devozine*: www.devozine.org
- Guardian Angel Kids: www.guardian-angel-kids.com
- *Highlights for Children*: www.highlights.com
- *Hopscotch*: www.hopscotchmagazine.com
- *Humpty Dumpty*: www.uskidsmags.com/magazines/humptydumpty
- *Inteen*: www.urbanministries.com
- *Jack and Jill*: www.jackandjillmag.org
- *Kids' Imagination Train*: www.kidsimaginationtrain.blogspot.com
- *Leading Edge*: www.leadingedgemagazine.com
- *Live*: www.gospelpublishing.com/store/startcat.cfm?cat=twritguid
- *The New Era*: www.newera.lds.org
- *Partners*: www.clp.org
- *Pockets*: www.upperroom.org/pockets
- *Shameless*: www.shamelessmag.com
- *Shine Brightly*: www.gemsgc.org
- *Skipping Stones*: www.skippingstones.org
- *Sparkle!*: www.gemsgc.org
- *Spellbound*: www.eggplantproductions.com
- *Spider*: www.cricketmag.com, www.spidermagkids.com
- *Sports Illustrated Kids*: www.sikids.com
- *Stone Soup*: www.stonesoup.com
- *Story Mates*: www.clp.org
- *Take Five Plus*: www.gospelpublishing.com

- *Teen Graffiti:* www.teengraffiti.com
- *Turtle:* www.uskidsmags.com
- *YARN:* www.yareview.net

Adult Poetry Markets
- *Absinthe:* www.absinthenew.com
- *AGNI:* www.agnimagazine.org
- *Alive Now:* http://upperroom.org
- *America:* www.americamagazine.org
- *American Book Review:* www.americanbookreview.org
- *American Literary Review:* www.engl.unt.edu/alr
- *Amethyst Arsenic:* www.amethystarsenic.com
- *Appalachian Heritage:* www.community.berea.edu/appalachianheritage/
- *Arkansas Review:* http://altweb.astate.edu/arkreview
- *Artful Dodge:* www.wooster.edu/artfuldodge
- *Art Times:* www.arttimesjournal.com
- *Ascent Aspirations:* www.ascentaspirations.ca
- *Asimov's Science Fiction:* www.asimovs.com
- *Authorship:* www.nationalwriters.com
- *Azizah:* www.azizahmagazine.com
- *Babysue:* www.babysue.com
- *The Bear Deluxe:* www.orlo.org
- *Bellingham Review:* www.wwu.edu/bhreview
- *The Bitter Oleander:* www.bitteroleander.com
- *Blackbird:* www.blackbird.vcu.edu
- *Black Warrior Review:* www.bwr.ua.edu
- *The Bloomsbury Review:* www.bloomsburyreview.com
- *Blue Mesa Review:* www.unm.edu/~bluemesa
- *Bluestem:* www.bluestemmagazine.com
- *Bogg:* www.depoetry.com/yymisc/bogg.html
- *Bomb:* www.bombsite.com
- **Boston Review:** www.bostonreview.net
- *Boulevard:* www.boulevardmagazine.org
- *Brick:* www.brickmag.com
- *The Brooklyner:* www.brooklyner.org
- *Bull Spec:* www.bullspec.com
- *California Northern:* www.calnorthern.net
- *Callaloo:* http://callaloo.tamu.edu
- *Calyx:* www.calyxpress.org

- *Canteen:* www.canteenmag.com
- *The Caribbean Writer:* www.thecaribbeanwriter.org
- *Carolina Quarterly:* www.thecarolinaquarterly.com
- *Catamaran Literary Reader:* http://catamaranliteraryreader.com
- *CelticLife:* www.celticlife.ca
- *The Chaffin Journal:* http://english.eku.edu/chaffin-journal
- *Charlotte Viewpoint:* www.charlotteviewpoint.org
- *Chattahoochee Review:* www.chattahoochee-review.org
- *The Christian Century:* www.christiancentury.org
- *Christian Communicator:* www.acwriters.com
- *The Christian Ranchman:* www.cowboysforchrist.net
- *The Christian Science Monitor:* www.csmonitor.com
- *Chrysalis Reader:* www.swedenborg.com/chrysalis
- *The Cincinnati Review:* www.cincinnatireview.com
- *Colorado Review:* http://coloradoreview.colostate.edu
- *Columbia: A Journal:* www.columbiajournal.org
- *Commonweal:* www.commonwealmagazine.org
- *Concho River Review:* www.angelo.edu/dept/english
- *Conduit:* www.conduit.org
- *Coping with Cancer:* www.copingmag.com
- *Cover of Darkness:* www.samsdotpublishing.com
- *Crab Orchard Review:* www.craborchardreview.siuc.edu
- *The Cream City Review:* www.creamcityreview.org
- *Creations:* www.creationsmagazine.com
- *Creative with Words:* http://members.tripod.com/creativewithwords
- *Cross Currents:* www.crosscurrents.org
- *CutBank:* www.cutbankonline.org
- *Denver Quarterly:* denverquarterly.com
- *Descant:* www.descant.ca
- *Desert Ashram:* www.light-of-consciousness.org
- *Double Dealer Redux:* www.wordsandmusic.org
- *Echo Ink Review:* www.echoinkreview.com
- *Eclectica:* www.eclectica.org
- *Ellipsis...Literature and Art:* www.westminstercollege.edu/ellipsis
- *Epoch:* www.arts.cornell.edu/english/publications/epoch
- *Euphony Journal:* www.euphonyjournal.com
- *Evansville Review:* http://evansvillereview.evansville.edu
- *Event:* http://eventmags.com
- *Feminist Studies:* www.feministstudies.org

- *The Fiddlehead:* www.thefiddlehead.ca
- *Fifth Wednesday Journal:* www.fifthwednesdayjournal.com
- *First American Art Magazine:* www.firstamericanartmagazine.com
- *Flint Hills Review:* www.emporia.edu/fhr/
- *The Florida Review:* www.floridareview.cah.ucf.edu/
- *Folio:* www.american.edu/cas/literature/folio/index.cfm
- *Forge:* www.forgejournal.com
- *Fourteen Hills:* www.14hills.net
- *FreeFall:* www.freefallmagazine.ca
- *Frigg:* www.friggmagazine.com
- *A Gathering of the Tribes:* www.tribes.org
- *The Gay & Lesbian Review*: www.glreview.com
- *Georgetown Review:* www.georgetowncollege.edu/georgetownreview
- *Georgia Review:* www.thegeorgiareview.com
- *The Gettysburg Review:* www.gettysburgreview.com
- *Grasslimb:* www.grasslimb.com/journal
- *Greatest Uncommon Denominator:* www.gudmagazine.com
- *The Green Hills Literary Lantern:* http://ghll.truman.edu
- *Green Mountains Review:* http://greenmountainsreview.com
- *The Greensboro Review:* www.greensbororeview.org
- *Gulf Coast:* www.gulfcoastmag.org
- *The G.W. Review:* www.thegwreview.weebly.com
- *Hanging Loose:* www.hangingloosepress.com
- *Harpur Palate:* http://harpurpalate.binghamton.edu
- *Hawai'i Review:* www.kaleo.org/hawaii_review/
- *Hayden's Ferry Review:* www.asu.edu/piper/publications/haydensferryreview/
- *The Hopkins Review:* www.press.jhu.edu/journals/the_hopkins_review/
- *Hunger Mountain:* www.hungermtn.org
- *Illuminations*: cofc.edu/illuminations
- *Image:* www.imagejournal.org
- *Indiana Review:* www.indianareview.org
- *Inkwell:* www.inkwelljournal.org
- *Inside Pennsylvania*: www.insidepamagazine.com
- *Iowa Review:* www.iowareview.org
- *Irreantum:* www.irreantum.mormonletters.org
- *Italian Americana:* www.italianamericana.com
- *Jabberwock Review:* www.msstate.edu/org/jabberwock
- *J Journal:* http://jjournal.org
- *The Journal:* http://thejournalmag.org

- *Kaleidoscope:* www.udsakron.org
- *Kansas City Voices:* www.kansascityvoices.com
- *Kelsey Review:* www.mccc.edu/community_kelsey-review.shtml
- *The Kenyon Review:* www.kenyonreview.org
- *Kerem:* www.kerem.org
- *Kestrel:* www.fairmontstate.edu/publications/kestrel/default.asp
- *Left Curve:* www.leftcurve.org
- *Lilith:* www.lilith.org
- *Limestone:* limestonejournal.com
- *Literal:* www.literalmagazine.com
- *Literary Juice:* www.literaryjuice.com
- *Literary Laundry:* www.literarylaundry.com
- *Literary Mama:* www.literarymama.com
- *The Literary Review:* www.theliteraryreview.org
- *Louisiana Literature:* www.louisianaliterature.org
- *The Louisville Review:* www.louisvillereview.org
- *Lullwater Review:* www.lullwaterreview.com
- *The Lutheran Digest:* www.lutherandigest.com
- *The MacGuffin:* www.macguffin.org
- *The Madison Review:* www.english.wisc.edu/madisonreview
- *The Malahat Review:* www.malahatreview.ca
- *Massachusetts Review:* www.massreview.org
- *The Maynard:* www.themaynard.org
- *Memoir Journal:* www.memoirjournal.squarespace.com
- *Michigan Quarterly Review:* www.michiganquarterlyreview.com
- *Mid-American Review:* www.bgsu.edu/midamericanreview
- *Midwifery Today:* www.midwiferytoday.com
- *The Minnesota Review:* www.theminnesotareview.org
- *Mississippi Review:* www.mississippireview.com
- *Mobius:* www.mobiusmagazine.com
- *Modern Haiku:* www.modernhaiku.org
- *Mountain Record:* www.mro.org/mr
- *Narrative:* www.narrativemagazine.com
- *Natural Bridge:* www.umsl.edu/~natural
- *Natural Life:* www.naturallifemagazine.com
- *Nebo:* www.atu.edu/worldlanguages/Nebo.php
- *Necrology Shorts:* www.necrologyshorts.com
- *Neo-opsis Science Fiction Magazine:* www.neo-opsis.ca
- *New Delta Review:* www.ndrmag.org

- *The New Guard:* www.newguardreview.com
- *New Letters:* www.newletters.org
- *New Orleans Review:* www.neworleansreview.org
- *The New Orphic Review:* www3.telus.net/neworphicpublishers-hekkanen
- *The New Quarterly:* www.tnq.ca
- *The New Renaissance:* www.tnrlitmag.org
- *Nimrod International Journal:* www.utulsa.edu/nimrod
- *North American Review:* www.northamericanreview.org
- *North Atlantic Review:* www.northeaglecorp.com/nar.html
- *North Carolina Literary Review:* www.nclr.ecu.edu
- *North Dakota Quarterly:* www.und.edu/org/ndq
- *Notre Dame Review:* www.nd.edu/~ndr/review.htm
- *Now & Then:* www.etsu.edu/cass/nowandthen
- *Obsidian:* http://english.chass.ncsu.edu/obsidian
- *On Spec:* www.onspec.ca
- *Orion:* www.orionmagazine.org
- *Oxford Magazine:* www.oxfordmagazine.org
- *Painted Bride Quarterly:* www.pbq.drexel.edu
- *Parabola:* www.parabola.org
- *Parenting New Hampshire:* www.parentingnh.com
- *The Paris Review:* www.theparisreview.org
- *Parting Gifts:* www.marchstreetpress.com
- *Passager:* www.passagerbooks.com/
- *Passages North:* http://myweb.nmu.edu/~passages
- *Paterson Literary Review:* www.pccc.edu/poetry
- *Pearl:* www.pearlmag.com
- *Peregrine:* www.amherstwriters.com
- *Phoebe:* www.phoebejournal.com
- *The Pinch:* www.thepinchjournal.com
- *The Pink Chameleon:* www.thepinkchameleon.com
- *Plain Spoke:* www.plainspoke.net
- *Planet:* www.planetmagazine.org.uk
- *Pleiades:* www.ucmo.edu/pleiades/
- *Ploughshares:* www.pshares.org
- *Pointed Circle:* www.pcc.edu
- *Porchlight:* www.porchlightzine.com
- *Portland Review:* www.portlandreview.tumblr.com
- *Potomac Review:* www.montgomerycollege.edu/potomacreview
- *Prairie Journal:* www.prairiejournal.org

- *Prairie Messenger:* www.prairiemessenger.ca
- *Praxis:* www.oneonta.edu
- *Prism International:* http://prismmagazine.ca
- *Provincetown Arts:* www.provincetownarts.org
- *Quarterly West:* www.quarterlywest.utah.edu
- *Ellery Queen's Mystery Magazine:* www.themysteryplace.com
- *Queen's Quarterly:* www.queensu.ca/quarterly
- *The Rag:* www.raglitmag.com
- *Rambunctious Review:* www.rambunctiousreview.org
- *Rampike:* http://web4.uwindsor.ca/rampike
- *Raven Chronicles:* www.ravenchronicles.org
- *Red Cedar Review:* http://msupress.msu.edu/journals/rcr
- *Red Rock Review:* http://sites.csn.edu/english/redrockreview
- *Red Wheelbarrow:* www.deanza.edu/redwheelbarrow
- *Reed Magazine:* www.reedmag.org
- *Reverie:* www.aquariuspressbookseller.net
- *Revolver:* www.around-around.com
- *RiverSedge:* www.utpa.edu/utpapress
- *River Styx:* www.riverstyx.org
- *Roanoke Review:* www.roanokereview.wordpress.com
- *Rockford Review:* www.rockfordwritersguild.com
- *Room:* www.roommagazine.com
- *Rose & Thorn Journal:* www.roseandthornjournal.com
- *Sacred Fire:* www.sacredfiremagazine.com
- *The Saint Ann's Review:* www.saintannsreview.com
- *Salt Hill:* www.salthilljournal.net
- *Sanskrit:* http://sanskrit.uncc.edu/
- *The Seattle Review:* www.seattlereview.org
- *Sewanee Review:* www.sewanee.edu/sewanee_review
- *Shenandoah:* http://shenandoah.wlu.edu
- *Sinister Wisdom:* www.sinisterwisdom.org
- *Slate & Style:* www.nfb-writers-division.net/slate_style/slate_style.cfm
- *Snowy Egret:* www.snowyegret.net
- *SN Review:* www.snreview.org
- *So To Speak:* www.gmu.edu/org/sts
- *The South Carolina Review:* www.clemson.edu/cedp/cudp/scr/about.htm
- *South Dakota Review:* www.usd.edu/sdreview
- *The Southeast Review:* www.southeastreview.org
- *Southern California Review:* http://dornsife.usc.edu/mpw/literary-journal

- *Southern Humanities Review:* www.auburn.edu/shr
- *The Southern Review:* www.lsu.edu/tsr
- *Southwest Review:* www.smu.edu/southwestreview
- *Spitball:* www.spitballmag.com
- *Stand:* www.standmagazine.org
- *Stone's Throw:* www.stonesthrowmagazine.com
- *The Storyteller:* www.thestorytellermagazine.com
- *Strange Horizons:* www.strangehorizons.com
- *Sub-Terrain:* www.subterrain.ca
- *Subtropics:* www.english.ufl.edu/subtropics/
- *The Sun:* www.thesunmagazine.org
- *Switchback:* www.swback.com
- *Sycamore Review:* www.sycamorereview.com
- *Tales of the Talisman:* www.talesofthetalisman.com
- *Tampa Review:* www.ut.edu/tampareview/
- *The Texas Review:* www.shsu.edu/~www_trp/
- *Third Coast:* www.thirdcoastmagazine.com
- *Tiferet:* www.tiferetjournal.com
- *Tin House:* www.tinhouse.com
- *TriQuarterly:* www.triquarterly.org
- *USHospice.com:* www.ushospice.com
- *Vermont Ink:* www.vermontink.com
- *The Virginia Quarterly Review:* www.vqronline.org
- *The Walrus:* www.walrusmagazine.com
- *Washington Square:* www.washingtonsquarereview.com
- *The Way of St. Francis:* www.sbfranciscans.org
- *Weave:* www.weavemagazine.net
- *Weavings:* www.weavings.org
- *West Branch:* www.bucknell.edu/westbranch
- *Western Humanities Review:* www.hum.utah.edu/whr
- *Whiskey Island:* www.csuohio.edu/whiskey_island/
- *Whitefish Review:* www.whitefishreview.org
- *The William and Mary Review:* www.wm.edu/so/wmreview
- *Willow Review:* www.clcillinois.edu/community/willowreview.asp
- *Willow Springs:* http://willowsprings.ewu.edu
- *Wisconsin Review:* www.uwosh.edu/wisconsinreview
- *The Worcester Review:* www.theworcesterreview.org
- *Workers Write!:* www.workerswritejournal.com
- *The Yale Review:* www.yale.edu/yalereview

JUST WHO WRITES FOR CHILDREN'S MAGAZINES? YOU SHOULD!

BY MARCIA AMIDON LÜSTED

Recently, on one of the children's writers chat boards that I visit online, someone asked the question, "Is anyone still writing for children's magazines?" At first the question made me indignant, as both the author of 400 magazine articles and as an associate editor for a children's magazine group. The question made it sound as if children's magazines are a dinosaur lumbering toward extinction. But then I became incredulous. Why wouldn't anyone be writing for children's magazines, especially today?

We all know it has been a rough five or six years as far as publishing and the overall economy are concerned. Even authors who have been well-published in the past have found it difficult to get book contracts, and publishers seem to be choosier about what they buy and how many books they put out a year. Many children's magazines have fallen victim to the recession as well. All you have to do is look at a current market guide and read the list of magazines that are no longer in business. But many, many magazines are still alive, kicking, and even flourishing, and they are still the best place for writers not only to get published for the first time, but also—if they develop the skills—to be published frequently.

Submissions Needed

Think about it: The average magazine for children publishes 9 to 12 issues a year, every year. An issue may have anywhere from 5 to 10 articles, plus activities, departments, book reviews, puzzles, or other content. Many magazines also now produce digital editions, to be read online, or on devices like tablets and smartphones. Digital editions may be an identical electronic version of the print magazine, but many also add content, since the publishers do not have to pay additional print costs.

My most recent market guide lists more than 600 publications for children's, parenting, educational, and related magazines. Think of the considerable amount and variety of content that these magazines need to come up with regularly—and the good writers needed to provide it. So even if you have never considered writing for magazines before, they are worth a look.

A very wide range of periodicals are published either for children and teens, or for parents or teachers. No matter what you are interested in or what genres you prefer, you are bound to match up with some of them. General interest children's magazines include *Highlights for Children*, all the Cricket magazines, *Jack and Jill* and the other U.S. Kids magazines, and *Girls' Life*. Religious magazines include *Pockets* and *Focus on the Family Clubhouse*. Among the niche magazines are *Horse & Rider*, *Kiki* (fashion), *Scholastic News*, and *National Geographic Kids* (science).

The only way to become familiar with the many possibilities is to purchase a good, current magazine market guide, and then dedicate time to reading the entries for each magazine thoroughly and marking those that seem like good possibilities for your specific style or type of writing. This also means that once you have narrowed down the choices, you will need to read copies of those magazines. This might include a trip to the library or bookstore newsstand, sending away for sample copies, or visiting the magazine's website to see if they have sample issues that you can read digitally. Research is vital to writing successfully for magazines, but too many writers skimp on time and effort given to this part of the process. If you want to avoid those dreaded rejection words "does not meet our present needs" (often a euphemism for "you didn't bother to research our publication and notice that we don't publish poetry/fairy tales/3,000-word stories"), then you need to have a clear understanding of what a particular magazine publishes and what it does not.

Evil or Exploding? Nonfiction

A word about that seemingly evil term that seems to strike terror into the hearts of many children's writers: *nonfiction*. So many writers seem to dismiss nonfiction writing outright, thinking of it in terms of those long-ago school term papers and preferring to write fiction. But today's nonfiction is vibrant and exciting and fun, and more important, it represents the fastest route to making money as a working writer.

Thanks to the new Common Core national curriculum standards and their focus on nonfiction, the market for nonfiction writing is suddenly exploding. Many magazines are finding that they can sell their nonfiction content to testing companies and curriculum developers, and in cases where writers only sell first rights to their articles, they may reap additional income when their articles are resold. (Note: Read your contract closely, though. Many magazines are buying all rights now.) Do not be quick to dismiss nonfiction writing, because it will help you make those magazine sales. Editors typically receive many more fiction submissions, even though they need more nonfiction. Articles will also build your writing credits, and even lead to nonfiction book writing.

On Themes

If you are ready to consider magazine writing seriously, you done your research well with a market guide, and determined some potential markets, what is next?

Let's start with themed magazines. These are magazine that focus on a particular subject in each issue. For example, *Faces*, which is a world culture and geography magazine, has recently published issues on the power of music, Germany, must-see cities, and Nigeria. This means that every article, department, and story in the issue relates specifically to that theme. Focusing on themes is a good way to start writing for magazines, especially nonfiction, because it gives you a helping hand with a subject.

Most nonfiction magazines require you to submit a query detailing what you want to write about for that issue, rather than writing an entire article. Why? Nonfiction articles in general tend to be submitted first as an outline or general summary, rather than a complete article. An editor may like your general idea but want to tweak the focus a bit. Nonfiction is more malleable than fiction in that you can take a specific topic and write it in a number of ways, depending on the publication and its audience.

Rosalie Baker, Editor of *Calliope* and *Dig* magazines, suggests to authors, "Read several issues of the magazine, choose a theme that really interests you, research the theme a bit, and then think of an angle that would be informative, engaging, and of interest to our readership."

Susan Buckley, Editor of *AppleSeeds*, agrees and adds, "Send in a well-thought-out query that gives details about your approach to a particular topic. And think about slants to a topic that will be unusual and kid-friendly." Avoid the most obvious ideas for a theme; for example, if the theme is "who did what on the frontier," the editors are likely to receive articles about cowboys or pioneers. Research to find a different topic—perhaps a job that we do not usually associate with the frontier—or take a different focus or approach to a well-worn theme, such as African Americans or women who worked as cowboys.

Meg Chorlian is Editor of *Cobblestone*, an America history magazine for kids ages 9 to 14. She is even more specific about her history themes and how writers can best approach them. "Queries that try to focus in on an interesting aspect of the issue's theme (rather than trying to provide a provide a broad overview) are more likely to get considered. I also like when writers make a suggestion about how they will begin an article. The opening sentence reveals a lot. I also like authors who express flexibility. For example, an author who indicates that he or she is willing to write either their specific query or another angle on the issue's theme gets put in the *consider* pile. If I don't have any queries for a specific article that I want to include, I'd turn to that author who showed a willingness to be accommodating to the issue's needs."

It also pays to be careful when writing query letters, since you are not only presenting an idea, but also giving an editor their first taste of your writing, both in content and mechanics. Many editors mention being put off by a query letter or outline riddled with typos. "If someone can't take the time to proof a query, it makes me leery of asking him or her to write an article," Chorlian comments.

Another frequent error writers make is not noting that a magazine is themed. Buckley says, "One of the biggest mistakes is when writers don't pay attention to the theme, or they submit queries that are far too general, with nothing to distinguish their query from others."

Baker indicates that she does not like queries that are too brief, with no information about the person querying. "They need to say why the topic is of interest to them and why they are, in some way, a good person to write for the issue." Sources are also extremely important in nonfiction writing. "When I see a bibliography where websites outnumber primary sources or vetted history books, I think twice about using the author," Chorlian says.

Another point: Try to give editors a few extras, such as links to pertinent websites, photos, or videos. Your article idea will be even more appealing.

For Fiction Submissions

As for writing fiction for children's magazines, while you may not need to worry about good primary sources or an interesting focus, as you do with nonfiction, research is still very important. Be absolutely sure the magazine you are targeting does publish fiction.

Read the writers' guidelines carefully. Is your story appropriate for the ages the magazine targets? Is it within the correct word length guidelines? Do not send a 1,500-word story to a magazine that only accepts fiction up to 800 words long. If the magazine is themed, or deals with very specific content, does your story work with those specifications? Do not, for example, send an overtly religious story to a magazine that is not at all religious in focus, or send a graphic, contemporary teen story to a religious magazine. Remember, too, that if you are submitting fiction, then you are facing much more competition from other writers than you would if you were submitting nonfiction. Some of the most popular, most well-known magazines for kids receive upwards of 800 queries and submissions a month. Your story must be as perfect as you can make it, and meet all of that magazine's criteria, to stand out against so many others.

Once you submit to magazines and begin selling your work, chances are pretty good that you can build a reputation for not only writing well, but meeting all guidelines and deadlines—in short, becoming someone an editor can rely on and is likely to use again. As Chorlian says, "We are always looking to add to our list of assignment writers, and someone who can write well and accurately for children, and who meets deadlines, will be added to my list after one good article. . . . Authors who can complete and assignment without a lot of handholding make my job much easier."

So is anyone still writing for children's magazines? If they are not, then they are doing their writing career a big disservice. So get out there, explore your local newsstand, the library, and online, and give it a try!

HELP YOURSELF, AND OTHERS, WITH SELF-HELP WRITING

BY CHRISTINA HAMLETT

"Change yourself," says a Portuguese proverb, "and fortune will change with you." People have always compared themselves to others, and looked for quick-fix solutions to remedy their perceived flaws. Why is their cave bigger than ours? Why does that guy have more friends than I do? Why can't I be as happy as she is? Why aren't our children as smart as theirs?

The proliferation of self-help titles in the marketplace—generating $13 billion annually—is a testament to our perpetual quest for self-improvement. Whatever the malady we think holds us back, someone has a magic elixir, first aid, or motivational pep talk that promises to make us better. In an age when anxieties are high, patience is short, and wallets are running on empty, it is little wonder that one in 10 nonfiction book purchases are about taking greater control of life and resources. Self-help books also offer anonymity, and cost less than professional help.

Here are some other facts about the lucrative self-help genre:

■ The first book in this category dates to 1859. Samuel Smiles endeavored to show people that if they learned to be thrifty and hard-working they could survive the newly industrialized Britain. It sold more than 250,000 copies.

- Self-help books fall into four overarching categories: finances, health/wellness, relationships, and spirituality.
- Women buy the majority of self-help books.
- U.S. self-help titles sell well in Australia, modestly in Japan, and poorly in the U.K.
- Consumers who buy self-help books tend to keep buying them.

While many self-help books are penned by professionals such as psychiatrists, fitness coaches, or religious or spiritual counselors, self-help or motivational is open to anyone with passion, expertise, or research and journalism skills.

Maybe that person is you.

Qualifications

A lack of academic degrees has never stopped anyone from publishing opinions and advice, but to be respected by prospective readers—and to sell self-help articles or books—writers do well to have professional or personal experience in their subject. But it is also possible to be a strong researcher in finance, health, relationships, or any other subject, and an insightful writer. Many aspiring writers in this field begin by pitching advice columns to newspapers and magazines; they may have never officially trained in any way to offer advice, but they can do the legwork in self-help guidance by interviewing experts and investigating their subject thoroughly.

Self-help writers must also have the ability to distill complex concepts into user-friendly, conversational information and advice that a novice can follow. This requires understanding the target audience thoroughly, including the needs and fears that fuel their desire for healthier, wealthier, happier lifestyles.

Market research is critical to put a fresh spin on existing books or self-help approaches. As this *Writers' Guide to 2014* is being prepared for publication, top-selling self-help titles on Amazon include *The Gifts of Imperfection: Let Go of Who You Think You're Supposed to Be and Embrace Who You Are* (by a research professor)*; E-Squared: Nine Do-It-Yourelf Energy Experiments That Prove Your Thoughts Create Your Reality* (by a freelance writer)*; Lean In: Women, Work and the Will to Lead* (by a Facebook executive)*;* and *The 5 Love Languages: The Secret to Love that Lasts* (by a pastor and radio host). If you have in mind a parenting self-help article or book, or one on eating disorders, or time management, what will be your unique angle? What do you have to offer?

Be careful, however. Catharsis is good for the soul but it may not be commercially viable if your self-help writing offers only your personal triumphs over adversity as a generic template for others. No one wants to read advice in the form of a self-indulgent memoir. Even if you will be sharing personal experiences, add other voices with firsthand stories to validate the advice; case studies are interesting to read. Taking this approach will also resonate with book publishers if you do not have specific personal credentials, like a medical degree.

Remember that you have to offer options or solutions that are truly available to your readers. Your own accomplishments in losing weight, trimming expenses, or becoming more confident may owe their success to getting a gym membership, finding room-mates, or joining Toastmasters—options not necessarily available to your average reader.

A self-help book must always be approachable, reader-centric, and impart the level of advice and encouragement you would want someone to give you or someone close to you. While some self-help authors have found success with a *tough love* stance that involves criticizing, disparaging, or trivializing a reader's weak-nesses, this strategy negates the true purpose of a book: to offer hope.

That said, a self-help book should not make unrealistic promises, especially if its focus is on large objectives such as conquering addictions, coping with grief, developing self-esteem, overcoming anxieties, acquiring wealth, and confronting fears. People often purchase self-help titles because counseling and treatment are cost-prohibitive; it is essential your book carry a disclaimer that the text should not be viewed as a substitute for professional consultations.

In developing self-help content, consider:

- Does it clearly define what a reader will learn? (i.e., how to create a household budget).
- Is the advice specific, with a reasonable starting point and goal? (i.e., how to overcome a fear of hamsters rather than how to overcome a fear of every creature in the animal kingdom).
- Are incremental action steps, relevant examples, and a self-evaluation element included, to measure progress?
- Will the book include resource lists?

Solving Today's Problems

Since the 1930s, self-help books have paralleled social and economic trends, shifting demographics, technological advances, and family dynamics. Many titles from this period, for example, focused on etiquette and table manners, how to find a husband, and how to run a smooth household. In the 1930s, in the midst of the Depression, Dale Carnegie's *How to Win Friends and Influence People* promised to help improve life, love, and making a living. Dr. Spock was the go-to authority for many a mother in the postwar baby boom.

Prior to the feminist movement of the 1960s, issues such as higher education and financial independence were not high on the advice list for female readers, nor was it expected that husbands and fathers would ever require guidebooks on how to set foot in a kitchen or assist with child-rearing. Victimization—blaming troubles on other people—was not socially permissible to talk about, much less discuss in writing. Conforming to the expectations of parents, peers, and bosses was touted as the only way to achieve goodness, make friends, be successful, or even have a satisfying sex life. But then in 1962, along came Helen Gurley Brown's *Sex and the Single Girl*.

In our current times, the seemingly unyielding problems of stagnant wages, unstable employment, and social insularity are giving rise to more titles for people seeking safe harbor. Social changes are another inspiration for self-help writing. Four groups in particular are fertile markets for self-help writing:

- *Teens*: In 1960, 1 in 20 babies was born to an unwed mother. That statistic is now 1 in 3. These young moms need self-help books on parenting, budgeting, and getting an education. In addition, today's teens (and tweens) need expert information on how to cope with bullying, school violence, and substance abuse.
- *GLBT:* The gay/lesbian/bisexual/transgender population is becoming more visible but still faces issues of discrimination and intolerance. And, as the marriage laws have changed, opportunities are increasing for self-help writing on everything from wedding planning to couples counseling targeted at this market.
- *Immigrants:* Changes in U.S. immigration law will bring more newcomers to American neighborhoods, schools, and workplaces. How they acclimate to their new surroundings and respond to the cultural tugs of their native countries will influence the market for books that literally

Book Publishers

- ACTA Publications: www.actapublications.com. Religion, parenting, relationships, grief.
- Adams Media: www.adamsmedia.com. Relationships, finance, parenting.
- Addicus Books: http://addicusbooks.com. Health and wellness.
- Bancroft Press: www.bancroftpress.com. Personal growth.
- Barron's: www.barronseduc.com. Business/finance, health/wellness, relationships, mind/body/spirit.
- Berrett-Koehler Publishers: www.bkconnection.com. Personal growth.
- Career Press: www.careerpress.com. Motivational.
- Entrepreneur Press: www.entrepreneur.com/entrepreneurpress. Finance.
- Free Spirit: www.freespirit.com. Self-help for children and parents.
- Findhorn Press: www.findhornpress.com. Mind, body, spirit.
- Foghorn Publishers: www.foghornpublisher.com. Health/wellness, finance, spirituality.
- Hazelden Publishing: www.hazelden.org. Addictions, personal growth.
- Hay House: www.hayhouse.com. Mind, body, spirit.
- HCI Books: www.hcibooks.com Addictions, personal growth.
- Hunter House: www.hunterhouse.com. Health/wellness, personal growth, family, relationships.
- Impact Publishers: http://impactpublishers.com. Health/wellness, relationships.
- International Wealth Success: www.iwsmoney.com. Finance.
- Jossey-Bass/Pfeiffer, John Wiley & Sons: www.josseybass.com/WileyCDA. Motivational, finance, relationships, spirituality.
- PS Avalon: www.willparfitt.com/psanew.html. Spirituality.
- Red Wheel: http://redwheelweiser.com. Health/wellness, finance, spirituality.
- Rockpool Publishing: www.rockpoolpublishing.com.au. Mind, body, spirit.
- Self-Counsel Press: www.self-counsel.com. Business, law, finance.
- Shambala Publications: www.shambhala.com. Health/wellness, spirituality.
- Sounds True: www.soundstrue.com. Health/wellness, spirituality.
- Sourcebooks: www.sourcebooks.com Relationships, personal growth, finance.
- Square One Publishers: www.squareonepublishers.com. Alternative health, finance.
- Wesleyan Publishing: www.wesleyan.org. Religion, spirituality.

SELF-HELP MARKETS

Magazines

- *AARP the Magazine:* www.aarp.org/magazine. Finance, health/wellness, relationships.
- *American Fitness:* www.americanfitness.com. Health/wellness.
- *BackHome:* www.backhomemagazine.com. Sustainable living, family, finance, community.
- *Backwoods Home:* www.backwoodshome.com. Self-reliant lifestyle.
- *Catholic Digest:* www.catholicdigest.com. Spirituality, relationships, family.
- *Delicious Living:* www.deliciousliving.com. Health/wellness, lifestyle, sustainable living.
- *The Dollar Stretcher:* www.stretcher.com. Finance
- *Experience Life:* http://experiencelife.com. Health/wellness.
- *Going Bonkers:* www.gbonkers.com. Health/wellness, relationships.
- *Grandparents.com:* www.grandparents.com. Family, relationships.
- *Grit:* www.grit.com. Do-it-yourself, family, community.
- *Guideposts:* www.guideposts.org. Inspiration, facing challenges.
- *Health Magazine:* www.health.com. Health/wellness, mind/body.
- *Ladies Home Journal:* www.lhj.com. Health/wellness, relationships, personal growth, family.
- *MASK (Mothers Awareness on School-age Kids):* www.maskmatters.org. Family/parenting, social issues, health/fitness.
- *Natural Life:* www.naturallifemagazine.com. Health/wellness, lifestyle.
- *Psychology Today:* www.psychologytoday.com. Human behavior.
- *SageWoman:* www.sagewoman.com. Spirituality, health/wellness.
- *Science of Mind:* www.scienceofmind.com. Spirituality.
- *Self:* www.self.com. Health/wellness, relationships.
- *Spotlight on Recovery:* http://spotlightonrecovery.com. Health/wellness, family, personal growth.
- *Strategy:* www.strategymagazine.com. Personal growth, finance.
- *Tathaastu:* www.tathaastumag.com. Health/wellness, spirituality.
- *Vista:* www.wesleyan.org. Spirituality.

and figuratively speak their languages.

■ *Older workers:* As if the stress of worrying whether they have saved enough for retirement weren't enough to keep baby boomers awake at night, consider an even more daunting scenario: being suddenly let go from their job 5 to 15 years earlier than they anticipated. The employment pool is quite a different one from the one they dove into as a new grad. Additionally, boomers are increasingly responsible for elderly parents and for adult children moving back home. Self-help finance books and titles regarding reinvention, retooling skills, and self-esteem will be in demand.

Marketing Pointers

Whatever the subject area of a self-help book, they all seem to have a special lingo for their titles. Editors, and readers, love titles with numbers. Numbers are all about bite-sized tips, tidy timeframes, and statistical assurances that the potential readers are not alone in whatever their state of need. Consider:

■ *2 Weeks To Your Best Body Ever!*
■ *45% Of Most People Are In The Wrong Job: Are You One of Them?*
■ *Win Your Ex-Boyfriend Back In 3 Days!*
■ *How To Become Debt-Free In 6 Months!*
■ *10 Ways To Find Joy!*

Consumers are also drawn to titles that provoke questions.

■ *The Monk Who Sold His Ferrari*
■ *Get out of Your Mind and into Your Life*
■ *Blink: The Power Of Thinking Without Thinking*

- *The Mother-in-Law Dance: Can Two Women Love the Same Man and Still Get Along?*
- *Your Immortal Reality: How to Break the Cycle of Birth and Death*

Whether you pursue traditional publishing channels or go the DIY route, a strategic and aggressive marketing platform is required. Most publishers will not even offer a contract unless the author has a following on Facebook, LinkedIn, and Twitter; a professional website; and a promotion plan in place. Self-help books also frequently rely on ancillary activities to generate sales. For instance, you will likely be expected to:

- write blogs and articles
- produce tapes and CDs
- create videos and infomercials
- do speaking engagements
- provide consulting services
- offer workshops
- pursue media opportunities

The more of these you can incorporate in your marketing plan, the greater chances of your book's sustainability in a highly competitive industry. To appreciate the power of this strategy, look to the heavy hitters in this category: Tony Robbins, Suze Orman, Deepak Chopra, Barbara DeAngelis, Dr. Phil, Jillian Michaels, and Shakti Gawain.

Popularity of that magnitude is not without its price. The more your image becomes synonymous with your brand, the greater the scrutiny of your core message.The media has no trouble exposing experts like self-help guru James Arthur Ray, whose practices resulted in the "sweat lodge deaths." Once an expert's ethics are discredited for not practicing what he or she preaches, it can sometimes cause readers to question the validity of the advice dispensed.

If you have a positive and innovative approach to a strong subject, an authentic voice that engenders trust, and a willingness to promote tirelessly, pitch your project to the right publisher. Self-help is a profitable field, to be sure, but one that also embraces an altruistic ideal: to make the world a better place, one reader at a time.

STYLE

KISS: KEEP IT SIMPLE, STUPID!

How to Write About a Complex Subject in a Simple Way

BY DEVYANI BORADE

I have worked in the information technology industry in various capacities for the last decade. As anyone who does not live under a rock will know, the IT field, along with biotech, space, and genetics, is one of the fastest-growing, changing, and revolutionary fields. From the invention of the wheel to the first cloned sheep to putting the *smart* into every single smart gadget available on the market today, we have come a long way in a relatively short period of time. Little wonder then that this progress needs, indeed deserves, to be documented accurately and engagingly. Who better to do the job than a writer with knowledge of the inner workings of the system?

Whether you are writing about the latest scientific advancement, or unveiling secrets of great historical pith and moment, or even jousting around different political perspectives, your audience has to be able to understand what they are reading. This means keeping things simple—writing about complicated stuff in an uncomplicated way for the benefit of the layperson. So how do you ensure that you have the know-how, as well as the can-do, required?

The Need to Know

To put it very bluntly, you cannot write on a complex subject unless you know what you are talking about. While this is true for most specialist industries like technology, manufacturing, legal, shipping, etc., this premise is especially true for any industry where the playing field is the whole world.

Thanks to the Internet, every Tom, Dick, and Hari from Ireland to India has access to a wealth of information on every topic. Which in turn means that every pair of eyes that reads your work will be scrutinizing it for mistakes. The true brains contributing to a field will analyze and either accept or reject your writing contributions. Unless you yourself are well-versed with a given topic, lack of experience will open you up to ridicule unless you are knowledgeable and accurate.

Know the lingo of your subject or field too. Complex industries rely heavily on jargon. For example, in the IT field, RAM is neither a male sheep nor a Hindu god. Make no mistake, if you slip up, you will get slapped down.

Focus

Often a subject may be so vast and intricate there is no way to write everything about it in a single article or book—or even in one lifetime anyway. With the advent of fast communication devices, news and views travel faster than it will take you to read through to the end of this sentence. While your fingers are laboring away on an 800-word article about what you think is the latest must-have gizmo, elsewhere in the world there have already been three more innovations made to it. By the time your piece actually appears in print, it has become outdated.

You need to concentrate on a very small aspect of a particular subject and write strictly within the scope of those boundaries. This is not just true for the fast-changing world of science and technology. It holds for political topics, and for more *traditional* subjects as history and art as well. So, for instance, you cannot cover the entire history of early American settlers in a thousand words. You can, however, address new issues on the topic of the Mayflower within that framework.

Selection Criteria

When it comes to picking an actual topic, there are no limits. To begin with, you can write about whatever appeals to you personally. Chances are you will share your interests with a fairly large readership, and there will be editors and publishers who will be interested in your article.

Gain fluency in a subject, subscribe to newsletters that discuss the hot topics of the day, and constantly stay attuned to possible subjects and how you might present them to a general, interested audience.

Angle

Just knowing what you are going to write about is not enough. You also need to know where you are going with it, what your goal is. Are you raising an objection to a well-known concept? Are you emphasizing a little-known aspect of a popular phenomenon? Are you debating the advantages and disadvantages of several different products or services? Are you aiming to align your loyalties to a specific school of thought?

Your article needs a clear slant. Readers should know what to expect from it when they start reading, and this expectation should be wholly satisfied at the end, with minimum distractions, tangents, and ambiguities. A title like "Five Ways to Use Social Media for Marketing Your Book" should give the reader five concrete, distinct, and useful ways to help them market their book. You should not suddenly begin a discourse about how

Twitter has brought about the degradation of the English language. Charm 'em, don't cheat 'em.

Provoke

A good article makes the reader think. A great one forces him to react. In the world of writing, which is all about communication, the mark of an expert is how much *buzz* or discussion his article generates, how many people weigh in with their opinions, what feedback is given and taken, where else the work is being bandied about. Complex subjects can easily become dry and dull if not handled carefully.

> A good article makes the reader think. A great one forces the reader to react.

Unlike fiction, nonfiction on layered topics has no characters to make the readers care about them, no twists in the plot to keep up audience interest, and no emotionally charged dramatic scenes to vary the pace of the narrative. So you need to make sure that either the topic you are writing about is sufficiently interesting to make your audience feel strongly about it, or the way you present it is unique enough to urge readers into some sort of action, whether it is vociferous agreement or vehement disagreement—anything but mild apathy.

Evoke

Evocative writing does not have to be the stranglehold of fiction. Complexities arise when ideas evolve to help people solve their real world problems. So writing about a complex topic can revolve around some practical issue faced by either you or a hypothetical user, and it can evoke a sense of consequence.

Often, opening an article with a problem statement written in simple language serves to hook and draw the reader in. Of course, the problem itself needs to be valid and as close to a genuine problem as possible, otherwise no one will bother continuing reading. Writing about how your local legislator campaigned for increasing cycle usage is acceptable; writing about how the increased cycle usage helps lower the income tax rate is stretching the imagination—and incredulity—a little.

Read the Reader

As with all other types of writing, complex articles have to be written with the reader profile in mind. For example, technology brings together people from various walks of life—the know-it-all geek, the keen amateur, the lost-without-my-phone college student, the what-does-this-button-do inquisitive child, the I-don't-understand-but-I-want-to grandfather, the employee steeped in drudgery charged with keeping himself up to date at the cost of losing his job, even the hair stylist next door who is into technology as a hobby by night. While it is not possible to imagine every kind of person who might come across your article, it is wise to have a general idea about whether you want to target the novices, the experts or the in-betweens.

The language in your article, specifically the use of jargon, should reflect the reading level of your audience. Everyone knows SMS refers to texting on their phone, not everyone knows that it is SCM that is the backbone of their online shopping. (For the curious, it stands for Supply Chain Management.)

You may market your article to a print magazine or a website that runs a blog. In both cases, you must understand their style, editorial requirements, production schedules, and work ethos, and tailor your article to align with these.

Supplementary information

Complex articles offer opportunities to supply additional information that both clarifies and expands on your topic. This might include:

- the leading players (whether business people selling a specific product, service or solution; tech types dealing in emerging technologies; scientists researching synthetic DNA; or art historians arguing the provenance of a newly discovered painting by a Renaissance master).
- sidebars discussing related topics that do not fit well into your article without complications
- sources for alternate views on your topic
- graphs and charts
- demographic profiles
- facts and figures
- hyperlinks for further reading
- even a cartoon or two depicting with a different take on the topic.

Authenticity & Authority

It goes without saying that you must verify your facts before you have your manuscript set out before public eyes. Confirm and record the salient features of your article.

The authority comes from external sources. Expert quotes lend gravitas to the point you are trying to make, and help you maintain accuracy. Articles that incorporate comment from experienced professionals in the field are always preferred to those that come from a single voice—the writer's—and that simply sound opinionated.

So just because an article on a complex subject necessarily deals with information that the reader may not yet know, it does not mean that the piece needs to be written in incomprehensible language. Some amount of jargon is accepted, even expected, but the bulk of the article text should be kept as simple and easy to digest as possible. Instead of impressing your readers, obtuse language only serves to confuse, distract, and put them off.

The structure of the article should lead your audience through to your conclusions with clarity. By using plenty of diagrams and real-life examples, your article can not only keep the interest of those reading, but also hook those who may not have otherwise been so inclined. Select your topic with care, keep your readers in mind, know what you're writing, and get a reaction—and your work will not only get acknowledgment but also accolades aplenty.

NOVELIST, EDIT THYSELF

BY CHRIS EBOCH

The fiction book market is more competitive than ever. Editors with mile-high slush piles can afford to choose only exceptional manuscripts. Authors who self-publish must produce work that is equal in quality to releases from traditional publishers. And regardless of their publishing path, authors face competition from tens of thousands of other books. Serious authors know they must extensively edit and polish their manuscripts.

Critique groups and *beta readers* (pre-submission readers who review your work, usually fiction, but who are not necessarily writers) can provide feedback and corrections. That might not be enough to perfect your work, however. Many critique partners will not want to read your manuscript through draft after draft. And unless they are experienced writers or writing teachers, *critiquers* may miss issues a professional editor would catch.

Hiring a pro is an alternative. Professional developmental editors can help writers shape their manuscripts and provide advice. Copy editors and proofreaders can catch inconsistencies and spelling or grammar errors. But even if you decide to hire a free-lancer, you will get more from the experience by turning in a draft you have already edited yourself. According to freelance editor Linda Lane, "Carefully preparing your manuscript for an editor rather than simply forwarding the latest draft saves dollars, because freelance editors often charge an hourly rate."

Regardless of how much help you have from others, self-editing is an essential tool for every writer in every genre and category.

The Big Picture

Wading through hundreds of pages trying to identify every problem in your book manuscript is at once intimidating and not very effective. The best self-editors break the editorial process into steps, and they develop practices that allow them to step back from the manuscript and see it as a whole.

Editor Jodie Renner recommends putting a manuscript away for a few weeks after the first draft is complete, except for sharing it with a critique group or beta readers. Ask your advisers to look only at the big picture: "where they felt excited, confused, curious, delighted, scared, worried, bored, etc.," Renner says. During your writing break, you can also read books, articles, or blog posts to brush up on your craft techniques.

Collect feedback from your readers and make notes, asking for clarification as needed. Consider placing everyone's comments on a single manuscript for simplicity. This also allows you to see where several people have made similar comments, and to choose which suggestions to follow. At this point, you are just making notes, not trying to implement changes.

Another technique is to make a chapter-by-chapter outline of the manuscript to see what you have in hand, but without the distraction of details. For each scene or chapter, note the primary action, important subplots, the mood or emotions, and expressions of theme. This novel overview, amounting to only a few pages, can help you identify trouble spots. Compare your outline to the traditional pattern of the *hero's journey* narrative, or a three-act dramatic structure, or other narrative foundations that you admire, to see if those expose any weaknesses in your story or inspire any improvements.

Next, review the scenes, paying attention to anything that slows the story. Where do you introduce the main conflict? Can you eliminate your opening chapter(s) and start later? Do you have long passages of backstory or explanation that are not necessary? Does each scene have conflict? Are any scenes out of order or repetitive, and might be cut? Do you need new scenes? Condense any? Make any more moving?

Colored highlighters (or the highlight function on a computer) can help you track everything from point of view to thematic elements to clues in a mystery. Highlight subplots and important secondary characters to make sure they are used throughout the manuscript in an appropriate way. Note where you might cut or combine minor characters.

Once you have an overview of the changes you want, revise the manuscript for big picture items—issues such as plot, structure, characterization, point of view, and pacing. Renner recommends rereading the entire manuscript, still focusing on the big picture. Depending on the extent of your changes, you may want to repeat this process several times.

During this stage of editing, consider market requirements. Is your word count within an appropriate range for the genre? Are you targeting a publisher that has specific requirements? If you are writing a romance, will the characters' arcs and happy ending satisfy those fans? If you have an epic fantasy, is the world-building strong and fresh? If your thriller runs too long, can it be broken into multiple books, or can you eliminate minor characters and subplots?

Once you have done all you can, you may want to hire a content editor. Find someone who will focus on content, structure, and stylistic weaknesses. Do not pay someone to fix your typos when

How to Get a Good Critique

Few people are good at analyzing their own work, so getting critiques is an important part of the editing process. To get the most useful feedback, clarify what you want from your audience. When working with a professional editor, this means discussing whether you need developmental editing, copy editing, or proofreading. When getting feedback from other writers or beta readers, let them know what type of feedback you want. Less experienced critiquers may benefit from having specific questions to answer. Freelance Editor Karen R. Sanderson offers this list to provide guidance to your critique partners:

- Critical: Please provide an honest response, not only compliments.
- Real: Does it feel real and does the dialogue read like people actually talk?
- Imagery: Can you imagine the scenes, places, and people?
- Timing: Did the timing of events, chapters, and character introductions make sense?
- Interesting: Did it capture your interest or were you ready to put it down after the first paragraph?
- Questions: Did you have questions? Were you unsure of what was happening or why?
- Unique: Is it unique or is it like a dozen other books you wished you hadn't purchased?
- Engaging: Were you engaged in the characters, the scenes, the events?

you might still have major changes to make. Communicate clearly with a prospective editor to make sure you know what you are getting.

You could also send the manuscript to new beta readers or critique partners. People who have not read the manuscript before might be better at identifying how things are working now. If you do not have critique partners, reach out through writing discussion boards or Goodreads author groups.

Fine Tuning

Once you are confident that your characters, plot, structure, and pacing are working, you can dig into the smaller details. At this stage, make sure that your timeline works and your setting hangs together. Create calendars and maps to keep track of when things happen and where people go. Then polish, polish, polish.

Bill Peschel, author of *The Complete, Annotated Mysterious Affair at Styles* (Peschel Press) and a former newspaper copy editor, says, "Reading with a critical eye reveals weak spots in grammar, consistently misspelled words, and a reliance on *crutch* words, such as *simply, basically,* or *just.* While it can be disheartening to make the same mistakes over and over again, self-editing can boost your ego when you become aware that you're capable of eliminating them from your work. It takes self-awareness, some education, and a willingness to admit to making mistakes."

This stage of editing can be time-consuming, especially if you are prone to spelling or grammatical errors. "Be systematic," Peschel says. "Despite all the advice on how to multitask, the brain operates most efficiently when it's focusing on one problem at a time. This applies to proofing. You can look for spelling mistakes, incorrect grammar, and your particular weaknesses, just not at the same time. So for effective proofing, make several passes, each time focusing on a different aspects."

One pass might focus only on dialogue. "Read just the dialogue out loud," Renner suggests, "maybe role-playing with a buddy or two. Do the conversations sound natural or stilted? Does each character sound different, or do they all sound like the author?"

Wordiness is a big problem for many writers, so make at least one pass focused exclusively on tightening. "Make every word count," Renner advises. "Take out whole sentences and paragraphs that don't add anything new or drive the story forward. Take out unnecessary little words, most adverbs and many

RESOURCES

Books

- *Writing It Right!* by Sandy Asher (Writer's Institute Publications)
- *Self-Editing for Fiction Writers,* by Renni Browne and Dave King (William Morrow)
- *Style That Sizzles & Pacing for Power: An Editor's Guide to Writing Compelling Fiction,* by Jodie Renner (Jodie Renner Editing)
- *Scene and Structure,* by Jack Bickham (Writer's Digest Books)
- *Manuscript Makeover,* by Elizabeth Lyon (Penguin)
- *Revision & Self-Editing,* by James Scott Bell (Writer's Digest Books)
- *Thanks, But This Isn't for Us,* by Jessica Page Morrell (Tarcher)
- *Advanced Plotting,* by Chris Eboch (Pig River Press)
- *Rivet Your Readers with Deep POV,* by Jill Elizabeth Nelson (CreateSpace/ Amazon Digital Services)

Online

- Resources for Writers, by Jodie Renner: http://jodierennerediting.blogspot.ca
- The Plot Outline Exercise from *Advanced Plotting,* by Kris Bock (Chris Eboch), www.krisbock.com/blog.htm
- The Other Side of the Story, by Janice Hardy: http://blog.janicehardy.com
- Jordan McCollum offers downloadable free writing guides on topics such as character arcs and point of view, at http://jordanmccollum.com/free-writing-guides.

Editors

- Chris Eboch, developmental editor, www.chriseboch.com
- Linda Lane, freelance editor, www.denvereditor.com
- Jodie Renner Editing, freelance fiction editor, www.JodieRennerEditing.com
- Karen R. Sanderson, "The Word Shark," proofreading, editing, and critique services, www.karenrsanderson.com

adjectives, and eliminate clichés."

Make additional passes looking for grammar errors, missing words, and your personal weak areas. For example, if you know you tend to overuse *just*, use the Find option in a program like Microsoft Word to locate that word and eliminate it when possible.

Even if you are not an expert editor, you may be able to sense when something is wrong. "Trust your inner voice" when you get an uneasy feeling, Peschel says. "It can be something missing, something wrong, something clunky, and if you stick to it—read it out loud, read it backwards, look at it from a distance—the mistake should declare itself."

Fool Your Brain

By this point, you have read your manuscript dozens of times. This can make it hard to spot errors, since you know what is supposed to be there. Several tricks can help you see your work with fresh eyes.

Peschel says, "Reading the same prose in the same font can cause the eye to skate over mistakes, so change it up. Boost the size or change the color of the text or try a different font. Use free programs such as Calibre or Scrivener to create an EPUB or MOBI file that can be read on an ebook reader."

Renner also recommends changing your font. Print your manuscript on paper if you are used to working on the computer screen. Finally, move away from your normal working place to review your manuscript. "These little tricks will help you see the manuscript as a reader instead of as a writer," she says.

"An effective way to check the flow of your story is to read it aloud or have someone read it to you," Lane notes. "Better yet, record your story so you can play it back multiple times if necessary. Recruiting another person to do this will give you a better idea of what a reader will see." Some software, such as MS Word

2010, has a text-to-voice feature to provide a read aloud. Lane adds, "If recording your story yourself, run your finger just below each line as you read to catch omitted or misspelled words and missing commas, quote marks, and periods. Also, enunciate clearly and *punctuate* as you read, pausing slightly at each comma and a bit longer at end punctuation. While this won't catch every error, it will give you a good sense of flow, highlight many shortcomings, and test whether your dialogue is smooth and realistic."

Some people even recommend reading your manuscript backwards, sentence by sentence. While this will not help you track the flow of the story, it focuses attention on the sentence level. Finally, certain computer programs and web platforms are designed to identify spelling and grammar errors, and in some cases even identify clichés. While these programs are not recommended for developmental editing, they can be an option for later polishing.

Now you are ready for final proofreading. Do a last read-through yourself if you are confident in your technical abilities, or pass the manuscript to a professional, especially if you plan to self-publish.

Looking at all the steps to successful self-editing may be daunting, but break them down into pieces, take a step at a time, and do not rush your revisions. "This whole process could easily take several months," Renner says. "Don't shoot yourself in the foot by putting your manuscript out too soon."

Each time you go through this process you will be developing your skills, making the next time easier. "Like anything else, self-editing becomes easier the more you do it," Peschel says. "When it becomes second-nature, you'll have made a big leap toward becoming a professional writer." And you'll give every manuscript its best shot at standing out in a competitive market.

A SEEK-AND-DESTROY MISSION: REDUCE THE PASSIVE VOICE

BY KATHERINE AYRES

In the old days, settlers built their homes to suit the geography. They situated a house in a location unlikely to flood, near a good water source, near transportation. They also employed a number of passive solar features that architects and designers still use today: planting an evergreen windbreak on a northern exposure, placing a deciduous tree at a southern window, or using brick or stone flooring to capture and retains the sun's heat. These passive techniques helped a home operate well, with no further action.

For writers, construction in the passive voice weakens the action of a story; it squelches conflict. It can also result in more telling than showing, eliciting yawns from the reader or editor. The most frequent perpetrator of passivity is the verb *to be,* in its many and various forms. Most writers understand the limitations of using the passive voice, but it can creep into a manuscript in insidious ways and work its wickedness. Seek and destroy passivity and welcome in active, vital prose.

Diagnostics

In a first draft, you may not concentrate on the subtleties of word choice. Using great images and power verbs, creating a setting that jumps into three-dimensions, and bringing to life characters who speak with clarity and authority take the lead in a first draft, not worries about repetitions or the dreaded to be verbs. Ride that rollercoaster of action from opening chapter to conclusion, just getting the story out on the page. First revisions attack structural issues. Why finesse a page or a paragraph or a chapter, if the story doesn't need it and cuts or drastic restructuring is? Later revisions address character, setting, voices, dialogue. Once those elements are in place, set the stage for powering up the language.

The find-and-replace function on your computer serves you well here. Locate all the various forms of *to be* and highlight them. For the writer who prefers to work on paper at this stage instead of on screen, changing the verbs to all caps works equally well. Make sure to change only whole-word finds, or great nouns like *werewolf* (were) and verbs like *inscribe* (be) will also show up. After the find-and-replace action the offending passivity will pop right up in bright, florescent yellow and stare you in the face. Most word processing programs also count the number of replacements made: I found 200 replacements in one document recently, and 97 in another.

In my manuscripts, the dreaded yellow words tend to cluster. Bunches appear on a page or two, then only in a few scattered places. Those trouble spots often describe settings or habitual actions rather than active, physical scenes. They need work, but at least they no longer hide like bedbugs, waiting to come out and bite me while I sleep.

Treatment

Diagnosis of the passive voice happens quickly. Treatment takes time and employs multiple strategies. Work on a chapter or two at a sitting, to keep your thoughts and language choices fresh. For a first cut, go after the easiest ones: *there were* phrases.

- "There were three baby robins in the nest" becomes "Three baby robins crowded the nest and cheeped for food."
- "*There was* a rickety plank bridge across the creek and I was scared to cross" becomes "Splintery gray boards bridged the creek. When I stepped on the first, it shifted under foot, and I stepped back fast. I can't swim.

In both cases, the revised version carries more description, more power and detail, and less telling. The changes also allow integrate description and action seamlessly. When I make such revisions, the character responsiveness increases almost naturally.

The second set of cuts is to passive forms consisting of a *to be* verb and an *-ing* verb form.

- "Missy and Anna *were sitting* at the lunch table and whispering, probably about me" becomes "Missy and Anna *sat* at the lunch table and whispered, probably about me. Like they did yesterday, last week, last month. Like they will tomorrow, next week, forever. Maybe I'll spill some milk on them. Chocolate."

Even if you want to make an action habitual (*were sitting* or *is sitting*), be aware that these versions of the verb are less powerful and more limiting. The substitution of the simple past tense (*sat*) allows the elaboration in this example—in the past was yesterday, last week, last month, and prompts more description and meaning. This type of revision carries me as a writer further into the story in ways I find fresh and unexpected. I had no clue when I sat to write this example that I would spill chocolate milk. It just happened. With a bit of luck, such energy carries the reader right along with me.

State-of-being verbs do little more than convey basic, boring information. They rarely offer details, specifics, or reasons for reader empathy.

- Jamie was sick. His head ached and he had a fever.

In this example, two sentences repeat some of the same information; the second gives details to flesh out the first. In such situations, I simply cut the first. Then, if I wish, I have room to elaborate.

- Jamie's head ached and he had a fever. His stomach felt like an overinflated balloon that might just erupt. He dragged himself to the bathroom.

Dramatic Potential

Think drama; think theater. Theater means *actors*, acting parts on stage, not *passives*, sitting quietly, unless the play is *Waiting for Godot*, and even there the characters do talk and disagree. Actors initiate stage business, most often conflict that results in dramatic scenes. Passivity implies receiving the actions of others, rather than kicking up one's own; it can imply victimhood, not power. Readers, like theatergoers, do not generally connect to passive characters that seem frozen and unable to act. They prefer characters that make choices, take chances, risk mistakes.

To make writing sing, and characters come to life, turn to active, *crunchy* verbs. If chosen carefully, power verbs can accomplish multiple purposes: They can show the action or situation with precision; they can characterize the actor; they can set the mood. In the examples below, two actions occur, an entrance and a response to a piece of furniture. The characters and moods and meanings vary greatly, and the reader develops certain expectations, due to the two simple verbs in each.

- Maria marched into the room and stomped up to the teacher's desk. Confrontation coming?
- Jason tiptoed into the room and crept up to the teacher's desk. A sneak thief?
- Emma stormed into the room and swept past the teacher's desk. Drama queen?

Each of the examples uses two verbs that describe moving through space. Using *went* and *walked*—rather than marched/ stomped, tiptoed/crept, stormed/swept—would lose the power and specific meaning. Verbs can activate writing.

We all need to refresh our vocabulary and stretch our minds and language sometimes. Try these two exercises to help. First, play thesaurus, and generate a long list of synonyms for a boring verb, like *went* or *walked*. Search your own mind for, in this case, fun and comfortable or not-so-comfortable means of perambulation. Even act out the verbs you choose. A second exercise is to attend cooking school in your mind. Think about a chef and scribble down all the verbs you can imagine a chef performing in a large restaurant kitchen, from blend to sauté to submerge to decapitate and beyond. Then look at novel ways to use such verbs in your own writing.

- The morning sun *baked* my shoulders as I climbed above the tree line.
- The big table *chopped* the room in half—good kids on one side, not-so-good on the other.
- All around him, creatures *stirred*, rustled, *spiced* the fall air with danger.
- "Go ahead, *fry* me. See if I care," Lucas told his mother. "I don't want to go to the stupid party anyway."

You can try the same exercise imagining a dentist's office, construction site, or farm—all active occupations that will help generate active, interesting verb lists. Use only those verbs you feel suitable for your writing; do not sound precious or uppity or forced. Honor and respect your own writer's voice. So, in most of my fiction, people do not actually perambulate; they run, scramble, scoot, or inch along.

Would You or Wouldn't You?

Writers often use *would* to describe general conditions, usually in the past, rather than the precise action of a particular moment. The word shows up frequently in backstory and can signal a passive information dump—lots of facts but little reason to care about them.

> ■ When I was in school, Daddy would always go on about getting good grades and achieving. I would always shrug and make some reply that looked like I agreed with him, and then quickly stuff food into my mouth. Now I've been accepted into medical school, but who knows if I can go the distance?

So what? This example presents no people in motion, no action. Good writing, on the other hand portrays specific moments in time, and can also convey that these moments represent a long stretch of actions and behaviors. To banish the *woulds*, build a mini-scene that will make the characters show their habitual behavior in a critical moment.

> ■ It began my first day of kindergarten. At the dinner table, Daddy started in. "How'd it go today? How many A's did you get? Who's the smartest kid in your class?"

I shrugged. I didn't know what an A meant and I didn't even know the names of the all kids yet. So I loaded up my fork and shoved in a ton of mashed potatoes.

He kept at it, all the way through high school and even when I went off to college. So now I've been accepted into medical school, and no surprise, I hate it. I want to quit.

As I wrote the second version, after losing the two *woulds*, I found myself growing more and more interested in the character. Male or female? Does this person have a weight problem after stuffing years' worth of mashed potatoes into the mouth? Will the field of psychiatry attract him or her, to help untangle a twisted psyche? How does the father behave at the current point in time and how does the offspring react? Have they ever experienced direct conflict?

The writing we all want to create and the writing we want to read focuses on the action, the scene, complete with dialogue; it feels like it takes place in real time rather than habitual time. So would I? Would I use the passive voice when the more active voice sings to me? No, I wouldn't.

(Note: I confess, I slashed, cut and otherwise destroyed many *to be* verbs in the construction of this article; I chose the ones that remain simply to provide negative examples.)

SECRET WEAPONS IN CHARACTER DEVELOPMENT

BY KATHERINE AYRES

In Greek mythology, Athena emerged fully formed from the head of Zeus, and took her place immediately in the pantheon as goddess of wisdom. The birthing process seems both amazingly easy (no nine months of waiting) and potentially excruciating. Athena's birth is an image of exactly what fiction writers hope for: a character who emerges from the brain, well-developed, fully formed, with strengths and weaknesses, and enough potential for interesting dilemmas to be ready to take her place in a plot.

Entire how-to books have been written on character development, with discussions of everything from what your character carries in his pocket, to backstory and family dynamics, to situational ethics that ask what your character would do in a series of imagined scenarios. When it comes down to it, the ultimate point is to know a character's secrets—the *things* that matter to him, the internal motivations, unspoken conflicts—and see where they lead.

Uncovering

In 1952, a television show called *I've Got a Secret* premiered. Its premise was simple: While four celebrity panelists were blindfolded, a person would enter and whisper a secret to the host, which would be revealed on the television screen for viewers. The panelists asked yes-or-no questions to try to discover the secret. During its original 21-year run, viewers consistently ranked the show in the top 30 on television—people love snooping about in other people's business, and particularly love uncovering a secret.

For writers, the devising and disclosing of secrets is a powerful tool that can help shape character and plot. The writer's job, however, is not to provide the quick pop of entertainment found in a 10-minute TV segment. It is to create and reveal fully formed characters. One technique for writing compelling fiction is to invent a batch of secrets and then determine what character owns which secret. As the story unfolds, the writer drops clues so the reader will begin to ferret out the secrets and make guesses about how the story might resolve.

We read fiction because we like to discover and connect with people, even if they are made up. As in real life, we like those people to be interesting, quirky, and not a hundred percent predictable. We like to see what happens when they are placed in tough situations and forced to endure hardship. Most often plot comes from character—strengths, weaknesses, life history, and of course, secrets.

The skillful writer will make use of a wide variety of secrets in constructing a dramatic piece of fiction, whether the secrets belong to the character instrinsically or behaviorally, were done to the character by others or by people in the past, and those the character discovers in other people.

Behavioral Secrets

Avoiding punishment, embarrassment, or shame is a powerful motivator for many people. When we have done something we think others will not condone, we are likely to hide the evidence, change the subject, keep silent, and even lie to avoid exposure. The worse the behavior, the more fiercely we try to guard our secrets.

Behavioral secrets have a developmental dimension; that is, in real life and in fiction, they can increase in toxicity as a person moves from childhood to adulthood. Snitching cookies can give way to stealing lipsticks to embezzlement. The first task of the writer is to select secrets appropriate for the character and for the tone of the book. Stealing those cookies might make an excellent secret for a young child character, who might then blame a sibling, stuffed animal, or imaginary friend for the loss. But cookie theft could also figure in a story for older kids—what if the shipment of Girl Scout Cookies disappears? Or the theft could be accomplished by a gang who hijack trucks and resell the contents. The consequences of discovery follow similar developmental paths— a scolding from Mom, getting kicked out of Scouts, time in the slammer. It is all a matter of scale.

A precise matchup between character and secret can be powerful. The member of the clergy who dabbles in witchcraft, the straight-A student who cheats, the elementary school principal who is discovered to have kiddie porn on his computer, the banker with a gambling addiction: These individuals have much to lose if their secrets come to light, and they will go to great lengths to protect themselves. In a well-written mystery or suspense novel such toxic secrets abound, casting suspicion on a wide range of characters, people who would embrace the dark side rather than have their own darkness revealed.

Historical Secrets

Sometimes our secrets are not fully our own, and are passed down to us. A famous real life example is the history of Thomas Jefferson and Sally Hemings. Various sources, including oral history and DNA analysis of descendents, point to an intimate connection between Jefferson and Hemings, a slave. If Jefferson himself did not father Heming's children, as some dispute, a close male relative of his surely did. Yet this particular secret has taken hundreds of years to emerge from the shadows.

Similarly, historical secrets can act as motivators of action or character qualities, even if the behavior is in the near or distant past. Does a man want it known that his grandfather was a Nazi? Probably not. Would such a life history cause him to espouse different political or social beliefs than the man whose grandfather helped people escape from the Nazis?

What baggage will a girl or young woman carry when she discovers that her mother was a prostitute and her father a client? Or that her father, whom she has been told is dead, is actually a serial killer? A priest? How will this knowledge impact her character if she discovers it as a child? As a teen? As an adult about to bear a child?

Most families have dark historic secrets, and ferreting them out can provoke equally dark actions in the present. Imagine then setting such a scenario in a small town or an intimate neighborhood where one person's history intersects with many others' over time. If decades ago, a gang of three boys set fire to a house, killing some of the occupants, and a present-day character discovers that her now-deceased grandfather was one of the boys, what will his co-conspirators or their offspring do to keep their identities hidden? What risk does the situation pose for the person doing the discovering? Secrets of this sort can have interesting plot consequences, as well as character building potential.

Secrets of Identity

It's not easy being green, as Kermit the Frog well knows. His essential froggy nature, however, is visible to all. Until fairly recently many people living in the gay, lesbian, bisexual, and transgender community spent much of their lives closeted; they kept their true sexual identities hidden from all but the most trusted of their friends and families. To come out of the closet placed people at risk in many ways: Occupational success, social interactions, even personal safety could be compromised by having such knowledge made public. Some people lived double lives—a public, conventional life and a secret, private one.

Even today, with same-sex marriage legal in more jurisdictions all the time, coming to terms with one's own sexual identity is a private and intensely personal journey, especially for teenagers who are in the midst of a broad process of self-discovery. Sadly, the newspapers report true stories about kids whose secrets are exposed before they are comfortable with themselves, with tragic consequences, including suicide. The fact of a suicide itself can be a closely held family secret.

Some secrets of identity also occur by choice, not by chance. There is a whole subgenre featuring people who secretly assume alternative identities for their life's work. The unmasking of a spy or a mole provides high drama in real life as well as in fiction, as character angst and plot development opportunities abound when a character holds a secret of identity. Or imagine a slightly less toxic situation in which a teenager assumes a novel and invented personality and life history during a summer camp experience—geek goes goth. What effects do such secrets of identity have on the internal life and the external actions of a person? To what lengths will the honorable Dr. Jekyll have to go to avoid public disclosure of his alter ego, Mr. Hyde?

Other People's Secrets

When a close friend confides a secret—I'm pregnant, I'm getting a divorce, I have a crush on Luke, I cheated on the math test—what happens next? Most people have an array of friends and over time they learn, sometimes painfully, which ones may be trusted with secrets and which are blabbers. If a person has news that is ready for full disclosure, the loose-lipped friends make wonderful town criers. The rest of the time, folks usually choose to whisper to someone who knows how to keep a secret.

Go beyond categorizing a character as either strong and silent, a gossip, or something in between. Find opportunities to *pressurize* a character and probe for his deepest moral convictions. Suppose a friend discloses to a high school boy that he is collecting weapons and building bombs. While teenagers have strong in-group loyalty, the wave of public violence and school shootings might cause the character to break that unwritten rule and rat out the friend before disaster occurs. Or perhaps the character keeps the secret and the disaster does occur. In either case, how does a person live with the results?

When dealing with other people's secrets, the writer has the opportunity to understand both the character's everyday person-ality and habits, and the choices he might make under great stress. If the character is inclined toward keeping secrets but feels morally compelled to tell a particularly toxic one, tremendous internal conflict is possible, which is great fuel for the writer. Alternatively, if a character is a talker, what will it take to keep silence—threats, personal danger, danger to others?

Discovering Secrets

Most of us seem to enjoy having privileged information, know-ing the dark, hidden facts that others do not. Another character type to explore is one who likes to ferret out secrets—a snoop. This comes naturally to most children. Visit Grandma's new house and all drawers must be opened, all closets explored. But many adults also snoop. Some may not have ever opened up someone else's bathroom medicine cabinet for no reason, but many have. Is my friend on birth control or using drugs? Does she have a serious illness that she hasn't told anyone about? Does a protagonist suspect snooping and develop prevention strategies such as a mostly empty medicine cabinet, or one filled with marbles that spill out and make a racket when the door opens—a great conflict-filled and humorous image for a plot.

More seriously, if a character does snoop, what will she do with the information gained? Suppose she finds prescription painkillers in a larger than expected quantity; will she confront the friend, suggest rehab, tell the boyfriend, broadcast it to the universe? Each of these options described a different personality, a different set of beliefs, in short, a different character.

A final example comes from one of the great American novels. In *To Kill a Mockingbird*, Atticus, Scout, and Jem Finch will carry the secrets of Boo Radley forever, a conclusion that is one of the many wonderful reasons to love their story. Some secrets are meant to stay secret. Even if discovery occurs during the course of a story, it may belong exclusively to the characters making it, and to the reader, but not to the rest of book's universe. What a delicious sense of being party to a particularly valuable secret.

CONSIDER THE SOURCE: FACT-CHECKING

BY CHRISTINA HAMLETT

An editor at the *New York Sun* famously received a question about Santa Claus from a little girl named Virginia O'Hanlon in 1897. Her father, she explained, had told her, "If you see it in the *Sun*, it's so." Francis P. Church's thoughtful response to Virginia— "Yes, there is a Santa Claus"—went on to become perhaps the most enduring newspaper editorial ever. And the story of Virginia, her father, and the editor reinforces the notion that certain information sources should be deemed incontrovertible.

I was reminded of this a few months ago when a ghostwriting client who insisted on doing her own fact-checking set forth a statement that rang false on multiple levels. "But I got it off of Wikipedia," she said, adding with childlike innocence (echoing a certain funny and successful State Farm television commercial with a "French male model"), "They can't post things on the Internet that aren't true." How then, I challenged her, could a designer friend of mine mischievously fib that he invented chiffon, a bogus claim that has yet to be challenged, seven years after he posted it?

Purposeful high-jinks aside, there is no shortage of erroneous content being touted as truthful floating around cyberspace. It can also be found in newspapers, magazines, textbooks, media interviews, back-fence gossip and even personal journals passed down through the generations. A rumor may be tweaked each time it is retold with innocent or tumultuous consequences in a family or community. Writers should have no tolerance: It is part of their profession always to verify the origins and validity of a "fact" before extending it to another audience in their work.

Shake the Family Tree

Throughout my childhood my grandmother regaled me with stories about how she and her siblings were adopted from a bleak and grimy London orphanage. This Dickensian tale made for a much more interesting narrative than saying her actual life begn on a Nebraska homestead. In fairness, hers could have been a false memory made by relatives she had no reason to disbelieve. Not until my husband did genealogical research into my family and discovered alternative information—facts—did I begin to wonder just how many other colorful myths had embellished my family tree.

As dearly as you may love them, you cannot take every family anecdote as truth. Every generation brings it own interpretation of events and causation to the table. As a writer responsbile for accuracy, you will always need to dig deep. For any kind of family history, whether you are investigating for a memoir or for an investigative journalism piece, or any other, many fact-checking resources are available for information about individuals, some free and some fee-based. Writers and others can accessing public information related to vital statistics, licenses, property deeds and mortgages, business registrations and incorporations, military service and criminal records. While many writers start genealogical sleuthing at Ancestry.Com and FamilySearch.org, additional sources for fact-checking include:

- Census Records: www.censusrecords.com
- Census Finder: www.censusfinder.com

- Cyndi's List: www.cyndislist.com/categories
- Death Records Online: www.myheritage.com
- Ellis Island Records: www.ellisislandrecords.org
- ObituariesHelp: http://obituarieshelp.org
- SearchSystems: http://publicrecords.searchsystems. net
- United States Vital Records Information: http://vitalrec.com/index.html

A cautionary note: The data you find in public records searches are, alas, only as accurate as the person who entered or transcribed the source document. Ellis Island records, for instance, are a reflection of port officials who sometimes took their best guess on how to spell the names of immigrants and the towns from which they came. Also problematic are scanned documents from faded ledgers in which it is difficult to discern whether a number is a 1 or a 7, a 3 or an 8. People also fudged marriage and birth dates to skirt any stigma of illegitimacy. Even the validity of a diary entry hinges on whether the author intended for it to ever be read by someone else.

Expert Testimony

If you were going to launch a new business, would you listen to the advice of someone who has actually started one too, or the recommendations of an avid blogger? Or listen more to the reports of a journalist interested in the process, who studied it for several years, but who has never actually worked in the industry at a high level? Or listen even more to the firsthand stories of employees of a new business? The authenticity of the data you collect depends on the quality of primary sources, but also on the qualifications of secondary source authors you rely on. For instance:

- Does the author possess expertise in your subject, including degrees, licenses, or certifications? Or has the author established journalistic expertise in the subject.

■ How many years has the author worked in this field? Has he or she won any awards?

■ Is the tone of the material unbiased and objective or is it written with a perspective that suggests sarcasm, chauvinism, or ethnocentricity, no matter how subtle?

■ Are claims and opinions in the source piece, whether primary or secondary, substantiated by reliable outside sources?

■ Are the cited sources from well-known institutions or government entities? (i.e., WebMD vs. a mommy blog about sneezes)

■ Was the research underwritten by an organization with a monetary stake in the outcome? (i.e., a drug study funded by a pharmaceutical company)

■ Have there been peer reviews of the source content?

■ Are your source's quotes consistent with what you know about the quoted individual's personality, knowledge base, and accessibility?

■ Have foreign phrases been accurately translated?

■ Does the material adhere to journalistic standards? (i.e., if it has spelling, grammar, and punctuation errors, does it come from a reliable organization).

The Rule of Three

A standard journalistic rule is to verify research findings with three independent sources. That does not include listing three books penned by the same author, no matter how good the reputation of a particular authors, because everyone is prone to error, misinterpretation, or bias. A college professor of mine would quip that the one fact in a document that always appears to be the most watertight is often the leakiest to begin with.

The rule of three supporting sources especially applies to newspapers and television stations that embrace strong political slants in reporting stories of the day. No better example of this is the ongoing clash between liberal and conservative media outlets when a candidate or elected official's competence is under scrutiny. Each side serves up its own mix of pictures, interviews, chronologies and syntax to justify its position and manipulate public opinion. As fervently as each side believes in the rightness of the views it espouses, however, the underlying motives can create distance from the truth. To make informed choices about what to write in your blog, article, thesis, or book, sift through the rhetoric, weigh both sets of arguments, and study the content. While relying on primary sources is essential, other sources that can help include:

- FactCheck.org: www.factcheck.org
- Politico: www.politico.com
- Snopes: www.snopes.com/politics/politics.asp
- ScamBusters: www.scambusters.org
- The Fact Checker: www.washingtonpost.com/blogs/fact-checker
- PolitiFact: www.politifact.com

Is a photograph, arguably a primary source, worth a thousand words of credibility? Not necessarily anymore. Today's digital image editing applications makes *adjustments* easier to do than ever. Anything can be Photoshopped. And episodes of using previously published pictures to support a later event—say, of protesters from a past controversy to illustrate an unfolding and completely different issue—are far from unheard of. So, fact-check your photographs too. Reverse image search engines such as TinEye (www.tineye.com) and Google's Inside Search enable you to research a photograph's origins and its modified versions as well. An excellent article on photo forensics can be found in the *Columbia Journalism Review* (www.cjr.org/the_news_frontier/

detecting_fake_photos_with_dig.php?page=all.).

Even eyewitnesses to historical events tend to view things through a subjective lens, especially the perceived impact events might have on their personal lives. Ascribing motives to individuals who lived in the 1820s, for example, is futile and bound to be inaccurate when measured from a twenty-first-century perspective. Also be aware of individuals' changing perspectives. Consider how many autobiographies you have read in which the authors devote multiple chapters to their childhoods. Would a four-year-old really have the awareness and sophistication to psychoanalyze the adults that peopled his or her childhood? Or is the emotion in those chapters, whether humor or pathos or anger, a rearview rationalization of an author now in midlife? Unless there are other family members or friends to corroborate the *facts*, many memories must be measured before they are fully believed.

Numbers, Names, & Roads to Nowhere

Whenever you decide to incorporate recent or historical dates, never rely 100 percent on your own memory. Check, double-check, and then triple-check. Again, always rely on primary sources and follow the rule of three. But the following websites will help you get your bearings, and provide cross-references to arts, science, politics, discoveries, and pop culture:

- Historical Timeline: www.historicaltimeline.com
- HyperHistory: www.hyperhistory.com/online_n2/History_n2/a.html
- Animated Atlas: www.animatedatlas.com/timeline.html
- This Day in History: www.history.com/this-day-in-history

The memory and perspectives of historians, scientists, and others also need confirmation. What is the year of publication on that textbook you found in the library? In his latest release,

Founding Myths: Stories That Hide Our Patriotic Past, author Ray Raphael says that although newer books are careful to be inclusive and reflect multicultural outlooks, but that has not always been the case. Folkloric legends and political and social *correctness* sometimes undermined truthful accountings. For instance, FDR was never portrayed as wheelchair bound, most likely to convey the strength of a leader during the Depression and Great War. To reconstruct an accurate picture of the past requires that multiple narratives, written at different times, be considered and weighed.

Even numbers can be deceptive, or just wrong. If you tell your readers that Eli Whitney invented the cotton gin in 1793 and then go on to say how much his invention changed Southern cotton production 250 years ago, check your math.

Percentages and lists can be tricky territory, too. Does your "Top 10 Tips for Auditions" really contain 10, or only 9? If you read a survey that identifies a voter population as 63 percent Republican, 31 percent Democrat, and 11 percent undecided, how much of that break-out can you really trust if it the numbers do not total 100? Nor can you rely on the accuracy of cookbook authors who, despite exact measurements in a test kitchen, will sometimes instruct readers to add butter, herbs, or a garnish not included in the list of ingredients.

Details matter. If you are writing about real people and real places, there is no excuse for misspelling their names, especially when so many resources are available today to verify the correct version. Even after you have checked the correct spelling, however, how many times have you typed it three different ways in haste Johnson, Johnston, Johnsen—in the same document? To counter this problem, use the spellchecker function in Word or another word programming application to add the names to your computer's dictionary; the spellchecker can then catch any misspellings and make it easier for you to correct them.

Have you referred to someone in the present tense—"Marjorie Taylor loves a good bargain"—when, in fact, Marjorie died back in 1989? Even worse, have you labeled someone as *the late Marjorie*," when she is still very much alive? A colleague of mine who writes celebrity news swears by a quirky but factually accurate website called Dead or Alive (www.deadoraliveinfo.com), which allows her to confirm who is still among us, who has passed on, and even causes of death.

Travel writers face yet another set of challenges in sharing accurate tips with fellow globetrekkers. That wonderful bistro on the Left Bank where he or she had a delightful lunch two years ago may now be out of business. The rail service that was such a cheap way to get around has tripled its fees in response to fuel costs. And what about Mother Nature wreaking havoc on seaside communities that have yet to rebuild?

While no one has a crystal ball to keep pace with changes both here and abroad, directing readers to websites that have not been maintained or phone numbers that have been disconnected is a sure way to jeopardize your credibility. As time-consuming as it is, always verify phone and fax numbers, email addresses, and website urls before you put them into your article or book. It is also essential that you match the right currency with the right country (www.nationsonline.org/oneworld/currencies.htm). Giving directions? Drive the route yourself; online mapping has its perks but rarely will MapQuest, Google Maps, and Bing agree with one another on the best way to get somewhere.

There is no substitute for thorough research. Time and persistence are your most valuable tools in establishing a fact's plausibility. All it takes is one error to cast doubt on an entire body of work, whether yours or someone else's. In the words of Albert Einstein, "Anyone who doesn't take truth seriously in small matters cannot be trusted in large ones, either."

BUSINESS

WE'RE ALL JUST PEOPLE: BUILDING GREAT EDITOR–WRITER RELATIONSHIPS

BY LESLIE J. WYATT

There was a time when editors courted budding authors, labored with them as they grew, stuck with them through thick and thin. This is not that time, and the publishing world continues to change rapidly. Yet writers and editors still collaborate in a synergistic mixture of respect, creativity, and literary discernment. With some insight into their world, cultivating good relationships with editors is not complicated for writers. To this end, we have asked a variety of editors and writers to comment on their working relationships.

■ **Writer's Guide**: *What do you wish writers knew about an editor's job?*

Chris Ryan, Editor at Portland, Oregon-based *Fresh Cup Magazine*: "Editors get tons of emails—some of these are from freelance writers, but we're also getting press releases, emails from colleagues at our publication about internal business, and much more. As such, we aren't always able to respond to queries immediately."

Carol Saller, Senior Manuscript Editor at the University of Chicago Press, author, and an editor of the *Chicago Manual of Style*: "You aren't my only author—at any given time I'm working with between 10 and 20 other writers. If I can't immediately recall something we discussed, it's not always because I'm an idiot (although I might be). When I change something in your manuscript, it isn't necessarily because I think my way is better or that you are wrong. Often it's because I'm following your publisher's style manual. I might even prefer it the way you wrote it. I'm probably willing to negotiate it. Also, a big chunk of the work I have to do on a text involves wrangling the word processing the writer used. I love writers who resist getting fancy with fonts and shading."

Cheryl Matthews, Associate Editor at Boyds Mills Press: "As a children's publisher that accepts unsolicited manuscripts, [our] editors review every project that is received; therefore, it can take up to three months before the author receives a response. The most common reasons for which we send form rejections include: The project didn't fit within our future publishing list; the guidelines weren't followed; the writing wasn't polished; and, surprisingly often, the content wasn't for children. . . . Our response to a manuscript always reflects our own perspective, and we hope that authors understand that another publishing house may view their work differently."

Kelly Milner Halls, critically acclaimed author specializing in quirky, well-researched nonfiction for reluctant readers: "First and foremost, remember your editor is a living, breathing human being, just like you are. She (or he) is trying to do the best job she can coordinating a very complicated editorial process—juggling the demands of her authors, her illustrators, her art department, the marketing team, and sales. Keep that in mind before you get too antsy about response times or tones."

Patricia Hermes, award-winning author, lecturer, and speaker: "This is a professional relationship. The editor is not your best friend and should not be treated as such. He or she might become a friend during the course of working together; that often happens. But initial contact should always be professional."

■ Writer's Guide: *What do you wish writers knew about editors in general?*

Hermes: "Remember that there is no such thing as *editors in general*. Each editor is unique, as different in his or her likes and dislikes, as different in personalities as authors. This is why a manuscript might be sold to one editor, after having been rejected by 10 previous editors. (Think Madeline L'Engle!)"

Ryan: "We may have a slight power advantage in the writer-editor relationship, but there is no need to be sycophantic toward us. When I get an introduction to a query, I much prefer a matter-of-fact, friendly tone to one that calls me 'Mr. Ryan' and thanks me profusely for my time."

Matthews: "Although unrealistic, editors would still love to publish all the projects that cross their desks, because we know that the author's heart and soul lives in each submission. We truly enjoy the process of bookmaking, from the first read, through its many revisions, to the wonderful aroma of a freshly printed book. Even though the submission pile seems like it's too overwhelming to tackle, editors do it anyway—because this is where we find buried treasure."

Halls: "Editors are very creative people, but they are creative in a different way than you are. They are not competition. They are editorial partners, so it's important to make a good match when it comes to working together on a book. That's why you shouldn't take a rejection personally. You don't want an editor who can't fall in love with your project, so it's a professional courtesy when the wrong editor admits it's not her cup of tea, so you can move on to the right choice."

Saller: "[Editors] aren't all sticklers. They aren't all frustrated writers. They do mostly wear glasses."

■ *Writer's Guide: How can a writer cultivate a good relationship with an editor?*

Ryan: "[For *Fresh Cup*,] Send a friendly introductory note before sending a query. We get so many queries that it's hard to give them all equal attention. Having a personality behind a query can go a long way toward an editor giving it extra consideration. Send friendly—but not pressure-filled—check-ins between assignments. Editors often have so many freelance writers that someone can slip through the cracks, so these reminder emails are a huge help. Establish a thorough understanding of an assignment before taking it on. This can mean more work from me at the outset in explaining what I'm looking for, but it almost always pays off when the writer turns in a story that doesn't need to undergo huge rewrites."

Matthews: "Consider the three R's: *Respect* time. *There aren't enough hours in a day* is true for all of us, and editors are no exception. Since many projects are being cultivated for future publishing lists, editors are working on several projects per season for as far out as four years. The editor is moving the author's work along the book-making path as quickly as possible.

Return phone calls, emails, and revised manuscripts in a timely manner. This almost always ensures the continued momentum of the project.

Revise. This is a necessary task for all manuscripts. Keep an open mind to the suggestions and comments from the editor. Remember that there are many possible approaches to any challenge. If you disagree with your editor's suggestion on something, you may find your own, different approach to solving the challenge."

Halls: "Don't take editorial requests personally. Your editor isn't calling your baby *ugly*. She's working hard to make it as perfect as it can be. She's fine tuning with an expert eye what you've created, no matter how painful it sometimes seems. So look at her editorial notes as positive steps toward launching a successful book. Your book may begin as a solo effort, but it continues as a team project, and you want to be known and respected as a good team player."

Saller: "Remember that the goal is collaboration on making a great experience for the reader. Accept that even if you have a PhD in English, you may be clueless about your publisher's house style and developments in grammar and style since you last studied it. Also, don't get competitive or defensive. Although it might feel as though the copy editor is marking your text as *wrong*, she doesn't feel superior doing it. You're the writer—your editor knows it's much easier to tweak writing than to put it on paper in the first place. You have complementary and overlapping talents that can combine to benefit the work."

Hermes: "Very occasionally, one might meet up with an editor who is not pleasing to work with, not compatible. That can be true of any job. Just do your best; maintain your dignity and calm. Resolve not to work with him or her again. And when the project is finished, don't gossip!"

■ **Writer's Guide**: *What do you admire about your complementary colleagues—editors or writers?*

Ryan: "The ability [of writers] to meet deadlines, which is hugely, hugely important and makes life much easier for me; turning in clean copy that doesn't need a ton of edits; and the aforementioned pinning down of exactly what the editor is looking for from the story at the time of the assignment."

Saller: "Well (ahem), I am also a writer, so I don't want to sound fatheaded. But in writers who aren't me, I admire great prose styling. When someone writes elegantly, with thoughtful word choice and rhythm, I'm happy to keep the red pencil in check and just stand out of the way."

Matthews: "Courage. Writing is such a personal journey, whether it's the writer's first book or twentieth book. It takes guts to send a manuscript out into the publishing world, knowing that it will be measured and scrutinized.

Imagination—this is where the story begins.

Tenacity. It's a writer's middle name. Tenacity keeps the author working under any and all circumstances. It empowers the author to keep sending out manuscripts in the face of rejection; it enables a writer to hone his or her skills. Without the unyielding tenacity of the writer there would be no written word."

Halls: "I admire how an editor can step into something you've managed for three to five years and see it as new. I admire how she carefully weeds someone else's garden, and slowly, patiently makes it her own, too. I admire the gentle way an editor weaves a powerful team to transform words to beautiful books. I admire their vision and determination, and the way [children's editors] reach out to kids to be sure that vision is clear and well-informed. Editors are remarkable people."

Hermes: "They work hard for very little money!"

■ **Writer's Guide**: *Any further advice?*

Saller: "Be warm and honest, and be open to a genuine collaboration. In a perfect relationship, the writer loves my suggestions, but also argues with a few, and we have some stimulating back-and-forth parries as we figure out what's best. We each learn something; in the end the book has as few errors as possible; everyone is happy with it; and the writer puts in the acknowledgments that she couldn't have done it without me, which of course is untrue, but nice to hear anyway."

Hermes: "Never, never, never gossip or bad-mouth another editor. You might find yourself working with that editor someday. Also, be timely. If you say you'll have a project completed on a certain day, have it completed on that day—or even better, a week early."

Ryan: "Many of us are doing the copy editing ourselves, so we're eternally grateful for well-written copy. We are most likely to take to pitches that resonate with our readership, so please know the publication before you pitch to them. In the case of our magazine, know coffee or tea at least a little bit."

Halls: "I think it's really important not to get a preconceived notion in your head about how [the] editorial relationship should look. Just let each one bloom as it does, and find its individual beauty. Respect is a valuable element of your editorial relationship. Don't argue. Listen with an open mind."

Matthews: "Stay open to honing your craft. There are so many ways the writer can do this: online courses, local workshops, conferences, and joining critique groups. Even seasoned authors continue to attend venues where they are students. Writers are never too old or too published to learn from others. The most important task [for children's writers], if you call this a task, is to read, read, read children's literature, including poetry and all other genres. Read your work aloud. By joining a critique group you allow others to read your work. Hearing your own writing read by someone else gives you a different perspective. And, most important, write, write, and write some more. And then revise, revise, and revise again. Then submit. Your editor will recognize how serious you are by your writing, your willingness to revise, and your enthusiasm to ride the waves to publication."

Onward & Upward: The Art of the Elevator Pitch

By Christina Hamlett

The last thing you expected to see as you walked down an empty stretch of beach was a brass lamp sticking out of the sand, its distinctive shape instantly reminiscent of *The Arabian Nights*. Without thinking, you give the lamp a vigorous rub and are totally caught off-guard when a genie emerges from the spout and offers to grant you three wishes.

Do you actually have three wishes at the ready? Or are you going to shift from one foot to the other, scratch your head, and agonize over whether you should wish for a million dollars, a new car, thinner thighs, or world peace? In the meantime, this particular genie is not one to suffer fools. You can tell because his nostrils are flaring, his eyes are glaring, and his muscular biceps look even more ominous as he folds them in a gesture of major impatience. If you don't speak quickly, your ticket to all things magical will vanish.

Fast-forward to reality. The last person you expected to see as you entered the elevator in a corporate high-rise was the one person whose endorsement of your writing talents could pave the way to publication or production. You have 30 seconds or less to make a stellar impression that will knock his or her socks off, either pitching an idea or promoting your book or brand. Do you really want to waste it talking about the weather or scrambling to compose an intelligent précis that could potentially make your dreams come true?

You may not literally need to make a big, passionate sell in the time it takes to ride an elevator to the twentieth floor, but master the concept behind an elevator pitch and you can use it at publishing conferences, workshops, and at other relevant gatherings. And your query letters, and even social media promotions, will benefit as well.

Conversations on the Rise

The term *elevator pitch* was coined in 1995, but the premise of a short, pre-scripted speech has been used by salespeople since the 1950s. Recognizing that they had only a short window of opportunity to hook prospective customers, entrepreneurs began crafting savvy *sound bites* (a term developed in the 1970s) that (1) were succinct, (2) imbued mystique, (3) projected empathy, and (4) invited a call to action.

While the original purpose was to pitch products such as vacuum cleaners, the latest cosmetics, or life insurance policies, the technique of an elevator pitch could also be used to interview for a job, attract the favorable notice of the media, and in the case of authors, court the interests of editors, agents, and producers. Today, opportunities for a quick pitch may also arise online, letting you connect or start a meaningful dialogue with someone who might be interested in your writing. The volume of digital communication today makes it important for authors to be able to distinguish themselves in a virtual elevator pitch. In the age of Twitter and Facebook, it is a valuable skill to be able to compose a *grabber* that accommodates an average human attention span of about eight seconds, but also suggests depth or uniqueness.

An effective elevator pitch should never be construed as an

aggressive, hard sell that backs the listener into a corner. It should, instead, arouse curiosity, invite questions, and subliminally promote an idea or project that the listener will remember long after the pitch is over.

Speed Dating 101

To hone your elevator pitch skills, think about being on a speed date. For those unfamiliar with the concept, speed dating originated in 1998 as a way for Jewish singles to mix, mingle, and decide in 5 to 10 minutes whether anyone they met at the event was a potential soul mate, or at least worth a dinner date. Not everyone who goes to a speed dating event is there for the same reason, to find romance. But they are collectively eligible. The purpose of the event is clearly to promote their best qualities, get to the point, and find a match.

The correlation to publishing is that putting yourself in a receptive environment—among literary agents at a writers' conference, for example—usually yields a higher rate of return than a what salespeople would call a *cold call*. As with digital communications, however, everyone is competing in the same arena for the same prize and with similar merchandise. You need to have that elevator pitch that sets you apart. It's a technique that not everyone uses.

As at that publishing speed-dating opportunity, sharpen your observation skills in sizing up receptivity to your pitch. If the person in your functional equivalent of an elevator (writers' conference, or writing course, and so on) does not make eye contact, smile, or exchange any social pleasantries, they probably just cannot wait to get where they are going. If their eyes start to glaze over in the middle of your spiel, do not keep pushing. They have let you know they are not interested and, have done you a twofold favor by saving you time and showing you that your pitching techniques need more rehearsal.

Ask Not What They Can Do for Your Book

To paraphrase the late President John F. Kennedy, the emphasis of your elevator pitch should be on how your project can meet the needs of your audience, not how they can meet your needs as an author trying to make a sale. But you can and should work to establish yourself as a credible expert, or skilled writer, especially if you are directing your pitch to a member of the media.

Let's say you want to get booked on a local talk show. The worst thing to do is announce, "I have a book to sell and I want you to help me do that." This only tells the media outlet that you are fishing for a free commercial rather than packaging yourself as a media-worthy event that will appeal to their target audience. If you are going to pitch a local radio or television station, or gathering of people who might be interested in your writing, your phone call or email must succinctly demonstrate (1) your familiarity with the show/event's format, (2) the types of guests it invites, and (3) the needs and concerns of its core followers. If you know these three things, the essence of your pitch can then focus on the take-away value your presentation will offer. Examples of elevator pitches:

- "I've been following your series about returning to the workforce after retirement and have identified the 10 best companies hiring seasoned workers. Would you be interested in my sharing them with your viewers?"
- "Your weekly segment on Fast & Frugal meals always makes me hungry! My signature cheesecake is simple enough to make blindfolded. Is your co-anchor, Niles, up for an on-air challenge?"

You will notice that neither of these pitches even mentions there is a book involved. The initial contact is strictly to whet your target's curiosity about a topic that will resonate with the people who regularly tune into the show. If your moment in the spotlight is entertaining, informative, inspirational and memorable, you will accomplish two things: intrigue the audience into checking out what you have published, and encouraging the media entity or event coordinator to invite you back.

Less Is More

In the pitch session workshops I teach, I always tell authors that if they cannot describe their book in 25 words or less, they probably do not know what it is about. Despite all the time they have invested in producing content, they are not adept at distilling its central message.

Whether a pitch is delivered in person, on the phone, or in print, the listener or reader should not have to slog through meandering verbiage to discern whether the book is of interest. Inherent in the art of brevity is recognizing the difference between story and plot, words too frequently used interchangeably.

Suppose someone asks you what your novel is about. You reply, "It's about a homecoming queen who loses her crown" or "It's about a parrot that likes to herd sheep" or "It's about a high school dropout who goes to live with his grandfather." Whenever you say, "It's about," you're delivering a one-liner summary of the type of tale it is going to be, without giving away any of the specifics on where the characters came from or where they are going next. When you can explain the gist of your project in one sentence, you are talking about the *story*.

Assuming your listeners are intrigued, they may ask, "How did she lose her crown?" "Where did the parrot learn to herd sheep?" or "Do the two of them get along?" Any question that asks how a situation happened to come about or how it is going to unfold in the future is answered in terms of the *plot*.

Your objective is to entice listeners to request more information, not overloading them with too many details up front. In other words, do not volunteer the *how* unless they actually ask.

Propping up the Pitch

If the man standing behind you in the checkout line at Safeway was dressed as a pirate, or if a woman in a Gothic laced-bodice dress with a velvet steampunk jacket and hat was reading a magazine at your neighborhood Starbucks, they would get your attention. You might be interested enough to react, and make the first move by commenting on their attire. This is exactly what they want to happen because it allows them to make the second move—to talk about the new play they are in or explain that donning a costume helps them get into the mindset of a character in the novel they are writing. At this point, is someone really going to say, "Oh, that's interesting," and walk off? Unless they are in a hurry, they are already hooked to hear more.

The key to this strategy is artful nonchalance which, in turn, creates mystique. Nothing is more seductive than someone who is confident and who has successfully fashioned a career that other people only dream about.

For those reluctant to go the full-fledged costume route, there are other ways to accessorize your presence when you are interested in attracting attention to make a pitch. Consider, for instance, a distinctive piece of jewelry; a hat or cap; a canvas tote bag sporting a logo of your book cover; or a lapel pin that asks a question ("Could your business survive a hurricane?"), cites a real or faux statistic ("27% of writers are extraterrestrials"), or features a catchphrase from your book ("The secret lies with Ethel.").

You should also never be without business cards or oversized glossy postcards courtesy of design companies like VistaPrint. Postcards, incidentally, are especially helpful to distribute at pitch fests because they memorialize all of the elements that listeners may not have time to jot down during your face-time session.

Revise, Review, Refresh

Remember also that your nutshell presentations, whether live or typed, cannot be practiced too much. You will probably go through multiple versions before you find a pitch that sounds both spontaneous and conversational.

Along with staying abreast of current events and trends so as to keep your patter fresh and relevant, take note of any follow-up questions you are asked. What if, for instance, someone asks you how your post-apocalyptic zombie novel differs from the competition? All that prep that went into crafting a spot-on sound bite to grab their attention will be for naught if your reply is, "Um . . . uh . . . I don't know."

Elevator pitches should also be customizable to different circumstances. Consider how your pitch about a book on home-based businesses would differ in vocabulary, scope, and visual imagery if your listeners are college students, housewives, or retirees.

Lastly, never underestimate the staying power of a great anecdote. Whether it is used to open your pitch or conclude it, a story that is funny, surprising, or nostalgic has a spellbinding effect on listeners to keep conjuring that elevator time after time.

It's a Whole New World

Submissions in the Electronic Age

By Katherine Swarts

A glance at any recent market guide confirms it: Publishers without an online presence are now extreme exceptions. "Submitting is so different today," says children's author and host of a popular writers' forum, Verla Kay. "Back in the *dark ages* there were no cell phones, Internet, or email; everything was done through snail mail and land-line telephones. Today publishers, agents, and editors accept email submissions, making the entire process much faster and easier. No longer do I need to make sure I have quality typing paper, lots of stamps and envelopes, a mail scale to weigh submissions. The one thing I miss is the self-addressed, stamped postcard."

"Once upon a time," says children's book author Linda Joy Singleton, "books were submitted only through the mail." In her early writer days, Singleton remembers "printing out hundreds of pages, figuring the right amount of stamps for my SASE, stalking my postal carrier for news. Rejections came through the mail and *the call* was made via phone. That's how my first sale happened in the 1990s: a phone call that rocked my world. By 2000, with fewer publishers and increasing submissions, the standard method shifted to the Internet, [especially] after the anthrax scares of 2001. I remember being surprised the first time I was asked to send my manuscript through email. Now it's rare to send a manuscript through USPS."

Steve Hussy, Co-Editor of *The Savage Kick,* a magazine published by Murder Slim Press estimates the current ratio of "email to postal submissions at least at 10 to 1. It may be closer to 20 to 1."

Don't Be a Blitzer

Querying with a click is a double-edged sword, however. Multitudes of writers now take the approach editors most hate: a blitz of submissions at questionable targets hoping the quantity will trump quality.

Stephen Mooser, President of the Society of Children's Book Writers and Illustrators (SCBWI) says of online submissions, "The biggest advantage [for publishers] is that you are no longer deluged with paper submissions stacking up on the floor. The biggest disadvantage is that you are still deluged since it is so easy and cheap for writers to flood the market."

"I have seen a huge increase in queries from overseas that don't [have a good grasp of English]," says Angela Hoy, Publisher of the *WritersWeekly* ezine and owner of Booklocker.com. "The editor will, of course, assume that the article will contain the same types of errors. I've also seen an increase in mass mailings that start with *Dear sirs*, some for articles completely unrelated to what we cover. I delete queries sent to *Editor* because that's a tell-tale sign they sent it to numerous other publications," probably did next-to-no research, and did not locate the editor's name. Many are sloppy in other ways: "A common mistake is when writers don't state up front that the piece has been published. When the editor finds out, he will likely feel that the writer tried to hoodwink them into paying for first rights," says Hoy. Note that blog posts count as publication.

Electronic submissions policies make it considerably easier for some writers to break through, says Hussy. "Murder Slim Press has published two people in prison; without email, I doubt they would have been able to get to us. The problem is, easier can mean lazier; there's nothing worse than [writers submitting] to a group address of 50 magazines in a kind of round robin. Let's hope most people will slowly realize that the freedom of email submissions doesn't mean you don't need to work at being a writer."

From the writer's side, Kay notes, "The advantage of snail mail is that I'm less likely to send something before it's really, truly ready. When I have to print it out, I see errors before it leaves my hands. When submitting electronically, I have to be extra diligent to make sure my stories and cover letters are error-free."

And yes, publishers still worry about technical problems. Says Mooser: "Many do not want attachments for fear of picking up a virus—for that same reason, many don't accept e-submissions except from those they are already working with. Certainly e-submissions are most convenient for the author, but any writer needs to abide by the publisher's preference, even if that means extra postage costs."

Surfing for Editors

Avoid being an inappropriate-submission pest by learning about each individual market. "Always check out the publisher's website," says Hussy. "Would you turn up to a job interview without knowing a little about the company?"

"Research your markets," agrees Kay. "Since it's so easy to write and send, slush piles are bigger and it's more important than ever to send only to people who would say, 'Wow! This is just what I need!' Find the guidelines. Check catalogues to make sure your story will fit into their list. Then send what they ask for, everything

Among the more popular submissions platforms are

- Contently: http://contently.com
- Drupal: http://drupal.org
- Ebyline: www.ebyline.com
- Google Documents: http://docs.google.com
- Kapost: http://kapost.com
- WordPress: www.wordpress.com

they ask for, and only what they ask for. Make sure you send your submission to the correct person, and address your cover letter to Mr. or Ms." Don't trust first names as infallible indicators. If you cannot find a photo or other gender identifier on the publisher's website, a quick Google search will turn up such information on almost anyone. Finally, "research what individual editors and agents love and hate. The more you know, the more appropriately you can target your submission packet."

For locating publisher websites and other information sources, Mooser recommends publications such as *Writer's Market*, (available with an online account) and its genre-specific sisters. SCBWI's own publications guide, *The Book*, is downloadable at www.scbwi. org/Pages.aspx/THE-BOOK--The-Essential-Guide-to-Publishing-for-Children. And do not forget the Marketplace section in the monthly *Children's Writer* e-newsletter, and the Writer's Institute annuals—*Best of the Magazine Markets, Book Markets for Children's Writers,* and *Magazine Markets for Children's Writers,* nor the rest of this *Writer's Guide!*)

Check writing websites for further recommendations. "I know

a number of sites that include details of what publishers want," says Hussy. "We get a bunch of submissions from Morgen Bailey's website."

"The Internet is fantastic!" says Kay. "The publishing industry changes so quickly that printed information can be woefully out of date in a few months. My personal [online contribution]—the Blueboard, now hosted by SCBWI—is a gigantic message board for children's writers and illustrators. Some of the most popular forums are the Market/Agent News & Discussion board and the Response Times boards for Agents, Book Publishers and Magazines." For still more ideas, "use your search engine. But remember, anyone can post anything on the Internet; just because it's out there doesn't make it true and correct. Make sure you get it from an official website you know is trustworthy. Also, check Preditors and Editors (http://pred-ed.com/) before submitting to any market you aren't a hundred percent sure about; this website is the Better Business Bureau of Internet submissions." And of course there is social networking: "Many people use Twitter to follow editors and agents and learn their personal likes and dislikes and how they operate their businesses."

Singleton says: "Networking online is a great way to connect. There are Twitter discussions for writers every week, usually at 9PM Eastern, 6 PM Pacific time, for #yalitchat, #kidlitchat, and #pblitchat. And I network via Facebook and some Yahoo writer lists."

The Sharpest Cutting Edge

Among all these online options, you will come across an increasing number of publisher websites that use online submissions forms with data fields. Or they may send writers to Submittable.com, SubMgr (www.submissionmanager.net), or ChristianSubmissionsManuscripts.com. And in these days of the cloud, many are going even further. "Instead of emailing in Word," says freelance writer Susan Johnston, who specializes in money and small business subjects, "a few clients now have me input articles into content management systems like Kapost, Ebyline, Contently, or WordPress" to streamline formatting and record-keeping. With most such systems, polishing before submitting takes on extra importance: "If I email a manuscript and later get a last-minute update, I simply email a new version. But when there's a content management system involved, I have to send my editor a message and they have to send the article back to me before I can update it. Google Documents is a bit different; you can edit it at any time."

Michelle Rafter, freelance business and finance writer and editor and a member of the FreelanceSuccess.com community: "I edit research reports and white papers; and I work for online publications and content marketing agencies, managing teams of freelance writers" and visuals professionals. "More and more, agencies and publications are asking writers to file stories into the agencies' own content systems" or into third-party content management systems. "Today, you really have to know at least the fundamentals of these systems. This is the way the industry is going. You can't be a technophobe."

Johnston agrees: "I suspect we'll see more of these platforms and more publications embracing them. At the same time, existing platforms will test out new features and simplify things. Most of these systems are already pretty user-friendly, but it's a good idea to get familiar with basic HTML and image editing. Some of the websites I write for have very specific requirements for image sizes and require the writer to upload photos. I use PicMonkey.com for resizing or cropping."

Writers tired of being paid on publication will root for at least one content-management feature to become standard: "On a

SUBMITTING DIRECTLY TO THE PUBLIC

Modern technology has streamlined more than the traditional submissions process. You may be wondering: How about self-publishing, in essence submitting your work directly to readers?

A detailed discussion of self-publishing is beyond the scope of this article. But everyone should know: Doing it well and profitably is not easier than with standard publishers. Never slack on your research, editing, or marketing in the fantasy that the public will instantly recognize your genius; do your homework and have a solid business plan.

Keep up with technology, but don't expect it to do your job. "Writing seems to persist through whatever technological advances," says Steve Hussy, of Murder Slim Press. But effective person-to-person communication inevitably remains at the heart of selling your writing. Beware of simply being one in "the plethora of vanity Kindle books."

Epublishing, though quick and inexpensive, works best with a long-term plan that includes eventual hard-copy options. "I am grateful for the new sales ebooks bring in," says author Linda Joy Singleton. "Before, my books went out of print [and] were gone for good." Nonetheless, "I still love the touch and experience of reading paper books. And a paper book doesn't need batteries."

There is no excuse for neglecting quality. Says author Verla Kay: "More and more truly well-written, well-edited, beautifully published books are being created through today's digital publishing methods." Your creations are your best testimonials!

system like Contently," says Rafter, "when I approve a story a writer has submitted, they get paid instantaneously via PayPal. There's absolutely no waiting," and "they don't even have to send an invoice. I like it because the writers like it, and they're happy to take more assignments from me."

Into the Future

Content management systems, and even newer options, will continue to expand. "One thing that could emerge," says Mooser, "would be a centralized site where people could post manuscripts by category—manuscripts that had gone through screening by agents or vetted volunteers. Editors and publishers could peruse the submissions and make offers, or request revisions before making an offer."

Whatever the technology, storytelling and quality of writing remain timeless arts. "Some things have stayed the same," says Kay. "What editors want changes from year to year and day to day, but a compelling manuscript without typographical errors will still eventually rise to the top. It's just as hard to find the perfect fit as in the past, but the more you submit well-crafted manuscripts to appropriate places, the more likely you are to find an editor or agent that says, 'I have to have it!'"

Successful writers embrace the new publishing world with equal enthusiasm. Kay concludes, "It's exciting to live today and to experience all the incredible changes that have evolved, and I'm in awe of what is yet to come."

SETTING GOALS & MEETING THEM

And Working Well With Others

BY VEDA BOYD JONES

Read any article or book on setting goals, and you will find the same wonderful advice:

- Write down your long-term goal.
- Write down medium-term goals that will help you reach your big goal.
- Write down short-term goals that will move you toward the medium goals.

Great suggestions, really. For me, following this advice means starting with daily to-do lists that I write out the night before, so I do not have to reconstruct tasks left from the day before.

But here is the thing. As writers we do work alone, yet goal setting and keeping on schedule to meet goals does not have to be a solitary endeavor. In fact, having someone you trust keep you accountable for your goals will help you reach them.

Find a Kindred Spirit

Ann Leach, who co-wrote *Goal Sisters* (New World Library) with Michelle Beaulieu Pillen, was not on the search for someone to keep her accountable for her goals. But she met Pillen at work and discovered they shared the same values, interests, even sense of humor. They confided their hopes and when both decided to make career changes, they encouraged each other by talking about the steps toward their individual goals, writing them down, and meeting each week to assess progress. Their goal-sister approach was born. Even though they now live thousands of miles apart, they still email, talk frequently, and meet every other year to discuss their goals.

The goal-sister approach is gender-specific, since men stereo-typically do not share their feelings as much as women, who open up with other women they trust. And trust is a key to selecting a goal sister. This person could be a close friend, but Leach has found that an objective outsider is not as attached to the outcome, even if this person eventually becomes a friend as a goal sister. Family members generally are not the best choices because they could be jealous if you succeed and they may not want to be part of something if you fail.

And there likely will be missteps. A goal sister celebrates both the successes and failures of your journey toward your goals and helps you learn from the failures. Analyzing a failure will show you what not to do.

"Holding the vision and celebrating the small steps are essen-tial," Leach says. "Noticing and acknowledging the little steps show that we are on the right path to our goals."

Leach has facilitated goal sister groups to spread the word on how the process works. Several years ago writer Bonnie Hinman, author of *Man vs. Mountain: Mount Everest* (Purple Toad Publishing) attended one of Leach's group sessions, which met weekly for six weeks, including an overnight retreat.

"My goals had writing in mind," Hinman says. "I liked the concept of sharing goals and providing support, but there was risk involved since I knew none of the other six women."

Leach had each woman create a vision board of how she wanted her life to be. Wanting something permanent, Hinman chose a canvas and affixed personal photographs, words drawn with colorful markers, and magazine images to her canvas and painted it with a clear sealant. It hangs in her bathroom so she sees it each morning when she brushes her teeth, and she can start her day with her goals in mind.

"Making the board and discussions with others helped me clarify and articulate my goals. I learned how to make goals that were realistic for me."

A writer's goals must not involve another's decision-making. Hinman could organize her time to devote more time to writing; she could set aside a time each day to market her work; but she could not set as a goal to sell her work to publisher X because that goal was not in her control. Instead she could set as a goal writing the best novel she could and sending it to publisher X. The buying-the-book part was up to an acquisitions editor.

"As a result of the goal sisters experience, my productivity increased and I learned that I could fix things in my life I didn't like."

Hinman occasionally communicates with women who were in her group, but because there were no other writers, she did not find a lifetime goal sister from that group. Still, she knew the concept worked.

Find a Lunch Bunch

After reading Leach's book, I realized I already have goal sisters in my life. For more than 25 years, I have met at a restaurant with four other working writers for Wednesday lunch. Although we know many details of each other's families, we do not socialize at lunch; we talk writing. We announce our acceptances and commiserate with each other over rejections and suggest other markets for our work. Rarely do we read each other's work, but at times we help with leads in nonfiction or discuss overall conflict in fiction. At times we dis editors, just for the fun of it, but we all know the value of a good editor.

Through the years the size of our by-invitation-only group has increased and decreased as we have met other writers and some moved out of the area. We have even had men attend our lunches, but they tend to be on a once-in-a-great-time schedule, by their choice and not ours.

Find an Overnight Group

At Wednesday lunch, we do not write down our goals. But every three months or so, two other writing friends and I meet for an overnight gabfest we call "Wine and Whiners," and we keep minutes of our meetings. Author Vicki Grove (*Everything Breaks*, Putnam) and author/illustrator Cheryl Harness (*Mary Walker Wears the Pants*, Albert Whitman), and I read our work aloud, make suggestions, and bring copies of our new books as they come out for the others to *ooh* and *ahh* over.

We encourage each other, and because we have wined and whined for well over 10 years now, we know how to talk with each other, and usually it is in a teasing manner. A typical conversation:

Veda: Woe is me. I don't know how to write, and I live in fear that editors will find out.
Cheryl: That's right. You don't know how to write.
Vicki: Why do we even hang out with her?

Or switch the speakers around and the same conversation will ensue. This may not sound like support, but it works for us.

We have spirited discussions concerning social media. Does it help with book sales? Is writing a blog a time waster? How can we find Internet sites where our books will be reviewed or we will be interviewed? Is this type of marketing busy work or helpful to sales? Do promotional materials like bookmarks and postcards help sales? We talk about school visits and how we say no to nonpaying speaking gigs, except the ones in our hometowns. Or even the ones in our hometowns. Is the expert always from out of town? Why are we not appreciated as much as authors in the place where people know us from the grocery store and the Little League field? Does membership in Society of Children's Book Writers and Illustrators, American Society of Journalists and Authors (ASJA), and the Authors Guild help, and in what ways?

Over breakfast, we decide when we can meet again, at whose home, and what goals we will meet by then. Our goals are directed by those scattered and disconnected topics. Vicki will get a Facebook page. Cheryl will design a postcard for a book. And I'll keep my membership in ASJA and start making time to visit the site each day to keep up on the industry. Those goals are written in the minutes, and when we meet again, we read the minutes and report on goals reached or not, and why not.

How Do You Find a Goal Partner?

As a member of a local writer's group, I also attend monthly meetings at the library and meet other writers. The library is a great place to start for writers looking for goal partners.

You know instantly if you hit it off with someone; there's quickly just a friendly, respectful response. When Vicki was speaking at a local school, I went to hear her. Afterward, I introduced myself and told her how much I enjoyed her presentation. I ran into her at writer's conferences, and we started talking. She invited me to her home and although it was a three-hour drive, I went and there I met Cheryl, who had also driven a couple hours to get to Vicki's country home. The Wine and Whiners were born.

MOTIVATIONAL THOUGHTS

- "You don't always get what you wish for; you get what you work for." *Anonymous.*
- "You manage what you measure." *Paraphrase of scientist William Thomson, First Baron Kelvin*
- "One way to keep momentum going is to have constantly greater goals." *Editor and author Michael Korda*
- "People with clear, written goals accomplish far more in a shorter period of time than people without them could ever imagine." *Author Brian Tracy*
- "If you have a goal, write it down. If you do not write it down, you do not have a goal - you have a wish." *Author Steve Maraboli*
- "Where there is no vision, there is no hope." *Scientist George Washington Carver*

"It's a tonic," Cheryl says of our overnight visits. A real inspirational tonic. When two of us happen to be at the same litfest or conference, of course we talk, talk, talk, but when the three of us are together, it is magic.

Hinman has found a goal partner by joining online writer's groups and following a few blogs. Again, she just felt a connection when she learned she and another person shared the same values. She has yet to have face-to-face meetings with her goal partner, but through email they keep each other accountable for their goals and encourage each other.

Do You Need a Goal Partner?

No. You can absolutely set goals all by yourself. I did when I started writing because I did not know another writer, and I did not think about goal-setting with *normal* people—although that would work perfectly fine. And although I did not write down goals, I set them. I had a certain time to write each day, and by meeting that one daily goal, I made steady progress on a novel, day by day, until it was completed.

Once I met other writers, it was fun to talk about our dreams of writing a bestseller and being interviewed on the morning news shows. But those were dreams, and when we got down to talking goals, those dreams did not make the lists. Those dreams involved other people, and we had no control over how much promotion money a publisher put into a book or who the booking agent liked for the *Today Show*.

Length of Goals

Each year at the January meeting of my local writer's group, which is open to any writers, we write down our goals for the year. Again, we cannot put on our list things that are out of our control. We write down goals that involve only us. "I will get an agent" can't go on the list because it involves someone else's decision. "I will query five agents a month" can go on the list. Then we put our lists in an envelope, seal it, entrust it to the group's president, who opens it the following January and distributes the folded lists back to the writers, who may share them if they wish.

We do not have to be accountable to others, but just having the goals in writing helps us see what we were thinking a full year earlier. Then we write down the goals we want to reach during the year ahead.

These one-year goals are not as long range as five-year goals, which give you a long-term vision of your future writing career. But in a year you can crank out a 365-page book if you write a page a day. You can write several short stories and articles. You can revise a book manuscript several times in a year. And you can certainly send your work to a multitude of agents and editors.

Medium-term goals, like a six-month goal and then shorter

one-month goals, will keep you looking ahead. Then decide on a short-term goal: What will you accomplish in one week? All the tasks that fit in a day are your extreme short-term goals. Those little daily steps will lead you toward that big goal.

Setting goals keeps you motivated and keeps you moving forward. Your self-confidence is boosted when you meet one of your short-term goals and takes a giant leap when you reach a medium-term goal. Every goal you meet makes you more determined to meet the next one. So set those goals and strive toward the great vision. And remember, there is no reason to do it alone.

Promotion: The Scary, In-Person Kind

By Veda Boyd Jones

I was trembling.

It is not that I had not done TV promotions before. I once filmed a commercial for the March of Dimes, and I have been a spokesperson for community programs. But this time I was promoting my ebook, *Joe's Ghost*, set in my hometown of Joplin, Missouri, which is why I thought the local afternoon television show might be interested in interviewing me in the first place.

Because it was *me* on the line, *my* words someone might read, I was scared.

Of course, the chilly studio was staged for deception. Two cameras aimed at the small marble table where the host and a woman guest were talking about art projects in front of a fake stone wall. In another part of the studio was the weather center, big blue screens with TVs off to each side. In the center was the news anchor desk. Through a narrow window in a door, I could see into another studio, with a cooking area that resembled a kitchen and a fake living room setup.

The producer signaled a commercial break, the art woman got up, and I stepped over thick electric cords running across the floor and took her place behind the round table. I shifted in the uncomfortable, but comfortable-looking, chair and thought of what I had read about performing, because that is what this was. I was only slightly less phony than my surroundings; my smile was a little wider than normal, but I hoped without the forced look. I glanced at the host when he directly asked me a question, then pretended the camera was a friend and I was talking to it. My words came easier when the book cover was flashed on the screen above the camera. The screen to the side of the host was a distraction, and I hoped I would not be caught glancing at it from time to time in Nixonesque, eye-shifting, debate mode.

I knew my novel's plot, of course, but I will admit to a few brain freeze moments in my past, and the thought that one could occur on camera had me purposefully focusing on how I had done the local research for the novel and used local landmarks the viewers would know. After all, I had to make the host glad he was letting me fill five minutes of his airtime.

When my segment was over, I took deep breaths, and took great pleasure when the producer walked me out and said they would love to have me on the program again. One of my sons watched the video on the station's website and texted, "You did great!" I replied that I was glad he thought I did okay. He texted right back, "Not okay. *Great!*"

I watched the clip, posted it on Facebook, and watched it again and again. I did do *great*, I say with humility. I mentioned my website and where my book was available—twice, but without sounding like an infomercial, which would have been taboo. I laughed at the right times. I used my hands for appropriate motions; when I mentioned the story arc, I made a sign of the rainbow.

It was like watching a confident stranger.

I had successfully faked it. Somehow I had fooled myself into believing I was comfortable talking to the host and the camera. None of the quaking writer came through in that interview.

And I am guessing none of the insecure writer came through when I wrote the producer an email and told her about my book set in our town. I played on the local connection with this book, and I also mentioned that ebooks do not have book signing launch parties. So I got the gig.

My Top Three Rules

For this in-person promotion, I dressed in a red, form-fitting, shiny jacket and black pencil skirt, something I felt good in and thought would look good on TV. For me this was all about building my confidence so I would look like a self-assured author. I also knew enough about TV not to wear an eye-crossing hound's-tooth or busy plaid top, although as it turned out, I could have worn jeans and the red jacket since only the top of me showed, but I didn't know that going in.

Looking my best is my first rule of in-person promotions. Of course, I write wearing jeans, but I want to look more professional than I do at work in the privacy of my upstairs office (aka a former bedroom).

My second rule is to know my audience. Whether speaking to a group of young student authors or to adult writers at a writing conference, to a local civic club or an in-service for English teachers, I feel I must leave them with a take-away they can apply to their own lives. Sure, my goal is to sell books, but to get the speaking gig, I have to deliver something (besides the opportunity to purchase my books) that will enrich my listeners' lives.

My third rule parallels my second one, and that is to know what I am talking about. That means I need something on paper to keep me on track. We can all talk about ourselves and our writing, but I have found out the hard way that if you are going to deliver something specific for your audience, have a plan.

Booking a Speaking Tour

Speaking tours are not a thing of the past, but publishers tend to organize them only for their best-selling authors. So, many authors act as their own publicists, which means plenty of secretarial duties.

Romance writer Terry Zahniser McDermid, got an idea for a library tour after being asked to speak at an area library for the February celebration of Love a Library Month. Since she was speaking to a community group, she needed to provide something more than a buy-my-book speech about writing. McDermid has lived in several places, and she started listing the many libraries in her life.

"The libraries I remembered were renovated old houses, a majestic Carnegie Library, a storefront library, and up-to-date libraries with modern technology. As I listed them, I remembered the different aspects of my writing life that I learned at each place. One library helped me learn about research—and I could bring up specific materials and books from that location. In another library, I discovered the many options for writers, from fiction to nonfiction to periodicals. Soon, I had a road map of my writing journey—library by library.

"After I did the first talk, I wanted to see if my memories were accurate, especially about the way the library looked during my time there. I called each library and was directed to a librarian who could give me help with the history of the library. While we were talking, I asked about speaking to their patrons about my writing journey, with specific emphasis on their particular library and my experiences in that city or town. I sent information about my talk, my writing credentials, and my tie to the library and community to the contact person. A few times, if I was in the area I stopped by the library and asked to meet with the person who arranged programs. If the person wasn't available, I left my business card, a copy of one of my books, and a short description of my talk. I then called or emailed as a follow-up."

At each place that would be in her library tour, McDermid asked her contact person if she would be allowed to sell her books or if someone from a local bookstore could have her books there for a signing.

Once McDermid had set the tour, she put information on her Facebook page and on her website. She shared the date and time on writing loops that allowed self-promotion. After her first library visit, where she found that her talk was listed on the calendar page of the local paper but had no other details to bring folks to her event, she started doing her own publicity. "I sent a standard press release, giving time, place, and content of my writing talk, and then included information that emphasized my personal connection to the community, any work experience in the location, and any other involvement I had there. In a few places, I was invited to do a short visit to an early morning talk show. I also contacted anyone I knew who lived in the area."

McDermid's library tour sparked her current work-in-progress, *Libraries I Have Loved: One Writer's Journey.*

What About Radio?

Dona Lee, co-author with Al Musitano of *Published! The Complete Guide to Nontraditional Publishing,* hosts a segment on a local Florida radio show called Ask the Author. She chats for about 10 minutes with an author. Her advice is for authors do their homework before going on a radio program.

"They should have their website information on hand and make sure they get it out during their on-air time. If possible, ask the station to post it on the station website. Promote the interview on social media and ask people to listen in and maybe have one or two call in. It shows interest; the stations love it and might even ask you back . . . soon!"

Lee suggests authors call local stations and radio and television stations in areas they intend to visit and tell them how their books can help people. This works especially well with nonfiction. "Stations love to have subjects to discuss on air. They might even put you on a list as a *specialist* and call you when something comes up they think you can weigh in on."

Authors should also be aware of innovative Internet talk radio, which has a growing worldwide audience, says Lee. For example, *The Author Connection* has aired on www.radioearnetwork.com for more than five years. Each week two authors are interviewed about their books. The show is accessed in 148 countries and has more than 15 million listeners. Podcasts can be accessed anytime. The show went into syndication in 2013 and has been having reruns on many public radio stations.

Lisa Collier Cool has given radio interviews around 200 times about her books, articles, and blog posts. She is the co-author, with Ralph Sarchie, of *Beware the Night: A NYPD Cop Investigates the Supernatural* (St. Martin's), which is being made into a movie by Sony Screen Gems. Many times radio shows have tracked Cool down to discuss her topic. "I make myself easy to find via website and social media."

Book Fairs, Book Signings, Readings

There is a reason politicians traditionally go door-to-door to meet and greet people. The personal connection translates into votes, and for an author, the personal connection can translate into sales and to speaking engagements that pay well.

Always take advantage of a book fair near you. If the organizers ask you to speak, then speak. The more people who see you and hear your voice and make a connection to the book you are holding up, the more sales you will make. Most book fairs are attended on your own time and your own dime, rather than the publisher's, but book sales can pay your way, and business travel expenses are tax deductible. Rewards are name recognition and word-of-mouth advertising of your books.

Make friends with the folks at your local bookstore for book signings. Believe me, I know that sitting at that book signing table can be like running a garage sale in the rain, but publicity is publicity. Get your name out there. Get your face out there. Get your voice out there. One connection can lead to something big.

Many writing conferences have open-mike times slotted for those brave souls who will read from their works. Be one of the brave. Time slots are short, so read the best passage you have written to get others interested in buying your book. Coffeehouses are often open to readings, so do some Internet research, or better yet, ask in person about being a guest reader.

Use Any Opportunity

I know a writer who was pumping her own gas when she struck up a conversation with the man at the other pump, and convinced him to buy a signed copy of her book as a Mother's Day gift for his wife. She kept copies in the car. Now, that is in-person promotion!

Of course, my doctor knows I am a writer. The last time I was at his office I told him I had a genuine ebook in this high tech world, and I gave him a printer-made card featuring the cover. He later dropped me a note and said his book club was reading *Joe's Ghost*. I was once asked to speak to a book club that was reading one of my books, but I did not pursue the thought of going to my doctor's club. Maybe that was a mistake, a case of not opening the door when opportunity knocked.

All this in-person promotion is hard work, and it is not in my nature to put myself out there. It is the part of writing that I did not sign up for, but it is now a bigger part of the writing game than it has ever been before.

You need to do it. So take a deep breath to still the shivers, then get out there and smile big.

Stepping Into the World of Social Media

By Mark Haverstock

"Today everyone can have 15 megabytes of fame."
— Robert Greenberg

This twist on Andy Warhol's famous quote reflects the universal availability of Internet platforms to showcase yourself, your talents, and your ideas. Blogs, social media, and social networks have effectively bypassed the traditional gatekeepers of fame and influence, and leveled the playing field for most of us.

Modern electronic media allow everyone to express themselves globally in a variety of formats, from pictures to video to varieties of text. No longer do you need to beg a book publisher for access to readers. You can now self-publish and place your book on Amazon for little or no up-front costs, and promote it yourself.

"The challenge now is not having access to the media because social media has provided the tools and means to take control," says Jeff Bullas, author and social media marketing expert (www.jeffbullas.com). "They are now your media and you have control. You just need the passion and the motivation to make it happen."

According to Bullas, the real challenge now is breaking through the conversations and clutter of billions of personal publishers in an increasingly online world. Writers must figure out how to establish themselves among the tens of thousands already out there and, more important, how they you develop relationships with readers and fans effectively.

Arguments for Social Media

Why should you blog, Tweet, create Facebook content, or build networks on social media? Is social media just a superficial exercise in connecting with others, or does it go much deeper than that? "Social media has touched something in human consciousness that goes beyond just online conversations," says Bullas. "It has provided a global connectedness that is culture- and nation-changing. It has given us as individuals control over our lives and how we express ourselves."

On his blog, Bullas cites 44 reasons for tapping into the power of social media. Here are a few that should appeal to the writer:

- Take control of your publishing
- Take control of your marketing
- Make a difference
- Become well-known or even famous
- Build an online asset that will show up in Google search results for years
- Grow your own network of influence
- Change others' lives and your own
- No longer have to worry about the fear of rejection

Wikipedia lists more than 200 major social networking websites, and more pop up every month. You cannot be on every platform, and you need to be selective. Bullas suggests looking at your intended audience and where they hang out. Choose the major or biggest social networks used by your target audience. As a

SETTING UP ACCOUNTS

- Facebook
  - www.wikihow.com/Set-up-a-Facebook-Account
  - www.ehow.com/how_2081063_set-up-facebook-account.html
  - Fan page: https://www.facebook.com/about/pages
- Tumblr
  - www.wikihow.com/Create-a-Tumblr-Account
  - www.tumblr.com/register
  - http://digitalsherpa.com/setting-up-your-tumblr-account-and-getting-started
- Twitter
  - http://michaelhyatt.com/the-beginners-guide-to-twitter.html
  - https://support.twitter.com/articles/100990-signing-up-with-twitter#
  - http://inkygirl.com/a-writers-guide-to-twitter
  - www.mitaliblog.com/2009/08/getting-started-on-twitter-quick-guide.html

writer, you will find that Facebook, Twitter, and Tumblr will likely be among those that will be most beneficial.

Facebook merits consideration from just about everyone who wants to be in closer touch with their clientele. Consider that nearly one *billion* people out there are sharing comments and conversations on Facebook. Given the massive potential audience, it would certainly be foolish not to examine the possibilities. The site is a good place to introduce yourself, and to set up fan pages once you have established yourself as a writer.

Twitter caters to both the busy and the attention-challenged, with a 140-word maximum microblogging format. It is a good

CREATE A FACEBOOK FAN PAGE

Having a personal page is a necessary start for writers creating a social media platform, but setting up a fan page adds another dimension beyond a circle of friends. The fan page is accessible to anyone on the web, whether or not they are Facebook members; no one has to be on your friend list to access it.

Author Kelly Milner Halls made a fan page for a book series she loves and contributed to, the Uncle John's Bathroom Readers for Kids. "I wanted teachers, librarians and readers on my Facebook account to learn about the quirky fun books," she says, "so I created one but quickly realized, 'if you build it, they will come' only works in Kevin Costner movies. No one came until I started asking them to come on my original Facebook page. So it seems important to bang the drum if you want your fan page to get fans."

It is also important to offer more than the opportunity to buy a book. Halls posted sample pages from the Uncle John's books on the fanpage, along with photos from contributing authors and weird videos related to some of the topics in the books. "My goal is to make it a fun place to visit—a place to go if you want a lift during your Facebook day," Halls says. "*Give* is the key word in successful social media, not *get*."

Will the fan page help Uncle John's Bathroom Reader get more play? Or help your book? Give it a try. If you are ready to set one up, here are a few resources to get you started:

■ Ten-step quick start: www.wikihow.com/Create-a-Facebook-Fan-Page
■ Detailed instructions: http://computer.howstuffworks.com/internet/tips/how-to-make-fan-page-on-facebook.htm

conduit for keeping your readers in the loop and is still growing by leaps and bounds, adding 500,000 users per day. It can be a valuable as a tool for you to keep informed about the writing business since Twitter has a huge network of writers and editors. "One of the reasons I decided to take Twitter seriously was because I kept hearing about various editors and publishers who were *tweeting*," says author and illustrator Debbie Ridpath Ohi. "And they weren't just posting promo items; they were also reading posts by other tweeters and sometimes replying to them."

Susan Orlean, a *New Yorker* staff writer and author of *Rin Tin Tin: The Life and Legend* (Simon & Schuster) and other books, is widely reported as having compared social media platforms to different kinds of parties. "Twitter is a noisy cocktail party, with lots of chatting and quick interactions, a kind of casual free-for-all," she says. "Facebook is a combination high school and college reunion, and therapy group."

Tumblr is a social media site where users can share anything and everything—blog text, pictures, videos, music files, links, and more. It is a bit like the Swiss Army knife of social media. If there is something to share, there is probably a way to share it here. Tumblr is also chock-full of inspiration. You can find anything from full-length blog posts, to poems, awe-inspiring pictures, music and links, to great sites all on this one social media resource. Tags allow you to give your posts a little extra exposure, so you can share them not only with people who follow you, but others who check out those tag threads—definitely a feature worth taking advantage of.

Be prepared to allocate time to your social media endeavors, but stick to your limits. Social media can become addictive and a great consumer of time. The average Facebook user spends 15 hours and 33 minutes a month on the site. If you are someone

SOCIAL MEDIA GROUPS

Facebook Groups are the place for small-group communication. Groups allow people to come together around a common interest, cause, issue, or activity to organize, express objectives, discuss issues, post photos and share related content. Some are publicly available for anyone to join, others require administrator approval for members to join, and some private groups accept members by invitation only. Like other Facebook pages, new posts by a group are included in the news feeds of its members, and members can interact and share with one another from the group.

Group pages can be a great resource for writers who want to make connections with others in the writing and publishing world. Many established writing groups are on Facebook right now. Here is how to find them:

1. Log into your Facebook page. Type "writing" into the search box.
2. Click on "See more results" at the bottom of the results page.
3. Look at "All results" and click on "Groups" to filter your results.

Facebook will produce a list of groups, complete with brief information about each. Try one of these, for starters:

- Children's Authors and Illustrators on Facebook
- Writers Helping Writers
- Writers Etc.

Cannot find one a group to meet your needs? Start your own. Go to your home page, click "Groups" on the left side, then click on "Create group."

Triberr is a close cousin to Facebook groups used in conjunction with Twitter. It is an online blogging and social media platform in which you join together with groups of other bloggers sharing similar interests. All agree to share each others' tweets and syndicate your content to your combined followers.

Bonfires are Triberr's community forums, places where members can interact with each other outside of their *tribes*. The name Bonfires was chosen because humans have gathered around such fires for as long as our species existed. Go to triberr.com for more details.

who is inclined to procrastinate, you could find your online time seriously eating into your writing time. Realistically, you should be able to handle your social media tasks in 15 to 20 minutes a day once you have become proficient with the platforms you use.

Be patient and realistic about your success. Your posts will not be found by the masses overnight. "It takes time to set up an audience," says author David Henry Sterry. "The sooner you begin, the more time you'll have to grow your fan base and start learning by studying your insight analytics."

Opening Communications

Part of using social media successfully is actually being social, like having a conversation with a friend. Sure, you will link to interesting things, post photos, and add comments. But it is also important to engage followers in order to keep them. As a writer wanting to gain a following, you have to try to keep everyone interested in you and what you have to say.

When you reach out to people through social media, make sure your personality comes through, no matter which platform you use. Temper your voice with a little diplomacy and common sense. Never post anything you will regret later, like sexist, racist, or demeaning comments. You never know what others may do with the content you post.

Offer something followers cannot get from your books, articles, or stories. Give some behind-the-scenes glimpses of what you do for research, including where you visit and to whom you talk. Share your travels if you do signings or school and library visits. Link to sites that relate to your book topics, things that interest you, and unusual or funny sites. Remember, you can also use video and photos or art.

In addition, you can share the process of putting together your current book under construction, or soon to be published. Share

SELECTED AUTHOR FACEBOOK PAGES

- Mitch Albom: www.facebook.com/MitchAlbom
- Paul Coelho: www.facebook.com/paulocoelho?fref=ts
- Neil Gaiman: www.facebook.com/neilgaiman
- John Green: www.facebook.com/JohnGreenfans?fref=ts
- E. J. James: www.facebook.com/ELJamesAuthor
- Stephenie Meyer: www.facebook.com/pages/Stephenie-Meyer/ 108380102517046?fref=ts (fan page)
- Kate McMullan: www.facebook.com/pages/Kate-McMullan-Childrens-Author/ 117156234963093?sk=wall
- Gretchen Rubin: www.facebook.com/GretchenRubin

excerpts, preliminary artwork, and other details, but always with your publisher's okay.

Not everything you post has to relate to your books or writing topics. John T. Edge, food writer and columnist for the *New York Times,* uses Twitter when he travels. He combines his genre with tweeting interesting facts that are not necessarily related to his writing. "I use it as a kind of diary to track things I saw, music I heard, food I ate," he has said.

Getting Personal

People are interested in you, your background, and what you have to say. But if you are thinking about Facebook or other social media as a direct sales tool, tread lightly. Social media is exceptionally good for the soft-sell, but it is not the best choice for a direct marketing tool. "No one likes to be marketed to on Facebook, at least not in that overtly obvious buy-my-stuff manner," writes Jane Friedman, social media expert and Web

Editor of the *Virginia Quarterly Review*. "And yet to approach it with no strategy at all could mean missed opportunities or wasted time." ("Five Principles for Using Facebook." http://janefriedman. com/2012/04/03/5-principles-facebook)

To understand what works best on Facebook, you need to realize that most people are seeing your posts in their newsfeed. Few people will actually visit your profile page unless they are researching you or may be curious about an item you have posted. Friedman suggests that you do not sweat the timeline too much. Fill out the information that you are comfortable sharing on the about page, but Friedman does not believe the profile information or timeline are important to marketing.

Instead, she argues that Facebook is a place to be informal, fun, and casual with people who have already expressed some level of interest in what you are doing. "If people friend or like you, they've given you permission to be in touch and offer updates," she writes. "Such people may not have any other alerts or notices about you, except for what appears in their Facebook newsfeed. Remember and respect that."

Find that sweet spot when it comes to number of posts you make. One of the biggest annoyances is that people or companies post too much too often, and the reaction is to mute or shut them off. "I'm a strong advocate of the 'less-is-more' philosophy when it comes to content and social sharing," says Friedman, because of the inundation of information everyone is exposed to online. The content you do include should be valuable in some way to those who follow you.

Taking the Step

If you have already signed up on one or more of the social media platforms, get into gear and start developing connections. Spruce up you profiles, change up your Twitter background, or even splurge on a premium Tumblr theme. Set up that fan page you have always been meaning to create.

If social media is new to you, however, take some time to acquaint yourself with the popular services available and how they work. There is hardly enough space in this article to give instructions on setting up accounts, or reviewing features in each of the sites covered. But you will find some resources in the sidebar to help you in your social media journey. Take a look at other writers' social media pages for inspiration.

Also be aware that you can interlink accounts between platforms. For example, a short comment on Facebook can automatically become a tweet by linking to your Twitter account, saving yourself a little time and also getting your message out to a larger audience. It is inevitable that some overlap may occur, since your followers will likely be active in more than one platform.

One word of advice: Avoid becoming preoccupied with how many people you influence through social networks. "Don't obsess about your number of followers," Orlean writes. "Just be genuinely engaged, and people will listen."

RESEARCH & IDEAS

PRE-MADE INSPIRATIONS FOR YOUR NEXT CAST OF CHARACTERS

BY CHRISTINA HAMLETT

In the decades that I have been interviewing published authors across all genres, nary a one has ever said that his or her characters sprang forth from thin air. More often than not, the fictional players that populate stage, page, cinema and television reflect aspects of the writers' own personalities, composites of friends and relatives, or are modeled after specific actors, politicians, rock stars, or criminals. The longstanding advice of "write what you know" translates aptly to "write *who* you know" and what their actions reveal about their character, strengths and flaws, and motivations.

Consider the following:

- Louisa May Alcott and Laura Ingalls Wilder drew upon the nineteenth-century hardships faced by their respective families as the inspiration for *Little Women* and *Little House on the Prairie*.
- Harper Lee used her attorney father as the model for Atticus Finch in *To Kill a Mockingbird*; her childhood playmate, Truman Capote, became Dill.
- Tom Sawyer was the mischievous alter ego of Samuel Clemens; Huckleberry Finn was based on the son of the

■ What is the first aspect of personality you notice in strangers?

■ Are your first impressions usually accurate? Identify a time you were completely wrong and what it was that derailed your judgment.

■ Which attribute best describes your hero or villain? Define the influences that shaped his/her dominant trait.

town drunk in Clemens's hometown of Hannibal, Missouri.

■ Christopher Robin, of *Winnie the Pooh*, was none other than author A. A. Milne's son.

■ In *Peanuts,* cartoonist Charles M. Schultz patterned Linus, Frieda, and good ol' Charlie Brown after a trio of co-workers.

■ Ever have a teacher you thought would make an intimidating character in a fantasy series? J. K. Rowling trolled the depths of classroom memory to transform her former chemistry professor into Severus Snape. Sir Arthur Conan Doyle found Dr. Joseph Bell's intuitive skills worthy enough to create Sherlock Holmes.

■ And let us not forget the recurring kooks from *Seinfeld.* J. Peterman, Jackie Chiles, and the Soup Nazi were each a caricature drawn from real life people who wandered in and out of the imaginations of Jerry and co-writer Larry David.

Chances are that your own world—encompassing your commute, your doctor's office, and the place where you always eat lunch—is replete with individuals who would make reluctant heroes, snarling villains, supportive helpmates, or plucky comic relief. To do so is just a matter of honing your observation skills and discerning which elements best lend themselves to the characters you want to create.

Personality

The first time we see or meet new people, we typically make snap judgments about what they are like based on the external clues they project. For example, people may come across initially as:

aggressive	bubbly	charming
defensive	gloomy	honest
nervous	nurturing	shy
boorish	carefree	creative
egotistical	gregarious	impulsive
nit-picky	reserved	surly

Initial impressions can be deceptive, however, because we are only observing people in the context of a specific moment—a timid mother putting on a brave face to calm her frightened children, a lazy job-seeker exuding enthusiasm, a smarmy salesman feigning sincerity.

Keep in mind that *personality* is a set of mental attributes that influenced by environmental factors and genetic inheritance. For your characters to be credible, ascribing a tag is not enough; you must also know the backstory that made them *that* way.

Character

While often used interchangeably with personality, *character* is the internal compass that guides a person's conduct or actions

CHARACTER EXERCISES

Exercise 1: Archetypes do not exist just in fiction. You can recognize their truths in your everyday life among family and coworkers. Choose any two archetypal opposites you know (someone outgoing and someone retiring, for example), and observe their best and worst traits, their common ground, and their most contentious dispute. Identify a conflict between two characters modeled on them that will require compromise. Develop a story line from there.

Exercise 2: A decade ago, the American Film Institute came out with its list of the top 50 Heroes and Top 50 Villains of all time (www.afi.com/100years/handv.aspx). Choose any three characters from each list and, based on what you know about their core beliefs and values, identify what they would do in the following situations:

- a family reunion
- a road trip
- a posh party
- a quarrel with a neighbor
- a delayed flight
- a jury summons
- a stalled elevator
- a terminal illness
- a break-up
- a lost wallet

and that derives from a learned set of beliefs. It is a more predictable measure of behavior because the individual's core values consistently carry over from one circumstance to the next. If, for example, your hero has always been betrayed by those he loves, his internal defensive mechanisms preclude trusting anyone's word, even if logic encourages otherwise. On the flip side, someone who has embraced a lifetime mind-set of kindness, piety, and personal accountability will not be tempted to cheat, rob, or harm another human being, regardless of any promised reward. Unlike real-life first impressions where we assess people within a matter of minutes (even seconds), fictional character evaluations take longer and require considering placing your character in a diverse spectrum of situations.

Character is frequently tied to *archetypes*—universal roles, categories, and symbolic motifs into which the players in your plot will fall. Some of these archetypes include:

Mentor	Nurturer
Free Spirit	Lost Soul
Warrior	Professor

(For a more extensive list, see www.tamicowden.com/archetypes. htm.)

When varying archetypes are put together, the dynamics that ensue are predicated on what each character wants and needs from one another, and on the respective strengths and weaknesses that will forge alliances, fuel contempt, escalate conflict, elevate awareness, inhibit growth, and promote empowerment.

Looks

Years ago I attended a Romance Writers of America conference and happened to observe two women standing ahead of me in the author registration line. One was a cute twentysomething blonde in a red bustier with fringed jacket, denim mini-skirt, and stilettos. The other was 60+, bespectacled, wore her grey-streaked hair in a severe bun, and was attired in a lumpy tweed pantsuit with a pair of sneakers. Based on a first glance, which one would you guess wrote the erotic bodice-rippers involving pirates and which one wrote YA sweet romance for teens and tweens?

Authors, just like their books, cannot accurately be judged by their covers.

Distinguish between archetypes and stereotypes, which are frequently perpetuated when we meet someone new. Question these in yourself as you create characters from real life people. For instance:

- Do all short men have a Napoleon complex?
- Are all redheads hot-tempered?
- Is every Asian good at math?
- Is every Scot a cheapskate?
- Are people who wear glasses smarter than those who do not?
- Are all actors gay?
- Is every professor absent-minded?

While common sense tells us there are no absolutes in categorizing people by gender, age, height, weight, hair, ethnicity, social status, or occupation, people nevertheless have an uncanny predilection for noting positive or negative traits and then manufacturing expectations of positive or negative behaviors. If you believe all redheads like to fight, you could end up construing even their most harmless comments as a verbal dare. What makes for multi-layered characters is allowing them to *play against type* and, like the elderly writer in tweed, project contrasts and deliver surprises no one sees coming.

Predispositions

We are constantly forming opinions about people based on their outward appearance, and processing information about them that is volunteered by others.

Let's say you're starting work at a new office. Before you even

ARCHETYPE EXERCISE

Exercise 1: Choose a setting where you can watch and get to know the same group of people over multiple encounters (fellow students, fellow tourists, restaurant wait staff). Jot down your initial assumptions about their lives. At the end of the observation period, review what you have actually learned from interactions and compare it to your original assessment.

Exercise 2: Park yourself at a coffeehouse for an hour and create detailed character bios for the patrons you observe based on (1) their clothing and footwear, (2) what they are doing (studying, reading, phone calls), and (3) body language if they interact with others. This is also a fun exercise to do at the airport; it allows you to speculate whether the passengers are traveling for business or leisure, what is in their carry-aboards, whether they are leaving or returning home, and what they do for a living.

go on your first break, the odds are high that someone will tell you in confidence, "Watch your back around Peggy. She's a certifiable snake who will try to take credit for everything you do." Yes, Peggy may have struck you as wonderfully pleasant and even showed you how to work the cappuccino maker, but will your Spidey senses start tingling when the boss assigns you to work on a project with her? Although you personally have no history with Peggy, and no evidence of her duplicity, you just cannot dislodge that coworker's warning, well-meaning or not, from your mind.

To establish the validity of an insider scoop, you need to consider the integrity of the person who provided it. Are you going to take the word of your Uncle Thatcher, who is the most trusted individual you know? Or that of a fellow employee you met a scant two hours ago, who may have an agenda stemming from jealousy that Peggy stole her promotion?

The same strategy works in reverse. Have you ever been told,

PREDISPOSITION EXERCISE

Exercise 1: Ah, celebrities! If they stopped behaving badly and getting caught in compromising positions, how would the supermarket tabloids ever stay in business? For this exercise, you will need three friends and the latest gossip magazine. At random, pick any story that puts an actor, an athlete, a royal, or a politician in a negative light. Working independently, two of you take the position of vouching for that person's character while the other two take the position of condemning it. Drawing from what you know, what you believe and what you have heard, create a character profile to defend your viewpoint. Compare the four results.

Exercise 2: Choose any famous literary character from the following list:

- Emma (*Emma*)
- Captain Ahab *(Moby Dick)*
- Miss Havisham (*Great Expectations*)
- Jo March (*Little Women*)
- Dr. Watson (*Sherlock Holmes*)
- Scarlett O'Hara (*Gone With the Wind*)
- Daisy Buchanan (*The Great Gatsby*)
- Nick Charles (*The Thin Man*)
- Inspector Javert (*Les Miserables)*
- Holden Caulfield (*The Catcher in the Rye*)
- T. S. Garp (*The World According to Garp*)
- George Smiley (*Tinker, Tailor, Soldier, Spy*)
- Celie (*The Color Purple*)
- Roland Deschain (*The Dark Tower*)
- Lisbeth Salander (*The Girl with the Dragon Tattoo*)
- Professor Umbridge (Harry Potter books)

As applicable, write down how they would be described by (1) their parents, (2) their teachers, (3) their romantic partners, (4) their next-door neighbors, and (5) their co-workers.

"Oh, you're just going to love Caroline! She's smart, she's funny and you're going to be the best of friends!" If this is coming from someone whose judgment is impeccable, you are primed to click before you and Caroline exchange your first hello. Granted, you might have warmed to Caroline on your own, but the effusive endorsement by someone who knows both of you puts an instant spotlight on her best qualities while diminishing any scrutiny of flaws.

When you are introducing new characters in a story, third-party commentary or author narrative can speak volumes before the players actually appear. Readers will naturally assume that the author's voice is the truthful one; the set-up remarks of the character's fictitious contemporaries, however, must be taken assessed only after enough chapters have passed to discern whether they are speaking to us from a position of love, hate, or neutrality. As in real life, if multiple people independently return similar analyses about someone's character, the chance that their collective judgment will be accurate is higher than if relying on a single opinion.

Believable characters are crucial to the craft of storytelling. Whether you borrow traits from your own life or that of others, the most plausible characters are born of a deep understanding and attentive observations of human nature—the quests, fears, triumphs, setbacks. And even if they are seemingly unlike anyone who has ever existed, readers will accept your characters if they behave consistently within the parameters of their ascribed traits and the fictitious world you have invented for them.

FIND GREAT PHOTOGRAPHS FOR YOUR ARTICLES & BOOKS

BY MICHAEL COOPER

They all might not be worth a thousand words, but good photographs can certainly help your articles and books win over publishers. Acquiring photos does not have to be expensive. A surprisingly high number of free, high quality photographs are available for anyone to use.

For more than 30 years, I have been doing photo research for my own and for other writers' books. In the old days, I spent hundreds of hours in the New York Public Library, the Library of Congress, and other archives, sorting through folder after folder of historical images. I was looking for images that were both relevant to the topic and eye-catching. Of course, photo quality is important too, but that does not mean every photo has to be perfectly focused or the lighting just so. It is more important for the image to be interesting.

Today, rather than donning ill-fitting white gloves and spending days in some musty archive I am more likely to look for photos by poking around on the Internet. That is easier in many ways, but it also has its downside. I tend to obsess about finding the perfect photo; the Internet has made it possible to never stop looking.

Free for All?

Before starting your photo research, you need to know the technical requirements for a publishable image. You will need at least 12 MB, or 300 dpi (dots per inch). The more dots, the sharper the image. For most book and magazine reproduction 300 dpi is fine. If the photo is going to be enlarged, say for a book cover, the dpi should be higher.

All photos come at a cost. At the very least that will consist of the amount of time and effort finding them. Depending on the source, a photo may entail reproduction fees or usage fees. Three terms you should know: *Royalty free* means that after paying a one-time fee, the purchaser can use the photo in various unspecified ways. *Right-managed* means a fee is charged and the photo can only be used as specified in an agreement. *Rights-free* means freely available for use, or in the public domain.

Tens of thousands of images on the Internet are free for the downloading. Here are three popular online sources, all somewhat different, for rights-free images.

■ Wikimedia Commons (commons.wikimedia.org) has more than 18 million images, with hundreds more being added by the minute. The Commons' public domain section contains only images with expired copyrights or images released by the owners or creators into the public domain. The Commons was originally created so that Wikipedia contributors would have good, free images to illustrate the tens of thousand subjects covered by the online encyclopedia which, it seems to me, has an entry for nearly everything. Most Commons' images are available in various dpi sizes.

■ The major search engines, such as Google Chrome, Bing, and Yahoo, all have image-searching features. One of the most popular is Google Images (www.google.com/imghp), which has indexed some 10 billion images. The user enters a search term and the browser turns up hundreds of images associated with that term. For example, enter the phrase "Klondike gold rush" and some 800 images pop up. Google also has a reverse image search that allows users to drop in a photo to see similar photos or to locate that specific image if it is on the Internet. This is quite handy if you have forgotten where you found a photo.

■ *Flickr* (www.flickr.com) is an image-hosting Internet site owned by Yahoo. It has more than 51 million registered users who have posted more than 6 billion images. This site contains a variety of images, from pet and vacation photographs to historical and news-related images.

Be careful here. Some Flickr users free up their photos under a Creative Commons license, and you are free to use them, generally with attribution, though sometimes there are restrictions on commercial use. Other Flickr sub-scribers maintain copyrights on their personal photos and do not want them used. Check which "default license" the owner of the photography has chosen.

Flickr also has a "no known restrictions" section with high-quality images free for the downloading. The National Archives, Boston Public Library, Smithsonian Institution, the George Eastman House, Library of Congress, and many other institutions have posted photo streams of thousands of images from their collections on Flickr.

Institutional Sources

Many libraries and historical societies, such as the New York Public Library and the Chicago History Museum, once provided

Photo Sources

- AP Images: 450 W 33rd Street, New York, NY 10001.
  www.apimages.com.
- Corbis Images: 710 2nd Avenue, # 200 Seattle, WA 98104.
  www.corbisimages.com.
- Flickr: www.flickr.com
- Getty Images: 605 Fifth Avenue South, Suite 400, Seattle, WA 98104.
  www.gettyimages.com.
- Google: www.google.com/imghp
- Library of Congress: 101 Independence Ave SE, Washington, DC 20540
  www.loc.gov/pictures
- National Archives: Still Picture Reference, Special Media Archives Services
  Division, National Archives at College Park, 8601 Adelphi Road, College Park,
  Maryland 20740. www.archives.gov
- Wikimedia: commons.wikimedia.org

low-cost images, but their fees now rival those of commercial agencies. The usage agreements from these institutions tend to be less restrictive, however.

An abundance of low or no fee institutional sources remain. While looking for 100 photos for my most recent book, I ran across Cornell University's Kheel Center for Labor-Management Documentation and Archives. According to its website, the center is one of the "most venerable archives of its kind in an academic institution." I was looking for photographs of the 1911 Triangle Shirtwaist Factory fire and the Kheel Center had lots of them. I paid only $43 for 12 excellent photographs.

In another case of search engine serendipity, while looking for images of nineteenth-century firefighting equipment I found the Hall of Flame Fire Museum in Phoenix, Arizona. It has one of the country's largest collections of firefighting equipment. Dr. Peter Molloy, the Fire Museum's director, wanted to promote his museum so he sent me a CD with 12 images of antique fire engines at no charge, not even for shipping.

Federal agencies such as NASA, the U.S. Forestry Service, and the National Park Service can be good sources for free or cheap photographs. Among the photographs I used in my book were two free photos of Naval helicopters fighting a wildfire in southern California. These came from the public affairs office of the U. S. Central Command, the organization in charge of providing military resources for public use.

Two of the biggest and most used federal sources for low-cost images are the Library of Congress and the National Archives.

The Library of Congress's Prints and Photographs division (www.loc.gov/pictures) has about 14 million photos and prints. Many of them can be browsed and purchased online. Locate the images you want and fill out an online order form. You will quickly receive a confirmation of your order and a bill. If a digital print of the image already exists, the cost is only $22 per image. If a digital print needs to be made then the cost is $50. A few days after paying the bill you will receive a link good for one week to download the photos you ordered. Or, for an additional fee, the photos can be put on a CD and mailed to you. You can also do things the old-fashioned way and order prints. This is much slower and slightly more expensive. It usually takes three to four weeks to receive the photos. Shipping rates start at $13.50.

It is sometimes possible to acquire Library of Congress images for little or no cost. When you browse the collection online you will sometimes see a notation that the larger images that are suitable for publication are available only at the Library of Congress. Anyone can visit the library by registering for an identification card. People doing research there can download the larger images to their laptops for free.

Another way to get inexpensive prints from the Library of Congress is to photograph the images. You can do that in the Prints and Photographs reading room. The library on Capitol Hill occupies three buildings and Prints and Photographs is in the John Adams Building on Independence Avenue. If you do not have a steady hand, it might be a good idea to take a camera stand.The Prints and Photographs Division is protective of its collection, as it should be. No flash is permitted because, over time, the bright light will damage the photos. For the same reason, photos cannot be scanned and older photos cannot be photocopied.

The Library of Congress emphasizes that it is up to the user to determine an image's copyright status, but most of the prints and photographs in its collection do not have copyrights. Some of the newer photos, such as those from 9/11, are copyrighted and usage rights have to be negotiated with the copyright holder, usually the photographer.

The National Archives system is different. The Still Pictures Research Room at the modern branch facility, Archives II, in College Park, Maryland, has some 8 million photos from a variety of government agencies. The subjects include natural resources, science and technology, and social programs. Archives II is a particularly good source for photos of America's wars, beginning with the Civil War. The National Archives has posted some 12,000 images on Flickr (www.flickr.com/photos/usnationalarchives). These include photos by Lewis Hine, who spent a decade in the early twentieth-century documenting child labor. There are also images of U.S. naval ships from 1775 to 1941 and photographs of the American West from 1861 to 1912.

People who cannot travel to Archives II for research can hire a local researcher. A list of researchers is posted on the Archive's website. There's also a list of vendors who, when provided with a photo's reference number, will make duplicates deliverable either by mail or Internet. These services are not affiliated with the Archives, so fees and other terms need to be negotiated directly with both researchers and vendors.

Photos from the Archives can be free or quite cheap. Unlike at the Library of Congress, researchers can scan high-resolution images onto their laptops. A copier is available for a dollar an image, and it makes prints good enough for publishing.

Fee-based Sources

Three of the largest fee-based photo sources are the Associated Press, Corbis, and Getty. These services typically charge rights-managed fees that are determined by how the image will be used—in a book or magazine, or for other purposes, such as an exhibit or advertising. When purchased for use in a book, the print run and the size of the photo (quarter page, half page, etc.) also determine the fee. Be prepared to pay $150 and up for an image.

The Associated Press, or AP (www.apimages.com), which is a news collective started in 1846, has the rights to some 10 million photos. Researchers are assigned to an account executive and then given access to the collection online. Once an image is purchased it can be downloaded immediately.

Corbis (www.corbisimages.com) was founded in Seattle in 1989 by Bill Gates. It has a collection of over 100 million images. These include the famous Bettman Archives, with its 19 million images, many of them well-known historical photos. Corbis also has exclusive rights to some 40,000 Ansel Adams photographs. The Corbis collection includes art photography from renowned institutions such as the London Museum of Art and the Philadelphia Museum of Art.

Getty (www.gettyimages.com) is another Seattle-based stock photo company. It has 80 million images. Among its treasures are the Michael Ochs archive, which was described by the *New York Times* as "the premiere source of music photographs in the world." And it has 15 million images from the British media dating back to the nineteenth century.

As you can see, there are hundreds of millions of images available, often for free, to illustrate your books or articles. The trick is to find the right ones, the ones worth a thousand words.

EXPERTS: BORROWING THE KNOWLEDGE YOU NEED

BY SUE BRADFORD EDWARDS

Whether you write what you know or delve into subjects that intrigue but are new to you, editors want primary sources. For some subject areas, such as history, this means locating letters, journals, maps, and other contemporary documents. For science and other academic topics, writers can turn to research studies and professional journals. For almost any topic, experts sources are among the strongest of all. Experts can expand on material located in journals, settle controversies, and give you access to the latest information in their field.

Despite this, many writers avoid contacting experts. Some hate cold calling. Others are not sure where to find experts or how to contact them. Still others worry about having to pay these sources. To put these concerns to rest, we interviewed a group of writers who connect with experts to bolster their manuscripts. The first piece of advice they gave us? Do your research.

Research First

Research is still essential, even when you are going to consult an expert. "I take advantage of as many public sources of information as I can," says author Melissa Joulwan. "That way, I don't waste interview time covering basics and can jump right into asking questions that garner new information or dig into details that might need more explanation. I've been the subject of interviews, and I find it a bit disrespectful when the interviewer hasn't done sufficient homework to have a basic understanding of my work and areas of expertise."

Do research first to make the best possible use of your expert resource. This way you will recognize when you are being told something new. "I do a great deal of research before I interview an expert for two reasons," says Kelly Milner Halls. "I want to confirm that published information is true—or is false, if that's how things play out. But I also want to hear what's new and not yet widely known. My job is to unearth new material to excite and inform young readers about my topics. So I do a lot of research first. As a secondary benefit, being so well versed in an expert's work makes the interview easier. The expert doesn't have to stop to explain as often, because I've already done my homework. Being well-prepared helps you come across as a trusted professional."

Just how much time you spend on research will vary depending on your background and topic. Melissa Stewart often writes about science for educational publishers. "I have a science degree, so it usually doesn't take too much time to get up to speed on the scientist's area of expertise," she says.

Finding the Pros

Another reason to research first is because the research itself will lead you to the experts to interview. "I read magazines, published scientific papers and books," says Hall. "I watch documentaries. As I do, certain names come up again and again as the true experts in any subject. Those are the people I want to interview."

Once you have a name, a Google search can lead you to the

expert. Many have their own websites. Others can be found through the universities and museums where they work.

If a search engine dump does not yield this information, look for contact information for the publisher or producer of the book, site, or documentary that was your original lead. "If I can't find contact information online, I contact the organization that published the material and ask," says Hall. "I've almost never failed to find my contacts using that technique."

Author Mary Roach often searches journal article databases such as PubMed or Google Scholar. "Put in a keyword and you have at a glance the people who are doing work in this area," she says. Unfortunately, the journals she finds sometimes are available to her only through PubMed. "You have to pay $30 to download the article," Roach says. Even if this is the case, take a look at the abstract and any other information that is publically available. "You can usually get the contact email without paying this fee. This is how I start to find people who are relevant."

Social media can also help you locate possible sources. "If I feel like I don't personally know someone who is right for the subject I'm covering, I turn to the experts I follow on Twitter and Facebook," Joulwan says. "I've also had good luck asking my Twitter and Facebook followers for recommendations and introductions to people they think would make good sources."

Last but not least, ask the experts themselves. "Everyone I talk to, I ask who they would recommend," says Roach. "People in the field are the best resource for who's who and who to talk to. It is always really valuable to pick an insider's brain."

Creating the Questions

Once the preliminary research has resulted in a list of names, prepare your questions.

Do not compose questions about topics, facts, or details that

WHAT IF I CAN'T USE AN INTERVIEW?

One very real worry is that you will take an expert's time and then not be able to use the information in the finished piece. Author Carla McClafferty has an answer. "In my very first communication I am totally honest about what I need from them, where I am on the project, and that I will thank them on the acknowledgment page of the book," she says. "I always tell them I don't know exactly how much of their work, if any, will be in the final version of the book—because I don't know how it will all go together in the end."

This gives McClafferty the flexibility to create the best possible piece of writing without trying to finagle a quote into the final piece to mollify an expert. "For example, take my new book, *Fourth Down and Inches: Concussions and Football's Make-or-Break Moment* (Carolrhoda)," she says. "I blend the cutting-edge medical and scientific research with the love of the game of football. My first interview was with Dr. Ann McKee at the Center for the Study of Chronic Encephalopathy (CSTE) at Boston University. Dr. McKee is the brilliant neuropathologist that is often interviewed on the news about this topic. I interviewed many other people for the book. While Dr. McKee and a few others are prominent in the text, not everyone I interviewed appears there, but I do list them in the acknowledgment page—as I promised."

Not every quote will make the final cut, but every one you do include will make for a stronger finished piece.

you could have gotten from your reading. This is the time to go beyond. "By the time I interview them, I've read everything I can about their work," says author Carla McClafferty. "I ask them questions that I cannot find the answers to any other way."

Avoid questions with one-word answers. Instead, ask questions that allow your sources to tell about their work, to give examples and to expand. "Ask questions that will allow your expert to share the heart of their passion for their field of expertise," says Hall. "Ask new, smart questions that will expand the informational exchange. It's more fun for you and for your subjects."

When it comes time to do the actual interview, do not be afraid of a little quiet in your phone or face-to-face interview. "It's important to ask open questions that give the interviewee room to expand, tell stories, share details, etc.," says Joulwan. "Let there be silence. It's in the quiet spaces that the juicy bits are revealed."

Stewart agrees. "Sometimes the best information comes when you let the interviewee just talk," she says.

Be ready to follow up one question with another if you need more information. Sometimes the treasures come from something other than specific questions. "I'm not locked into any particular thread of questions," Roach says. "I have a list of topics."

If you have a problem understanding what the expert is saying, ask for clarification. "It can be challenging when a scientist doesn't know how to talk without using academic jargon," says Stewart. "Some interviewees have trouble explaining things in a way that my young readers will understand. When this happens, I ask the scientist to imagine he or she is talking directly to a child. If that doesn't work, I might suggest suitable analogies or comparisons until the expert begins to get a sense of how to communicate with kids who have a limited knowledge of science."

Making Contact

Right about now, after the questions have been prepared, some writers start to panic. Introverts dread the thought of making a cold call and asking someone to do an interview. The solution is simple. Do not make a cold call.

"I make initial contact through email," says Roach. "You can bring them up to speed on the project and include a one-paragraph bio so they see you're legitimate. With an email, you aren't putting them on the spot like with a cold call."

Because you want the expert to say yes to your interview request, use this email to your best advantage. Introduce yourself. Explain a bit about the project. If you have a contract for an article or book, that is an important fact to include. You can also include sample questions you have already written so that they can get a better idea of what your slant is. This is vital when you are writing about something a little offbeat, such as Roach's *Stiff: The Curious Lives of Human Cadavers* or *Bonk: The Curious Coupling of Science and Sex* (both from W. W. Norton). "When I wrote *Stiff*, people were 'What is this? Is it a textbook?'" Roach says. "I don't want to mislead them. It gives them an opportunity to see the type of writing I do and the types of books I do. They feel more confident about saying yes."

Make the interview process as painless for your experts as possible. Give them several options when it comes to doing the interview itself. You can continue the exchange through email. The benefits of email are flexibility—you do not have to mesh your schedule with that of your expert—and a factual record— you have their answers in writing. You can also interview over the phone or via Skype. A phone interview allows for more spontaneity and makes follow up questions a bit easier.

"I tend to offer up a list of questions when I make email contact so, if they want, they can respond via email and our telephone call can be for follow-up questions," says Halls. "But I'm happy to discuss the questions on the telephone, too, if that's the interview source's preference. My job is to make it as easy to talk with me as possible. They are doing me a favor. So I bend over backwards to address their needs, rather than worrying about my own."

Many writers worry that experts will want payment. "The only experts that I've heard about wanting to be paid are Apollo astronauts because they are so besieged with interview requests," says Roach. "I've never had anyone request to be paid. I have offered to compensate someone if they seem very busy and reluctant to speak to me, but they've never taken me up on it."

Halls has never paid someone for an interview. "Only once in 20 years has an expert asked for payment," she says. "I simply found another expert. If someone insists on being paid, go down to the second expert on your list. Or ask that expert if his or her graduate assistant would be willing to discuss the topic without exacting a fee. They'll probably say yes, and the grad students do half the hard work anyway."

Doing an interview is not a shortcut and it may take considerable nerve to contact that first expert, but interviews are one of the best ways to gather the primary data that can enhance your writing and add lines to your résumé. Why not start looking for an expert for your next article or book?

READING TO WRITE

Ideas From the Inspiration of Other Writers

BY CATHERINE WELCH

The first question most writers are asked when people find out what they do for a living is how they get their ideas for short stories, novels, or nonfiction projects. If you are like me, you must actively search for ideas. I struggle to be creative. I am a logical thinker, which helps with certain stages of writing, but I tend to be a rigid thinker. I need an activity that shakes things up in my brain and gets me thinking in new directions.

I could seek out thrilling new experiences like dangling from a zip line to stir creative thoughts, but I would probably just end up with a migraine. So I choose to read—often, voraciously, and eclectically.

When reading I do not look to *steal* another writer's ideas or copy another writer's work. I view the ideas in others' work as springboards for my own new, unique creations. Here are examples of what I might read and how I brainstorm ideas for future projects.

Read Magazine Articles for Ideas

In the May/June 2013 issue of *American Spirit*, Courtney Peter opens her article, "The Coast Guard: Always Ready Since 1790," with the fact that the United States Coast Guard protects 95,000 miles of shoreline. That amazing fact gets me wondering about which of these miles is the most difficult to protect. This might be worth researching. I also wonder what it is like to be on a Coast Guard ship in the waters off Alaska. Does the water washing aboard the ship freeze?

Peter also includes information about the early life-saving stations along the country's waterways. When the water was too rough, the men shot a line to a wrecked or stranded vessel. That line was connected to a line that pulled a "submarine-like life car." People got in that car and were pulled to safety. The car held enough air to keep 11 people alive for 3 minutes. Imagine writing a short historical fiction story from the viewpoint of one of the 11 people.

In "The Better to Fool Others" (*Discover*, June 2013), author Paul Raeburn writes about self-deception. He focuses on the work of evolutionary biologist Robert Trivers, who studies why we lie to ourselves. The ideas in this article about deception are great starting points for fiction and nonfiction works. One concept is that those who deceive themselves can more easily deceive others. Consider that as a theme for fiction, or the motivating force behind a protagnoist or secondary character.

Another idea is that the ability for deception may be genetically determined. If this topic excites you, you might do research about the genetics of deception and write an article about current scientific findings. You might write a nonfiction book about the great deceivers in history or literature.

Raeburn's article also gives me this idea for a novel: What if a secret criminal society or terror group actively recruits expert deceivers and places them in government positions? Or I might think about writing a humorous picture book. What if a traveling salesperson (a clever deceiver) convinces an entire town that his special odor-eater lamps can rid the air of toxins?

As Raeburn points out in his *Discover* article, self-deception can result in loss of lives. He gives the example of a 1982 plane crash that might have been prevented if the pilot had believed the instruments, which suggested the plane did not have enough speed for takeoff. Why didn't the pilot believe the instruments? We do not know what the pilot was thinking, but this shocking bit of information should get you thinking. Why might a character in your short story or novel refuse to believe facts presented to him or her? Who might die as a result of the self-deception?

If you never read personal experience pieces or essays, consider doing so. In "No Turning Back" (*Bicycling*, July 2013), we follow author Mark Levine as he embarks on an 18-mile bike ride. Before he leaves home, his wife warns him it is supposed to rain, but Levine presses on. (Hmmm. Self-deception?) Early in the ride, he sees a dark storm cloud and another biker who turns around and heads back to town, but Levine continues pedaling. It takes thunder, lightning, flying debris, and hail to convince Mark he should take shelter in a bank doorway. He ends the article by asking himself why he feels compelled to ride during a storm. He guesses that he is "chasing the sensation of being fully alive."

The ideas in "No Turning Back" get me thinking about motives for people's actions. How many people go through life chasing something because they want to feel fully alive? For adult and young adult fiction or nonfiction, you might explore the topic of people engaging in risky behavior. What compels someone to swim with sharks, build a house at the base of a semi-active volcano, or become a housekeeper for a woman who is suspected of killing five other housekeepers? Why do some people never feel fully alive? Do some people lack a spiritual component to their lives? Or does it just come down to genetics? Perhaps some people's brains are lacking something.

Read Short Stories for Ideas

In the anthology *Shadow Show: All-new Stories in Celebration of Ray Bradbury* (HarperCollins) is a story by Charles Yu. After reading Bradbury's story "There Will Come Soft Rains" from *The Martian Chronicles*, Yu was inspired to write the short story, "Earth (A Gift Shop)."

In Bradbury's story, a fully automated house continues its daily routine after the people have died from a nuclear explosion. In Yu's story we see a future Earth, when fossil fuels are depleted and civilizations have collapsed. Most humans have long gone to other planets with some people returning to Earth for vacations. The narrator of the story tells how some of those who remain on Earth try to reinvent themselves. First, they try selling Earth as a museum, which travelers find boring. Then they try marketing Earth as a theme park and gift shop for travelers. It turns out the park rides are too expensive and dangerous, and the travelers just want a souvenir to take home. So "Earth: The Gift Shop" is the final stop for the planet.

What ideas from Bradbury's and Yu's stories get your attention? I love the idea of people reinventing themselves. I think of the teens who hope to recreate themselves once they leave high school and go to college. It might be fun to follow a teen's journey of reinvention. Does the reinvention include going so far from home that the teen's new friends will never have to meet his or her family or old friends? How many lies might a teen be willing to tell for this reinvention? (Deception. I see that idea is attached to my brain like a leech!)

Reinvention can also be a topic for a picture book. What if Raccoon Randy, who is habitually late for events, decides to be on time (or even early) for every town event? What if he drives everyone crazy trying to always be on time? Maybe the town people prefer the Raccoon Randy who is always running late.

SUGGESTED READING

- *After: Nineteen Stories of Apocalypse and Dystopia,* edited by Ellen Datlow and Terri Windling (Hyperion).
- *Baseball: A Literary Anthology edited by Nicholas Dawidoff* (The Library of America). Includes stories, memoirs, poems, news reports, and insider accounts about all aspects of baseball.
- *The Book of Virtues: A Treasury of Great Moral Stories,* edited by William J. Bennett (Simon & Schuster).
- *The 50 Funniest American Writers: An Anthology of Humor from Mark Twain to The Onion according to Andy Borowitz* (The Library of America).
- *How Did You Get This Number?* by Sloane Crosley (Riverhead Books). In this book of essays, the author takes the reader to Paris, Portugal, Alaska, and New York City.
- *Life on Mars: Tales from the New Frontier.* An original science fiction anthology edited by Jonathan Strahan (Viking).
- *Read It and Eat: A Month-by-Month Guide to Scintillating Book Club Selections and Mouthwatering Menus* by Sarah Gardner (Hudson Street Press).
- *Shadow Show: All-new Stories in Celebration of Ray Bradbury,* edited by Sam Weller and Mort Castle (William Morrow). Includes author notes that explain how Bradbury's work inspired each author's story.
- *Tripping Over the Lunch Lady and Other School Stories,* edited by Nancy E. Mercado (Dial Books).

I also keep thinking about Bradbury's idea of a fully automated house continuing its daily routine after the people have died. I might make this idea my own by first taking technology out of the picture. What if human servants of a mansion continue maintaining a house after the homeowners die? Why might human servants do this? How did the homeowners die? What might happen if a lost traveler spends a night at the mansion?

In the May 2012 issue of *Highlights for Children* is Jean Reagan's humorous story, "Mom Isn't Fancy." In this story, Jane finds her mom a source of embarrassment. Jane's mom, unlike the fancy-clothed moms, often wears gardening clothes, laughs too loudly, hums, and whistles. Jane has a change of heart about her mom during a class hiking trip, when Mom catches a snake that the fancy moms fear.

The idea of a child or teen being embarrassed by a family member is not a new one. Many writers have and will use this basic idea in their own stories. How can you put your own spin on it? What if a child's stay-at-home dad has a part-time job walking the neighbors' dogs. Imagine Dad walking the child, along with 10 dogs, to school each morning. What happens when all the dogs stop to poop? Yuck. How embarrassing!

In "Mom Isn't Fancy," Reagan shows Jane giving Mom a set of rules before the class hiking trip. In your story, you might *not* want to use this rules idea, to avoid writing a story that too closely resembles Reagan's story. The idea is to use the inspiration of the story but write your own, wholly original story, with your own voice, characters, and plot choices. I wonder what event causes the child to have a change of heart about his or her dog-walking dad? The child should be proud that Dad can handle so many dogs. I wonder how much one can make walking dogs? In Manhattan, a dog-walker might make quite a lot of money—and there is a topic for a nonfiction article.

Read Plot Summaries of Books for Ideas

If you hope to write salable nonfiction, novels, or even picture books, you need to read complete works. But when searching for ideas for story plots, you might also first try reading plot summaries, which can be found in anthologies and sometimes on the copyright pages of books.

In Nanci Milone Hill's *Reading Women: A Book Club Guide for Women's Fiction* (Libraries Unlimited), one plot summary leaps out at me. Donna Ball's novel *A Year on Ladybug Farm* (Penguin) is set in the Shenandoah River Valley in Virginia. This is the story of three middle-aged friends who try to reinvent their lives after the children are grown and husbands are gone by purchasing and renovating a run-down mansion. In reinvention (here is that idea again) I see a new twist for my story of the college-bound teen. What if three college-bound teens work together to reinvent themselves and form a clique on campus? For a nonfiction article, some aspect of home renovation might be a good topic.

Even if you are not a fantasy writer, you might like to take a look at the plot summaries in Ruth Nadelman Lynn's *Fantasy Literature for Children and Young Adults* (Libraries Unlimited). Vit Horejs's *Pig and Bear* (Macmillan) has an interesting plot. In this book for young readers in grades one to four, Pig and Bear struggle to run a pawn shop, having no prior experience running such a business. This idea of running a business with little knowledge is one that can be used in stories for picture books, chapter books, novels, and nonfiction for many ages, including adults. Brainstorm a list of interesting businesses: catering, pest control, lobster fishing.

Roger Norman's novel *Albion's Dream: A Novel of Terror* (Delacorte), for readers in grades 6 to 10, tells the story of an English boarding-school student who discovers that whatever happens on the board of an old game called Albion's Dream also happens in real life. What ideas do you get after reading this plot summary? What if the billboard in the center of a town keeps changing? What if the commercials on TV affect the lives of people in a town?

Now, I leave you with a choice. You can head for the nearest adventure park and knock your socks off on the zip line, or you can find a cozy spot in the library and start reading—and then writing.

On the Road: Geography & Travel Research

By Mary Northrup

One of the rewards of reading is being transported to another place. If your writing involves other places, you will want to do research on cities, countries, regions, and continents, plus what goes on in those places, including weather and climate, and the area's cultures and peoples. Perhaps you are interested in writing service pieces for travel magazines; a book about a life-changing journey to a foreign country; a children's nonfiction series to supplement the geography curriculum; or maybe an article about the geography and culture of a particular country.

Whether you need information on the location of a lake near a major city, a historic storm, the language spoken in a particular region, or the type of housing typical in a foreign city, you can find information in a variety of formats from sources that will help you make your writing accurate. For fiction and nonfiction, for articles and books, in writing for children or adults, the following sources will steer you to the right path as you travel through the world of information.

Starting Points

Many writers just like to get on the web, enter search words, and see what comes up. This is fine if you do not mind wading through millions of results. Just be sure to critically evaluate the sites you use. Typically, .edu and .gov websites are the most reliable, with .org sites as possibilities as long as you realize they probably have a bias. The .com sites, usually commercial, may be trying to sell something, although they may also contain some good information. Look for a list of authoritative sites later on in this article.

You may decide to start at your local library. Here you will find books, databases, and magazines that will aid you in researching geography and travel topics. If you have questions, ask a reference librarian, who will guide you to even more sources in whatever topic you are researching, and even point out local, specialized collections.

Get Going with Books

At the library, you can browse shelves to find books in specific areas.

- In the Dewey Decimal classification system, used in most public libraries, look in the 551s for books on weather and meteorology and in the 910-919 section for books on geography and travel.
- If you are at a large research university library that uses the Library of Congress classification system, browse in G-GF for geography, G149-180 for travel, and QC 851-999 for meteorology and climatology.

Besides browsing, you may want to use the online book catalogue to find books on your topic. Your library catalog may be connected to other branches or libraries in your area, so that you can request books to be sent on interlibrary loan. As you are searching in the catalog, try these subject headings:

- Travel, or Travel – name of country or city or area (Example: Travel – Costa Rica)
- Related subjects, such as air travel, bicycle touring, voyages, tourism, ocean travel
- Geography and related subjects, such as environmental geography, historical geography, maps, physical geography, urban weather
- Weather forecasting, or meteorology, and related topics, such as storms, droughts, winds

Rev Up with Reference Books

If you need a short definition, a long entry explaining a concept, or a fast fact, look for dictionaries, encyclopedias, and other volumes in your library's reference section. Here are a few standard sources that may be helpful.

- *The Columbia Gazetteer of the World*, second edition (Columbia University, 2008): This three-volume work contains 170,000 entries, defining every country, county, city, and physical feature in the world.
- *Encyclopedia of Climate and Weather,* second edition (Oxford University, 2011): These three volumes contain long entries explaining terms and places, each with a short bibliography at the end for further research.
- *Encyclopedia of Weather and Climate,* revised edition (Facts on File, 2007): Concepts in these fields are explained, along with appendices: biographies, top storms, laws, disasters, and discoveries.
- *Merriam-Webster's Geographical Dictionary,* third edition (Merriam-Webster, 2007): All political and physical entities are contained here, with maps. Lists at the back, in "Geographical terms in other languages" could be helpful.

- *The Weather Almanac,* twelfth edition (Gale, 2011): Many charts and graphs, summaries of climatological data from 1980 – present for 128 U.S. cities, and a timeline of meteorology for 9000 BC – 2000 AD make up this resource.

Atlases

Every library has a collection of these oversize volumes where you can find continents, countries, and cities and all their physical features.

- *National Geographic Atlas of the World,* 9th edition (National Geographic, 2011)
- *Oxford Atlas of the World,* 20th edition (Oxford University Press, 2013)
- *Rand McNally Road Atlas* (Rand McNally, annual)
- *The Times Atlas of the World,* 13th edition (HarperCollins, UK, 2011)

Moving on with Travel Guides

Some of the best sources for information on countries and cities can be found in travel guides. A number of companies have series; travelers and researchers usually find their favorites among them. For a semiannual roundup of new travel guides, see *Booklist* magazine, available at most libraries, with the travel listings usually appearing in the April 15 and the September 15 issues. Many public libraries have quite an extensive collection of these guides to check out; you may also want to visit their websites. Here are just a few of the most popular guide series:

- Fodor's: www.fodors.com
- Frommer's: www.frommers.com
- Insight Guides: www.insightguides.com

- Lonely Planet: http://www.lonelyplanet.com
- Rick Steves: http://www.ricksteves.com
- Rough Guides: http://www.roughguides.com

If you would like to write for these or other travel guides, consult the instructions for writers on their websites, usually under Contact Us or Work for Us.

Delving into Databases

If you have never used databases before, check out these great sources of reliable information, available at public and academic libraries. Many libraries also allow remote access, so you can search at home with access available using your library card number. Here is a sampling:

- ABC-CLIO U.S. Geography: Overview, with history and contemporary issues, for all states and regions; compare state rankings in a number of areas.
- Applied Science and Technology: Full-text articles from journals and magazines, including those on topics such as climate, meteorology, and weather.
- Columbia Gazetteer: Online version of the print reference source, with added information.
- CultureGrams: Information on the land, climate, and people of countries and states.
- Hospitality, Tourism and Leisure Collection: Articles from industry journals and magazines, travel guides, and newspapers; audio and video.
- Science in Context: Browse or search topics, including weather-related topics; articles, reference books, audio, websites.
- Science Online: See Weather and Climate section for

THE TRAVEL LITERATURE GENRE

If you long to follow in the footsteps of Sir Walter Raleigh, Graham Greene, Robert Louis Stevenson, or Mark Twain, you will find that a whole body of travel literature exists. Many historical travel writers were also explorers, and their writings can inspire as well as inform.

■ To investigate the field of travel literature and its famous authors, browse books such as *Encyclopedia of Travel Literature,* by Christopher K. Brown (ABC–CLIO), which offers entries on famous travel writers, explorers, and places.

■ To read about travel writing, check out *The Cambridge Companion to American Travel Writing,* edited by Alfred Bendixen and Judith Hamera (Cambridge University Press).

■ For examples of modern travel writing, see *The Best American Travel Writing* (Mariner/Houghton Mifflin Harcourt, annual).

entries from reference books; also images and videos.

■ Science Reference Center: Full-text articles and entries from reference books, including those on climate and weather.

■ Today's Science: Current news in science, plus an extensive glossary; search by keyword or browse the topic index.

■ World Geography and Culture Online: Facts and statistics for countries and states, from geography and weather to economy and education.

Stopping Along the Way with Magazines

Many of the databases above contain articles from magazines and journals, but you may also choose to browse the print magazines. Your local public library probably subscribes to one or more of the following.

■ *Condé Nast Traveler:* www.cntraveler.com

■ *National Geographic:* www.nationalgeographic.com

■ *National Geographic Traveler:* http://travel.national-geographic.com/travel/traveler-magazine

■ *Travel & Leisure:* www.travelandleisure.com

■ *Weatherwise:* www.weatherwise.org

Wend Your Way Through Websites

As with so many other subjects, there is no shortage of websites in the areas of geography, travel, and weather. The federal government (.gov) publishes many authoritative sites. Associations are another good source for accurate information from experts in the field. Try some of these.

■ The American Geographical Society: www.amergeog.org. An organization of professional geographers; find out about their publications and library.

■ Association of American Geographers: www.aag.org. An organization of geographers devoted to the advancement of geography.

■ Atlapedia Online: www.atlapedia.com. Information on geography, climate, people, statistics, religion, language, education, history, and economy for all countries, including physical and political maps for countries within their regions.

■ BBC News Country Profiles: http://news.bbc.co.uk/2/hi/country_profiles. An overview of each country or territory with a listing of facts, leaders, media, and timeline; information on countries and international organizations, such as OPEC, NATO, and the United Nations, plus audio and video from the British Broadcasting Corporation.

■ National Climatic Data Center: www.ncdc.noaa.gov. The

TRAVEL WRITING CAREER RESOURCES

Books

- *Make Steady Money as a Travel Writer: Secrets of Selling Travel Stories—Without Traveling,* by Jack Adler (Robert D. Reed Publishers).
- *Break into Travel Writing,* by Beth Blair (Hodder Education).
- *Travel Writing 2.0: Earning Money from Your Travels in the New Media Landscape,* by Tim Leffel (Splinter Press).
- *Travel Writing: See the World, Sell the Story,* by L. Peat O'Neil (Writer's Digest Books).
- *A Travel Writer's Handbook: How to Write—and Sell—Your Own Travel Experiences,* by Louise Purwin Zobel and Jacqueline Harmon Butler. (Surrey Books).

Organization

- Society of American Travel Writers: www.satw.org

world's largest provider of weather and climate data; maps and reports on climate in the United States.
- National Geographic Society: www.nationalgeographic. com. Browse through photographs and videos at this site, companion to the popular National Geographic magazine, with lots of coverage of geography and travel.
- National Oceanic and Atmospheric Administration (NOAA): www.noaa.gov. The government agency in charge of daily weather forecasts, storm information, and climate monitoring.
- National Weather Service: www.weather.gov. Part of NOAA; the place to check for current conditions, weather alerts, a variety of forecasts, past weather, and information on weather safety.

- Travel and Tourism Sites for U.S. States and Territories: www.usa.gov/Citizen/Topics/Travel-Tourism/State-Tourism. shtml. Links to the tourism websites of each state and territory.
- Tourism Offices Worldwide Directory: www.towd.com. Contact information for government tourism offices, visitors' bureaus, chambers of commerce, and other organizations where users can find free information
- U.S. National Park Service: www.nps.gov. Extensive information to learn about or visit historical and natural landmarks, from battlefields to coral reefs, seashores to mountains.
- U.S. Department of State Background Notes: www.state. gov/r/pa/ei/bgn. Current information on foreign countries as they relate to the U.S., plus links to much more.
- U.S. Travel Association: www.ustravel.org. Organization for those in the travel business. Look under "Research"; some publications are publicly available.
- Weather.com: www.weather.com. Sponsored by The Weather Channel; current weather and storm updates; how weather affects travel, health, recreation, home and garden.
- World Factbook: www.cia.gov/library/publications/the-world-factbook. Lots of facts and statistics, plus maps of regions and countries, sponsored by the Central Intelligence Agency.
- Google Maps: https://maps.google.com. Enter any address, city, country, or geographical feature.

The websites of historical societies in the city or state you are researching, or those of the city's Convention and Visitors' Bureau may also be good sources of information.

Travel Writing Markets

- *AAA Traveler:* www.aaa.com/traveler
- *AARP Bulletin:* www.aarp.org/bulletin
- *AARP the Magazine:* www.aarp.org/magazine
- About.com: www.about.com
- *Adirondack Life:* www.adirondacklife.com
- *Adventure Cyclist:* www.adventurecycling.org
- *Alabama Living:* www.alabamaliving.com
- *Alaska Airlines:* www.alaskaairlinesmagazine.com
- *Alaska Business Monthly:* www.akbizmag.com
- *Alaska:* www.alaskamagazine.com
- *Albemarle:* www.albemarlemagazine.com
- *Alternatives Journal:* http://alternativesjournal.ca
- *AMC Outdoors:* www.outdoors.org
- *American Angler:* www.americanangler.com
- *Among Men:* www.amongmen.com
- *Archaeology:* www.archaeology.org
- *Arizona Foothills:* www.arizonafoothillsmagazine.com
- *Arizona Highways:* www.arizonahighways.com
- *Arlington:* www.arlingtonmagazine.com
- *Aruba Nights:* www.nightspublications.com
- *Athens Parent:* www.athensparent.com
- *At Home Tennessee:* www.athometn.com
- *Austin Man:* www.atxman.com
- *Azizah:* www.azizahmagazine.com
- Babble.com: www.babble.com
- *Backroads:* www.backroadsusa.com
- *Bask:* www.baskmagazine.com
- *Bassmaster:* www.bassmaster.com
- *Beach:* www.modernluxury.com/beach
- *Best in Travel:* www.bestintravelmagazine.com
- *Better Homes & Gardens:* www.bhg.com

TRAVEL WRITING MARKETS

- *Big World:* www.bigworldmagazine.com
- *Blue Ridge Country:* www.blueridgecountry.com
- *Bonaire Nights:* www.nightspublications.com
- *BootsnAll:* www.bootsnall.com
- *Boundary Waters Journal:* www.boundarywatersjournal.com
- *Bowhunter:* www.bowhunter.com
- *Camping Today:* www.fcrv.org
- *Canadian Family:* www.canadianfamily.ca
- *Canoe & Kayak:* www.canoekayak.com
- *Cessna Owner:* www.cessnaowner.org
- *Charleston:* www.charlestonmag.com
- *Chatelaine:* www.chatelaine.com
- *Chesapeake Bay:* www.chesapeakeboating.net
- *Chesapeake Family:* www.chesapeakefamily.com
- *Christian Home & School:* www.csionline.org/chs
- *Cigar Aficionado:* www.cigaraficionado.com
- *Cigar & Spirits:* www.cigarandspirits.com
- *Cincinnati:* www.cincinnatimagazine.com
- *City & Shore:* www.cityandshore.com
- *Coast & Kayak:* www.coastandkayak.com
- *Coastal Living:* www.coastalliving.com/magazine
- *Coast to Coast:* www.coastresorts.com
- *Cocotraie:* www.cocotraie.com/the-magazine
- *Connecticut:* www.connecticutmag.com
- *Connecticut Parent:* www.ctparent.com
- *Connecting: Solo Travel Network:* www.cstn.org
- *Convention South:* www.conventionsouth.com
- *Cosmopolitan for Latinas:* www.cosmopolitan.com/cosmo-latina
- *Cross Country Skier:* www.crosscountryskier.com
- *Cruising World:* www.cruisingworld.com
- *Curaçao Nights:* www.nightspublications.com

- *Curve:* www.curvemag.com
- *DAC News:* www.dacnews.com
- *Delaware Beach Life:* www.delawarebeachlife.com
- *Diablo*: diablomag.com
- *Dirt:* http://dirt-mag.com
- *Dirt Rag:* www.dirtrag.com
- *Dirt Toys*: www.dirttoysmag.com
- *Dog Fancy:* www.dogfancy.com
- *The Dollar Stretcher:* www.stretcher.com
- *Family Circle:* www.familycircle.com
- *FamilyFun:* www.parents.com/familyfun-magazine/
- *Family Motor Coaching:* www.fmca.com
- *Fido Friendly:* www.fidofriendly.com
- *Fitness Plus:* www.fitplusmag.com
- *Florida Sportsman:* www.floridasportsman.com
- *FLW Outdoors:* www.flwoutdoors.com
- *Fly Fisherman:* www.flyfisherman.com
- *Flyfishing & Tying Journal:* www.amatobooks.com
- *Fly Rod & Reel:* www.flyrodreel.com
- *Game & Fish:* www.gameandfish.com
- *Georgia Backroads:* www.georgiabackroads.com
- *Georgia*: www.georgiamagazine.org
- *German Life:* www.germanlife.com
- *Glamour:* www.glamour.com
- *Go For a Ride:* www.gofarmag.com
- *Go* (NC): www.aaagomagazine.com
- *Go* (NY): www.airtranmagazine.com
- Grandparents.com: www.grandparents.com
- *Hampton Roads:* www.hamptonroadsmagazine.com
- *Healing Lifestyles & Spas:* www.healinglifestyles.com

- *Heartland Boating:* www.heartlandboating.com
- *Hemispheres:* www.hemispheresmagazine.com
- *Highway News and Good News:* www.transportforchrist.org
- *Highways:* www.goodsamclub.com/highways
- *Horizon Air:* www.alaskaairlinesmagazine.com/horizonedition
- *Houseboat:* www.houseboatmagazine.com
- *Hudson Valley:* www.hvmag.com
- *The Improper Bostonian:* www.improper.com
- *Indianapolis Monthly:* www.indianapolismonthly.com
- *Inland NW:* www.inlandnw.com
- *Inns:* www.innsmagazine.com
- *Inside Pennsylvania:* www.insidepamagazine.com
- *Insite:* www.insitebrazosvalley.com
- *The International Railway Traveler:* www.irtsociety.com
- *Interval World:* www.intervalworld.com
- *Invitation Tupelo:* www.invitationtupelo.com
- *Irish America:* www.irishcentral.com/irishamerica
- *Irish Connections:* www.irishconnectionsmagazine.com
- *Island Gourmet:* www.nightspublications.com
- *Jacksonville:* www.jacksonvillemag.com
- *Journal Plus:* www.slojournal.com
- *Kansas!:* www.kansasmag.com
- *Kansas City Prime:* www.primemagkc.com
- *Kashrus:* www.kashrusmagazine.com
- *Kearsarge:* www.kearsargemagazine.com
- *Kentucky Monthly:* www.kentuckymonthly.com
- *The Knot:* www.theknot.com
- *Lakeland Boating:* www.lakelandboating.com
- *Lexington Family:* www.lexingtonfamily.com
- *Life in the Finger Lakes:* www.lifeinthefingerlakes.com

- *Living for the Whole Family:* www.livingforthewholefamily.com
- *Long Island Woman:* www.liwomanonline.com
- *Louisville:* www.loumag.com
- *Lucky Peach:* www.mcsweeneys.net/luckypeach
- *Maine:* www.themainemag.com
- *Makeshift:* www.mkshft.org
- *Marin:* www.marinmagazine.com
- *Martha's Vineyard:* www.mvmagazine.com
- *Midwest Living:* www.midwestliving.com
- *Minnesota Conservation Volunteer:* www.dnr.state.mn.us/magazine
- *Mississippi:* www.mississippimagazine.com
- *Missouri Life:* www.missourilife.com
- *MotorHome:* www.motorhomemagazine.com
- *Natural Life:* www.naturallifemagazine.com
- *New Mexico:* www.nmmagazine.com
- *Newport Life:* www.newportlifemagazine.com
- *New York Family:* www.newyorkfamily.com
- *Niagara Escarpment Views:* www.escarpmentviews.ca
- *North Dakota Horizons:* www.ndhorizons.com
- *Northeast Flavor:* www.northeastflavor.com
- *Northern Breezes Sailing:* www.sailingbreezes.com
- *Northwest Travel:* www.nwtravelmag.com
- *Official Virginia Wine Lover:* www.vawinelover.com
- *Off Track Planet:* www.offtrackplanet.com
- *Ohio:* www.ohiomag.com
- *Oklahoma Today:* www.oklahomatoday.com
- *Ontario Out of Doors:* www.ontariooutofdoors.com
- *Orange:* orangemagazineny.com
- *Oregon Coast:* www.northwestmagazines.com
- *Our State:* www.ourstate.com

- *Palm Springs Life:* www.palmspringslife.com
- *Panama Days:* www.nightspublications.com
- *Parade:* www.parade.com
- *Parenting:* www.parenting.com
- *Pathfinders Travel:* www.pathfinderstravel.com
- *Pennsylvania Heritage:* www.paheritage.org
- *Pennsylvania:* www.pa-mag.com
- *Persimmon Hill:* www.nationalcowboymuseum.org
- *Philadelphia:* www.phillymag.com
- *Pink Corner Office:* www.pinkcorneroffice.com
- *Pittsburgh Parent:* www.pittsburghparent.com
- *Points North:* www.ptsnorth.com
- *Pontoon & Deck Boat:* www.pdbmagazine.com
- *Popular Anthropology:* www.popanthro.com
- *Portland Monthly:* www.portlandmonthly.com
- *Preservation:* www.preservationnation.org/magazine
- *Raising Arizona Kids:* www.raisingarizonakids.com
- *Recreation News:* www.recreationnews.com
- *Red Bulletin:* www.redbulletin.com
- *Reign:* www.denverreign.com
- *Reunions:* www.reunionsmag.com
- *Rider:* www.ridermagazine.com
- *River Hills Traveler:* www.riverhillstraveler.com
- *Road & Travel:* www.roadandtravel.com
- *RoadBike:* www.roadbikemag.com
- *Roanoke Valley Woman:* www.roanokevalleywoman.com
- *Robb Report:* www.robbreport.com
- *Route 66:* www.route66magazine.com
- *Ryse:* www.rysemagazine.com
- *St. Maarten Nights:* www.nightspublications.com

- *San Antonio:* www.sanantoniomag.com
- *The Saturday Evening Post:* www.saturdayeveningpost.com
- *Savannah:* www.savannahmagazine.com
- *Scuba Sport:* www.scubasportmag.com
- *Sea Kayaker:* seakayakermag.com
- *Sea:* www.Seamagazine.com
- *Seattle:* www.seattlemag.com
- *Serendipity:* www.serendipitygreenwich.com
- *Silent Sports:* www.Silentsports.net
- *Simply Buckhead:* www.simplybuckhead.com
- *S.I. Parent:* www.siparent.com
- *Skiing:* www.skiingmag.com
- *Slice:* www.sliceok.com
- *The Society Diaries:* www.thesocietydiaries.com
- *The South:* www.thesouthmag.com
- *South American Explorers:* www.saexplorers.org
- *South Dakota:* www.southdakotamagazine.com
- *Southern Boating:* www.southernboating.com
- *South Florida Parenting:* www.sfparenting.com
- *Southwest Airlines Spirit:* www.spiritmag.com
- *Spark:* www.al.com/spark
- *SpeciaLiving:* www.specialiving.com
- *Specialty Travel Index:* www.specialtytravel.com
- *Sports Afield:* www.sportsafield.com
- *Sunset:* www.sunset.com
- *Susquehanna Life:* www.susquehannalife.com
- *Syracuse New Times:* www.syracusenewtimes.com
- *Tallahassee:* www.tallahasseemagazine.com
- *Telemark Skier:* www.telemarkskier.com
- *Texas Highways:* www.texashighways.com
- *Texas Parks & Wildlife:* www.tpwmagazine.com

Travel Writing Markets

- *Tidings:* www.tidingsmag.com
- *Times of the Islands:* www.timespub.tc
- *Today's Chicago Woman:* www.tcwmag.com
- *Trailer Life:* www.Trailerlife.com
- *Trail Runner:* www.trailrunnermag.com
- *Trains:* www.trainsmag.com
- *TransWorld Snowboarding:* www.snowboarding.transworld.net
- *TravelAge West:* www.travelagewest.com
- *Travel + Leisure:* www.travelandleisure.com
- *Travel Goods Showcase:* www.travel-goods.org/travel-goods-showcase
- *TravelSmart:* www.travelsmartnewsletter.com
- *Tucson Woman:* www.tucsonwoman.com
- *Ulster:* www.ulstermagazine.com
- *UMM (Urban Male Magazine):* www.umm.ca
- *Vermont Life:* www.vermontlife.com
- *Via:* www.viamagazine.com
- *Virginia Living:* www.virginialiving.com
- *Virginia Wine Lover:* www.virginiawinelover.com
- *Wake Living:* www.wakeliving.com
- *Washington Family:* www.thefamilymagazine.com
- *Washington Flyer:* www.washingtonflyer.com
- *Washington Trails:* www.wta.org
- *Western Living:* www.westernlivingmagazine.com
- *Western New York Family:* www.wnyfamilymagazine.com
- *Where Toronto:* www.where.ca/toronto
- *Wisconsin West:* www.wisconsinwest.com
- *Women's Running:* www.womensrunning.com

Time for a Break: Research Leisure Activities

By Katherine Swarts

Reading for its own sake is many people's idea of a good time. But those with other leisure preferences still turn to articles and books for information on their own greatest pleasures. The writing opportunities in this category are endless.

Backyard soccer, crocheting, travel, window-shopping—if you intimately know your own favorite pastime, you have an immediate starting point. Any active hobbyist can be his or her own expert source. "Share your knowledge or experience with your reader," says Vivian Dubrovin, Editor of Storycraft Publishing. "If you have an advanced specialty, write about that."

If, however, you are a total greenhorn, or want to write about others' favorite leisure activities, everything starts with research, including market research.

First Steps

"Before you begin," says Dubrovin, "do a literature search. What has been done before? What is now needed? How will your information help? Whom will it help? Don't just do an Internet search of titles or reviews; study material close to the subject. It will give you ideas about what information to include, how to organize it, and how to define your message."

Once you have nailed a basic idea, pay attention to two information sources that no leisure-activities writer should ignore: those who do the activity all the time, and obtaining your own hands-on experience. "Contact organizations that promote the activities," advises Becky Newell, Editor in Chief of *American Quarter Horse Journal*. "Ask for names of people who are actively doing that activity, and ask for locations where you can try the activity."

For expert sources, interviews are virtually mandatory; do not try to get away with just reading books and press releases, although you should also read your chosen expert's work. "Do your homework," says Dan Kesterson, Editor of *Youth Runner*. "Coaches and other experts get interviewed a lot. Ridiculous questions will make them roll their eyes and want to cut it short." Interviewees are asked sometimes asked for information that is in plain view on their websites, or even in the email signatures they used responding to initial inquiries (like their exact professional titles). If you want to communicate to your sources that you see them as objects, mere tools for your project, go ahead and ask questions by the seat of your pants. It will be detrimental to your writing if you do, making your interviewee sound flat unless the real person has a chance to come through.

"Experts have heard all the basic questions before," says Dan Lucas, Editor of *Chess Life*, "and will quickly lose interest if they're asked the same" ones yet again. Do not ask yes or no questions either; they evoke few quotable responses.

"Don't expect the expert to teach you basics," says children's nonfiction book author Vicki Cobb. "Be knowledgeable enough to ask intelligent questions. Experts often are thrilled to share what they know with an intelligent layperson. I have watched reticent scientists become animated and blossom when I start interviewing them. I remind them of why they got interested in their field in the first place."

In-person interviews are always best if you want to show your subject's individuality. The more direct attention you give the person, the better. "Don't take notes," suggests Graham McCracken, Publisher of *Fibre Focus*. "Keep your eyes and attention focused on the person so you can go with the flow. Digital recording will give you an accurate record." While not every writer—or interview subject—would agree that notes are dispensable, every interviewer should look the subject in the eye and also take in the surroundings.

Phone interviews are the next choice, but increasingly writers are using email interviews. With some sources, says Kesterton, "We get better results with email questions, especially if you're not comfortable talking one on one with an intimidating expert."

Getting on the Field

As for hands-on experience, "Whenever you write about directions for doing anything," says Cobb, "it is imperative that you actually do the activity yourself. Even if you're a rank beginner, you get insights that are impossible if you only *arm-chair* what you're talking about. I have never published a science experiment that I haven't done." (Given that Cobb has been publishing entire books of children's science experiments since 1972, that is saying a lot!) "I think the most interesting books on sports were written by George Plimpton, who lived among professional athletes as if he were one. Read his book *Paper Lion* about his stint as a pro football player, or *The Bogey Man* about his travels with the PGA tour."

Adventure Cyclist, published for more than 30 years, specializes in bicycle travel, covering virtually any bike-tour-worthy part of the world. Most of its freelance articles are first-person accounts of specific trips. The magazine includes a Nuts & Bolts sections detailing hints "for readers as information useful to duplicate the trip," says Editor Michael Deme. This includes "what airlines serve the area, what policies they have about shipping bicycles, where a person could get maps, books available on the area, and any other useful information particular to that area or region." Naturally, the magazine prefers that writers personally make the bike trip they plan to focus on. Accounts of trips taken some years ago are acceptable, but writers should "have at least driven the route" more recently, says Deme, to note anything that has changed enough to make a difference to future travelers.

Your personal perspectives can also provide ideas for topic angles. "In the early days of my own writing," says Dubrovin, "I was given an assignment to write a series of third-grade books on sports. There weren't many books for that reading level, and the ones I found for older kids all had the same theme: 'If you try hard you can win!'" Dubrovin recalls that after studying several of those books, "I left the library to pick up my son at his summer track program. It was a hot day—over 100 degrees—and sweat was running down his face, and he had tried his hardest, but he would never come in first. He wasn't an athlete. I had my theme: 'You don't have to be first to win. There are many ways of winning.' Each book [in the resulting series] held a story of one way of winning. I still look for that message in books and stories today. Leisure sports are not meant to be competitive."

"I think the most authentic pieces are written by people who dream up creative angles that resonate with them," says Cobb. "What are the biggest training errors? Why is good form important in learning a sport? What are your best insider tips for the novice? When writing queries, make sure you pose an intriguing question and hint at the answer. You want to give editors who've seen it all something that will make them notice you."

Cobb continues: "It is sometimes fun to conflate a sport with some other activity or quest. As a woman who skied, I once thought of writing a piece for a resort magazine on how to *work* the mountain as a single woman, which I was at the time. It's a great way to meet guys, similar to speed dating. I had all kinds of tips on how to do it. Every time I went skiing by myself, I met someone. I met my husband at the bottom of the Avanti chairlift in Vail." Leisure activities come in many forms.

Resonating with Your Reader

If you already know your topic well—or once you master it—it can be easy to forget that everyone starts as a beginner. Insider jargon will make a newbie's eyes glaze over. "If you're an expert," says Cobb, "and you want to communicate something, chose a small tip that enhances performance. Don't try to teach too much. My husband taught himself to become an expert skier by reading magazine articles and first practicing the moves in his office. Ultimately he became extraordinary, someone everyone noticed for his perfectly carved turns."

Conversely, you may be a learning-as-you-go writer who suspects that your audience is well above your level. In that case, says Kesterton, "just be real. Most folks see through made-up technical jargon anyway, and if you really don't understand the topic, the readers that do know it will be turned off and never come back."

Interviewing an expert as an amateur has advantages, says Newell. Most interviewers "don't ask very good questions if you, yourself, already know all there is to know about the activity. Look at an expert interview as a way for them to fill you in. I think the writer has to be the one to break down what the experienced participant says, to make it understandable to readers of all skill levels. Ask the person to compare the activity to something.

E-Interviewing

Like self-publishing, e-interviewing is rapidly gaining respectability. And for good reason: It allows maximum scheduling convenience all around, minimizes accidental misquotation, and gives sources more chance to think before speaking. Email interviews work best when:

- The topic is not controversial and sources have no personal stake. If there is risk of someone protesting a quote, a voice recording is your best evidence.
- The expertise is what counts. If a source's actual personality is important, the more direct the contact the better.
- More than three sources are involved for an article, or more than seven for a book. In that case, the focus is probably on the topic and meeting a deadline, and the advantage of not having to juggle schedules becomes pronounced.
- The source requests it. Whenever possible, honor source preferences.

When e-interviewing, follow these hints for maximum effectiveness:

- To approach a new contact, send an introductory email of up to three short paragraphs, clearly explaining your assignment and why this person would be a valuable expert source. Be concise and descriptive in your subject line. For example: "Freelance writer needs expert sources on backgammon" or "[Mutual contact] recommended you as stamp-collecting expert."
- Send a well-edited list of 5–7 questions—specific and detailed, and not so many as to look like a survey.
- It is fine to include interview questions in the introductory message; it can save time all around. But put the questions after the signature, noting their presence in the message body.
- Always thank everyone who replies to an inquiry. If the answer is no, ask whether they would like to be considered for future articles.
- Definitely thank again all who do participate—and let them know when your project is published. If you can, send each source a free copy.

For example, in the quarter horse world, we compare the reining discipline to ice skating in that the horse and rider have a number of required maneuvers in a pattern, much like an ice skater has a number of required jumps and spins."

"A beginner can't write instructional articles," says Lucas, "but can certainly write a profile piece" or something in the interesting-news department. "A good way to break in is to look for anniversaries; an editor might not realize that in a few months the fiftieth anniversary of such-and-such will occur. All the better if the query includes connections that tie the piece to current events."

Whatever you do, do not be the writer who proposes an article on "the basic breeds of cats" to a magazine for seasoned cat-show regulars. Would you introduce a calculus curriculum with the basics of long division? "You've got to find an angle that will resonate with people who know more than you know," says Cobb. "That's exactly what Plimpton did."

Adventure Cyclist covers a broad range of reader expertise, notes Deme, from vicarious participants who have never even taken a bike trip to seasoned long-distance cyclists who "have traveled all over the world." Strictly speaking, the editorial in *Adventure Cyclist* "is not really about the bicycle; that's just the vehicle you use." It is about the person and the adventure. Hence, the magazine uses very few freelance articles that are heavy on techno-speak or focused on bicycle buying and maintenance. Rather than going to the experts for their articles' most important information, "the people who are writing the stories tend to be the experts themselves," says Deme, but the focus is on sharing a story with peers, rather than instructing others.

Which points up the number-one rule for any writer: "Never forget your audience," says Cobb. "Who are you writing for? The novice? The timid soul? The couch potato? The wannabe expert? That will shape the way you offer material and will give your

RECREATION & LEISURE MARKETS

Article Sources

■ *Adventure Cyclist:* Adventure Cycling Association, 150 East Pine Street, P.O. Box 8308, Missoula, MT 59807. www.adventurecycling.org/adventure-cyclist

■ *American Quarter Horse Journal:* American Quarter Horse Association, 1600 Quarter Horse Drive, Amarillo, TX 79104. www.aqha.com

■ *Chess Life:* United States Chess Federation, P. O. Box 3967, Crossville, TN 38557. www.uschess.org

■ *Fibre Focus:* The Ontario Handweavers & Spinners, Box 1444, Everett, Ontario LOM 1J0 Canada. www.onhs.on.ca

■ Storycraft Publishing: P. O. Box 205, Masonville, CO 80541. www.storycraft. com

■ *Youth Runner:* P. O. Box 1156, Lake Oswego, OR 97035. www.youthrunner.com

More Markets

■ *About Families:* www.aboutfamiliespa.com

■ *Adirondack Life:* www.adirondacklife.com

■ *Adventures NW:* www.adventuresnw.com

■ *AMC Outdoors:* www.outdoors.org

■ *American Snowmobiler:* www.amsnow.com

■ *Appaloosa Journal:* appaloosajournal.com

■ *Athlon Sports:* www.athlonsports.com

■ *AT Journeys:* www.appalachiantrail.org

■ *Backroads:* www.backroadsusa.com

■ *Bassmaster:* www.bassmaster.com

■ *BassResource:* www.bassresource.com

■ *Bicycle Retailer and Industry News:* www.bicycleretailer.com

■ *Boundary Waters Journal:* www.boundarywatersjournal.com

■ *Bowhunter:* www.bowhunter.com

■ *The Bridge Bulletin:* www.acbl.org

■ *Camping Today:* www.fcrv.org

- *Canoe & Kayak:* www.canoekayak.com
- *Cessna Owner:* www.cessnaowner.org
- *The Chronicle of the Horse:* www.chronofhorse.com
- *Cigar Aficionado:* www.cigaraficionado.com
- *City & Shore:* www.cityandshore.com
- *Club & Resort Business:* www.clubandresortbusiness.com
- *Coast to Coast:* www.coastresorts.com
- *Conscious Dancer:* www.consciousdancer.com
- *Convention South:* www.conventionsouth.com
- *Country's Best Cabins:* www.countrysbestcabins.com
- *Creations:* www.creationsmagazine.com
- *Cross Country Skier:* www.crosscountryskier.com
- *Cruising World:* www.cruisingworld.com
- *Dirt Rag:* www.dirtrag.com
- *Dirt Toys:* www.dirttoysmag.com
- *FamilyFun:* www.parents.com/familyfun-magazine
- *Family Motor Coaching:* www.fmca.com
- *Field & Stream:* www.fieldandstream.com
- *Fish Alaska:* www.fishalaskamagazine.com
- *Fishing Tackle Retailer:* www.fishingtackleretailer.com
- *FLW Outdoors:* www.flwoutdoors.com
- *Fly Fisherman:* www.flyfisherman.com
- *Flyfishing & Tying Journal:* www.amatobooks.com
- *Fly Rod & Reel:* www.flyrodreel.com
- *Game & Fish:* www.gameandfish.com
- *Go for a Ride:* www.gofarmag.com
- *Go (NC):* www.aaagomagazine.com
- *Go (NY):* www.airtranmagazine.com
- *Good Old Boat:* www.goodoldboat.com
- *Heartland Boating:* www.heartlandboating.com
- *Hemispheres:* www.hemispheresmagazine.com

- *Horizon Air:* www.alaskaairlinesmagazine.com/horizonedition
- *Houseboat:* www.houseboatmagazine.com
- *The International Railway Traveler:* www.irtsociety.com
- *Island Gourmet:* www.nightspublications.com
- *Knives Illustrated:* www.knivesillustrated.com
- *Lakeland Boating:* www.lakelandboating.com
- *Michigan Out-of-Doors:* www.mucc.org
- *MidWest Outdoors:* www.midwestoutdoors.com
- *Minnesota Conservation Volunteer:* www.dnr.state.mn.us/magazine
- *Missouri Conservationist:* missouriconservation.org/conmag
- *New York State Conservationist:* www.theconservationist.org
- *Niagara Escarpment Views:* www.escarpmentviews.ca
- *Northern Woodlands:* www.northernwoodlands.org
- *Northwest Travel:* www.nwtravelmag.com
- *Ocean:* www.oceanmagazine.org
- *Official Virginia Wine Lover:* www.vawinelover.com
- *Ontario Out of Doors:* www.ontariooutofdoors.com
- *Out & About:* www.outandaboutnow.com
- *Outdoor Canada:* www.outdoorcanada.ca
- *Outside:* www.outsideonline.com
- *The Ozarks Mountaineer:* www.ozarksmountaineer.com
- *Pennsylvania Game News:* www.penngamenews.com
- *Playground:* www.playgroundmag.com
- *Recreation News:* www.recreationnews.com
- *Reunions:* www.reunionsmag.com
- *Sail:* www.sailmagazine.com
- *Scene:* www.scenemagazine.info
- *Scouting:* www.scoutingmagazine.org
- *Skating:* www.usfigureskating.org
- *Skiing:* www.skiingmag.com

Recreation & Leisure Markets

- *SnoWest:* www.snowest.com
- *South Carolina Wildlife:* www.scwildlife.com
- *Southern Boating:* www.southernboating.com
- *Southwest Airlines Spirit:* www.spiritmag.com
- *Sunset:* www.sunset.com
- *Texas Parks & Wildlife:* www.tpwmagazine.com
- *Times of the Islands:* www.timespub.tc
- *Trail Runner:* www.trailrunnermag.com
- *TransWorld Snowboarding:* www.snowboarding.transworld.net
- *Washington Trails:* www.wta.org
- *Wisconsin Natural Resources:* http://dnr.wi.gov/wnrmag

work voice. Informational writing is never about the information so much as the human filter presenting it."

Remember that, and you and your readers can have a great time learning about leisure.

PINTEREST: THE GOOD, THE BAD, & THE DOWNRIGHT INACCURATE
Writers & Social Media Research

BY SUE BRADFORD EDWARDS

With 70 million users now pinning from their smartphones, tablets, laptops, and desktops, Pinterest has become home to a wide variety of images ranging from must-try hairstyles to Norman Rockwell posters. Books and blog posts tout this fast-growing social media site as a means to drive business, and numerous writers now use Pinterest for platform-building and marketing.

Marketing is important but Pinterest is good for much, much more. The astute writers we spoke with also use it for research, to organize their findings, and to inspire their work.

Researching Right

With so many images posted on Pinterest, it is becoming an increasingly valuable research stop for nonfiction writers whose work involves popular culture. "When I was working on a party planning article for the parenting magazine I edit, I browsed Pinterest for some fun party theme and favor ideas," says Renee Roberson, freelance writer and editor of *Little Ones*. "Pinterest also came in handy when I was working on a piece about how to make a child's lunchbox more eco-friendly. I wanted to get a sense of what types of products were out there and get an

RESEARCH & IDEAS 305

overview of cloth napkins, bamboo utensils, BPA-free water bottles, etc."

On Pinterest, writers can click on categories such as *food and drink* or *home decor* and immediately see the most popular posts in these topics. The ability to check trending posts is not only handy when writing a top-10 article, but also in adapting a trending idea to another area. A popular bridal craft might yield something for a princess-themed birthday party. Furthermore, knowing which Pinterest posts in crafts, classroom activities, and decorating cheats are trending can also reveal what topics editors in those areas have probably already seen.

Pinterest can be just as helpful for fiction writers who need to gather the specifics of a certain time and place. "When I was writing the first draft of a middle-grade novel set in the 1980s, I searched for images of summer camps that were located near Texas lakes, as well as posters and memorabilia from popular television shows during that time period," Roberson says. "I also pinned images of Walkmans, boom boxes and the neon fashions that were all the rage back then."

Pinterest images are not limited to Americana, so writers searching for something more exotic also stop by to see what they can find. "Since I write primarily Aztec-influenced science fiction, fantasy, and romance, I look for photography of Mesoamerican architecture and ruins, and artwork, including textiles," author Traci Morganfield says. "I keep an entire board of Central and South American textiles, so I can reference traditional patterns and clothing styles. In instances where my characters are historical figures or are based on mythological figures, I also look for artwork depicting them, to get ideas about small details to include in my prose descriptions." A *board* on Pinterest is where a subscriber *pins* all the images on a particular topic.

Like Morganfield, Nene Ormes's Pinterest searches also inform her characters. "My current work-in-progress is a gas-lamp fantasy," Ormes says. "I've used Pinterest for steampunk searches, for Victoriana, for old pictures of tourists in the East, and for pictures of people from different times and different cultures. Old photos have turned up and the people in them have made it into my story in different ways."

One of the best things about Pinterest is how one picture can lead to another. "What I particularly like about Pinterest is that if I find one image that is useful, frequently that user has a whole board of other related images. Often those are in areas that I wouldn't have thought to search for," says author Mary Robinette Kowal. To do this, Kowal simply clicks below the image on a link to the board where it is posted. There, she can see everything else on that board. Where these findings take her story is another matter altogether. "Recently, I was looking for an image of a World War I British captain's uniform and stumbled upon a group photo of Caribbean women in the British military," she says. "That gave me an idea which changed the outline of the novel I was working on."

To stay connected to an especially useful board, *follow* it with the click of a virtual button. "There are a number of wonderful pinners who are doing serious costume curation for various time periods, including Regency, medieval, and Renaissance periods," author Merrie Haskell says. "I follow them avidly."

In Plain Sight

As useful as Pinterest is in research, it is even more valuable in its ability to organize the material writers accumulate while working on a new project. "Pinterest has made my research gathering so much easier and changed how I keep my information," says Ormes.

As writers save images to Pinterest boards, they are not limited to pictures they find on Pinterest. Images from news feeds, blog posts, museum websites, and more can be pinned to their Pinterest boards as well. "I use Pinterest for organization and storage of images with links more than I do for searching," Haskell says. "If something comes across my feed that strikes me for a particular book, I will add it to one of my book boards."

Before Pinterest, writers had two choices. The paperless choice meant bookmarking websites to scroll through later, trying to find that one picture with the castle photos or the maps of Lisbon. Less patient writers often printed out material to have it on hand when they needed it, but that meant trying to locate a particular printout amid the chaos of a paper-strewn office.

Now writers simply pin their findings on a series of boards. Pinterest has anticipated the challenge of finding one particular pin. One recent innovation enables users to search just their own pins and find the castle amid the camels and crinolines they saved for future reference.

Inspire Me

While doing research for one article or book, it is not unusual to come across various images that might come in handy later. Many writers also keep inspirational boards of various kinds. "I keep large boards of clothing styles (*board:* Dressing for Past Lives), settings (*board:* Milieux), pictures that spark ideas (*board:* Story Ideas), characters (*board:* Character Studies) and quotes (*board:* Unsayable)," Haskell says. "When I start working on a book, I will wander through each of these boards and see if I get any shivers."

One board could be based on something an author always needs help with when starting a new project, such as setting. Another could be a category that acts as a writing prompt again and again, such as character. Once writers learn what helps them start a story, they can periodically search or simply browse the pins that have drawn their attention earlier or go looking for new ones.

"Occasionally, I just tool around, looking for something that will inspire or interest me based on key words," says author Shanna Germain. "My boards are organized into general gathering places first, with titles like Inspiration: Female Characters and Inspiration: Fairy Tales. Then they become something specific that I'm working on, like a novel in progress."

Some writers save inspirational quotes. Others pin peaceful locations. Still others collect creative bookcases, bookends, and bookmarks. When the time comes to start a new project, or when writer's block strikes, or when its time to transition into writing from another activity, these images and more help authors find their focus.

Writer Beware

If research, organization, and inspiration are the good, what then is the bad? "I love Pinterest, but it can suck you down the research rabbit hole more thoroughly than just about anything else," Kowal says. "All those pretty pictures, right there, waiting for me."

Not only can Pinterest become an elaborate electronic time drain, accuracy is another concern. Do a search on Mayan calendars and the vast majority of images returned are Aztec, one Mesoamerican artifact passed off as another. This is not the only example.

"When I did a search of Egyptian antiquities I found several descriptions that were just wrong," says Ormes. "The most blatant of mistakes was when the Pyramids were given the wrong names, and when Karnak temple was called Luxor temple. Even if they're close to each other, they are not the same thing. I wouldn't have

Pinterest Basics

For anyone unfamiliar with Pinterest, users *pin*, or save, photos to *boards,* which are not unlike web pages. Other users can view the images, *like* them, add their own comments, send them to others, or even re-pin the images to their own boards. As users follow each other's boards, they create networks that can take an image from obscurity to dozens of viewers in under an hour. Although quotations and other text blocks are posted, visuals drive Pinterest and quality graphics are a must for any successful post, even one based on a quote.

Writers on Pinterest:

Here is just a small number of the authors with boards to be found on Pinterest.

- Heather Blackwood: pinterest.com/heatherblackwood
- Eileen Dreyer: pinterest.com/eileendreyer
- Margot Finke: pinterest.com/margotfinke
- Shanna Germain: pinterest.com/shannagermain
- Merrie Haskell: pinterest.com/merrie
- M. K. Hobson: pinterest.com/mkhobson
- Mary Robinette Kowal: pinterest.com/maryrobinette
- Traci Morganfield: pinterest.com/tlmorganfield
- Nene Ormes: pinterest.com/lindorm
- Renee Roberson: pinterest.com/finishedpages
- Shiloh Walker: pinterest.com/shilohwalker
- Tiffany Trent: pinterest.com/tiffanyltrent

known the names were wrong if it weren't for my education as an Egyptologist."

The reason for errors is simple. "Since it's done by users, you can never be sure if the included information about the photograph is correct" on Pinterest, Morganfield says. "I find it less reliable than Wikipedia if only because Wikipedia has knowledgeable editors trying their best to fix inaccuracies, though it's by no means a reliable source either. I've often found artwork mislabeled or not labeled at all. There is no quality control on the metadata, so one has to be very careful about accepting anything at face value."

Verifying images for accuracy should not be difficult. "If you follow picture links to their original pages you can usually find out if the source is reliable or not," says Ormes. "It's much worse when a picture doesn't have a page link."

When someone pins a photo from a website or blog, the image links back to the original location. If the user uploads a saved image, they should credit the artist or photographer in the description because there is no external link. (Remember, if you want to use any photo found online, in Pinterest or elsewhere, you need to check who holds the copyright and if it is available for use. See the article "Find Great Photographs for Your Articles & Books," beginning on page 251.)

Another negative is that it can be difficult to trace an image pinned from a Tumblr account. "Where I run into problems is when I try to go back and look at the source material," says Kowal. "If they saw an image on the front page of a tumblr and pinned that, the url just takes me to the front page and the image may have already scrolled off of it."

To find information on a photo with no *home* or no attribution, Germain uses Tin Eye (www.tineye.com). "You upload the image and see who owns it or created it," says Germain. "Tin Eye doesn't have everything, so sometimes you search and can't find anything. But I'm surprised at how often it gives me an answer."

Google Image search (www.google.com/imghp?hl=en& tab=wi) is another option for tracking down the origin of a picture. Simply click on the camera icon in the text bar and follow the instructions to select the saved photo on your drive. Like any other source, Pinterest findings need to be checked for accuracy. Photo searches make this possible, but is Pinterest truly worthwhile?

The ease with which Pinterest enables writers to find and organize images is extraordinary, often inspiring them to collect more information than they might have done pre-Pinterest. This can bring unexpected benefits. "When I switched my current project from being set in the late 1800s to the early 1900s, the search for Edwardian dress, furniture, jewelry, and buildings gave me a feeling for the aesthetics of that era in a way my earlier research hadn't," Ormes says. "That number of pictures side by side gives an understanding that one picture with some annotation wouldn't have."

Pinterest has its limitations, but what other research tool can organize and inspire to this extent? These writers and many others have found Pinterest to be a tool worth exploring.

DRIVE YOUR IDEAS: 52 QUESTIONS TO RESEARCH & WRITE

BY SUSAN M. TIERNEY

Writing ideas come from many sources and directions. Some just come your way by chance. Others arise from specific calls for submissions, or editorial calendars or themes. Often enough, writers must go in a somewhat random pursuit of ideas to research and develop. The following questions, with their follow-up information and additional questions, are meant to help get the writing motor running so you can take off in new directions, on short trips or long, and arrive at an interesting destination.

Why is there such a strong link between smells and memory?
- What are the possible uses for a "telesmell" machine? See "A Camera That Captures Scent Instead of Sights," at www.slate.com/blogs/the_eye/2013/10/17/the_madeleine_ a_time_machine_for_olfactory_memories.html.
- What were Proust's techniques for invoking smells?
- How could a smell be at the heart of a plot solution, for a mystery, a romance, science fiction?

What is the Maker Movement?
- The Maker Movement comprises a "community of makers who bring a DIY mind-set to technology," according to

Make (makezine.com), which was launched in 2005 by Dale Dougherty. What are the origins of the movement, and what is its potential future?

■ The Maker Faire, the world's first, has been held annually in San Francisco since 2006. Participants bring their do-it-yourself creations, in a celebration of both arts and crafts and science and engineering. One of the goals of the movement is to improve young people's abilities in math and science. What are Maker Faires around the world producing? For example, the September 2013 faire in New York City was attented by 70,000 people and included a megaphone with guitar pedals, a percussive instrument made out of recycled items, workspaces to create LED pins and duct tape wallets, a robot dog, and lots of 3D printing.

■ The Maker Movement also involves *hackerspaces*, which are open workshops or labs for a community of people interested in coming together to share knowledge and resources while they develop software, hardware, or other technology. Hackerspaces arose in the 1990s in Germany, and have spread. They are also now not limited to technology, but have expanded to arts and crafts, still often using technology such as 3D printing. Today, hackerspaces or maker spaces include one in a high school in Sebastopol, California, where *Make* is published. The Fayetteville Free Library (http://fflib.org/fablab) in New York state was the first public library to open a maker space.

Which is more widely spoken, Mandarin or Cantonese?
■ In China itself, and around the world? (Chinese is the third most widely spoken language in the U.S.)
■ What are the histories of these languages? The cultural

differences they represent?

■ Who are famous literary figures in each?

■ How might variations in dialect in Chinese or any language play a part in a story plot, or in in forming a character?

■ Linguistically and historically, how have Chinese languages and Western languages intersected?

■ How are Chinatowns around the world the same and different? What plots might be set in them? For some leads, see "Chinatowns: A Little Bit Of Beijing, Wherever You Are," at www.npr.org/blogs/parallels/2013/10/19/ 236878193/chinatowns-a-little-bit-of-beijing-wherever-you-are.

What is the significance of loneliness in society today?

■ See an article on the condition as a social problem in Britain today, and a politician's take on it: "Jeremy Hunt Highlights Plight of 'Chronically Lonely,'" at ww.bbc.co.uk/ news/uk-politics-24572231.

■ What does loneliness mean for the most helpless in society, such as children and seniors?

■ What characters and conflicts might you develop out of the phenomenon of isolation and social loneliness?

How have different cultures, as well as scientists or medical professionals, seen mental illness and treated it?

■ Can we learn about mental illness from animals in some way? See an article on how hyenas are used in treatment in Somalia, "Where Hyenas Are Used to Treat Mental Illness," at www.bbc.co.uk/news/magazine-24539989.

■ How do definitions of mental illness vary from culture to culture? Use differing views as the point of conflict among characters in a story.

■ How have scientific views of *somatization*—experiencing psychological problems in physical form—changed, and how might the phenomenon be built into a fictional character and a plot? For example, *somatization disorder* was once called *hysteria*. Consider a contemporary story, and a historical story.

How many Springfields (or Greenvilles or Riversides) are there in the United States?

■ Where are they located, and what is each town like geographically, demographically, socially?

■ How might three different Springfields be depicted distinctly as fictional settings that inform the plot and characters of a novel?

■ What are some of the most unusual place names in the U.S., or around the world, and what was the genesis of each?

What classical fine art is available to the public online?

■ Who makes paintings and other art available for free online? In October 2013, the Getty Museum doubled the number of its digitalized works available for download by the public, to 10,000. (See www.theverge.com/2013/10/15/4841876/getty-doubles-open-art-collection-10000-pieces-studying-history.)

■ What other major museums digitalize art, and offer other online services? How might children study great art through collections offered in this way? In a time when the emphasis is on STEM (science, technology, engineering, math), what are the skills kids can develop through experience with the arts?

■ What are the current exhibitions at the Getty Museum, Metropolitan Museum of Art, British Museum or Tate Gallery, the Louvre, Hermitage, Prado, Guggenheim in Bilbao, or in other kinds of museums, like the Smithsonian, American Museum of Natural History, Mexico's National Museum of Anthropology, Egyptian Museum in Cairo, and so on? What articles or stories or books could be based on some aspect of an exhibition?

What is Tin Pan Alley?
■ What is the origin of its name, and the association with music? What other regional areas have had connections with music that have endured?
■ What other geographical areas have been associated with particular trades or industries, and have lent their names as *metonyms*? Consider Fleet Street, for journalism; Hollywood, for movie-making; Wall Street, for finance. What are some other examples?

Who plays vintage baseball today and how is it played?
■ What was the New York Knickerbocker style of baseball and what did it have to do with gentlemen's clubs? (See http://vbba.org)
■ Which nineteenth-century baseball players might be the basis for an interesting fictional character, or profiles?
■ In *Northanger Abbey,* Jane Austen writes about a 14-year-old girl playing cricket and baseball. What is the history of girls, women, and baseball?

Why has the age of the Earth mattered to people for so long?
■ How was it calculated at various times in history? From Greek and Roman theories to biblical estimates, to the

beginnings of modern science: See www.scientificameri-can.com/article.cfm?id=how-science-figured-out-the-age-of-the-earth. How did these various calculations reflect on the times and on religious and scientific beliefs?

■ What is the current science behind the dating of the Earth?

What new animals and plants have been discovered in the last year?

■ Are there still animals to be identified? See a National Geographic Society article on 400 new species identified in the Amazon, including a "purring monkey" and "thim-ble frog"). (http://newswatch.nationalgeographic.com/2013/10/25/purring-monkey-flamboyant-lizard-new-amazonian-species-are-totally-wild)

■ Would any of these sometimes unusual creatures or plants work in a piece of fantasy? What about at the center of a mystery?

What is cowboy culture and how does it manifest itself today, as society changes?

■ How did the American cowboy arise from the *vaqueros*?

■ How do century-old traditions merge with modern technology for today's cowboy?

■ What artists have portrayed and honored Western and cowboy life?

■ Who were the "cowboys of Westchester County" in the eighteenth century?

What is a wheatberry?

■ How is it used? What varieties of use does it have?

■ What cultures is it used in? What are its cultivation characteristics and place in agronomy?

- What are good recipes for using wheatberry? What is its nutritional value?
- What other foods are new to you, or new in general to the American palate?

What is the can-can?
- Where and with whom did it originate? What were its social origins?
- Who are the musical and other artists associated with it?
- What other, comparable, dances have had social or cultural impacts in history? The minuet, waltz, ragtime dances, the Charleston, the tango, the lindy, the twist, and so on.
- Where might any of these dances or others be used as part of fiction, as a theme, or as related to a character, a community, or a setting?

How does education and general knowledge shift over the decades, especially among young people?
- A Kent State study found a marked difference among college students in what they knew between 1980 and 2012. What did many contemporary students not know about that young people did a generation years earlier? Popeye. The name of the Lone Ranger's sidekick. Backgammon. Blubber. See "Kent State Research Shows Surprising Shifts in U.S. Knowledge," at www.kent.edu/news/newsdetail.cfm?newsitem=EF1F0097-AD5F-404E-1B2E67C70849C025.
- How has education changed over the last century, last two centuries? What was a *classical* education? (See, for example, the essay by Oxford-educated mystery novelist Dorothy Sayers at www.gbt.org/text/sayers.html.) Are

there arguments for classical education today, in the age of Common Core?

With all the threats of rising shores because of hurricanes, superstorms or global warming, what are the major coastal cities of the world doing in preparation?

■ New York City: In the aftermath of Superstorm Sandy, Mayor Bloomberg proposed adaptable floodwalls, levees, storm surge barriers, tidal barriers, dune systems, bulkheads, and a "seaport city." (www1.nyc.gov/office-of-the-mayor/news/201-13/mayor-bloomberg-outlines-ambitious-proposal-protect-city-against-effects-climate-change)

■ Venice: The city is building floodgates to protect the lagoon, and a new artificial island. (See "High-Tech Gates Will Hold Back Venice's Floods, at http://discovermagazine.com/galleries/2013/oct/holding-back-venices-floods#.Um1J5pT8krg.)

■ How have different regions and cultures adapted to coastal living across time? How might characters live in a futuristic coastal city?

Why was the biggest news in astronomy in 2013, the Comet ISON, of such importance?

■ What were Comet ISON's origins? How did comets of its kind help form the Earth? What set it on its path? (See "The Life and Death of Comet ISON," http://discover-magazine.com/2013/nov/11-comet-ison#.Um1EFpT8krg.)

■ Think of a science fiction or other story about why a particular location on Earth is being inundated with viewings of comets and meteors. For example, Comet ISON was observed in Russia in November 2013, and a meteor crashed and was recovered near Chelyabinsk, Siberia, in

February 2013. The famous Tunguska meteorite crashed in 1908. How many others and why? Or base a story on other major meteor crashes, like the one that landed in France in 1492—a famous year that perhaps was changed forever by the meteor for a fictional character?

When do children begin to develop math skills?
■ Do babies have innate math skills? Apparently some six-month-olds can distinguish between 10 and 20 dots. See a new study about the infant brain and numbers, "Babies Are Born With Some Math Skills," at http://news.sciencemag.org/ brain-behavior/2013/10/babies-are-born-some-math-skills.
■ In contrast, an Amazon tribe, the Pirahã, has no words for specific numbers or mathematical concepts and apparently never developed them. See "What Happens When a Language Has No Numbers?" at www. slate.com/blogs/lexicon_valley/2013/10/16/piraha_cognitive_anumeracy_in_a _language_without_numbers.html.

What was the origin of the legend of Atlantis?
■ What was Plato's purpose in discussing Atlantis? How did the legend expand over the centuries?
■ What other utopian societies have been the subject of literature or philosophy?
■ How might Atlantis be the setting of a modern story?

What have the Orkney Islands in Scotland revealed to archaelogists about neolithic life?
■ What has been learned from the huts of Skara Brae, the tomb of Maeshowe, and the Standing Stones of Stenness? What did the past decade's discovery and unearthing of

the Ness of Brodgar add to that knowledge?

■ What other great discoveries about neolithic and other prehistoric times have added to our understanding of the development of culture and history?

What is the Hasty Pudding Club?

■ What is hasty pudding?

■ What was the genesis of social clubs, fraternities, and sororities on college campuses?

■ What impact do these organizations have on the educational goals of college students?

■ In a piece of contemporary or historical fiction, consider setting the story amid a social club.

How is food culture changing in the U.S. today?

■ Celebrity has become a large part of general knowledge of food today. What are the social implications? See "Are Alton Brown's Recipes Any Good?" www.wired.com/ design/2013/10/celebrity-chef-smackdown/?viewall=true)

■ How is food culture the same or different from the past? Who were important figures in other times and cultures? Consider Amelia Simmons, author of the first American cookbook; Auguste Escoffier in the 1800s; and France's Guilaume Tirel (Taillevant) in the Middle Ages.

■ What will our current decade be remembered for in food? What will replace the typical tuna casseroles, cheese fondue, quiche, or pasta salads popular in other decades?

■ What cultures would you be interested in exploring for their food, perhaps those not considered stylish or modern today?

What is behind the piracy off the coasts of Africa? Where else does it occur?

■ The ICC Commercial Crime Services has an updated map of piracy all over the world at www.icc-ccs.org/piracy-reporting-centre/live-piracy-map. Also see "Pirate Attack Off Nigeria: Part of a Trend in West Africa," at http://energyblog.nationalgeographic.com/2013/10/ 25/pirate-attack-off-nigeria-part-of-a-trend-in-west-africa.

■ What is the history of piracy, and why was it more prominent at some periods of history than others?

■ What kind of character might you create as a pirate, but well beyond the stereotypes?

Just how old is social media really?

■ Author Tom Standage's *Writing on the Wall: Social Media—The First 2,000 Years* argues that social media is far from a new phenomenon. He claims that the distribution of political speeches in Roman times, Saint Paul's epistles, and Thomas Paine's pamphlets were forms of what we now call social media. See an excerpt at www.wnyc.org/story/social-media-pre-internet.

■ What forms of "instant communication" might play a role in a plot twist in a historical novel? What forms might develop in the future?

What have been the world's most important inventions?

■ The answer to that questions varies from one era to another, and among the people answering the question. But among the candidates: the wheel, nail, alphabet, paper, compass, eyeglasses, printing press, telescope, flush toilet, internal combustion engine, assembly line, penicillin, telephone, light bulb, refrigerator, automobile, electrocardiogram, computer, the Internet. For more ideas, see www.edinformatics.com/inventions_inventors, and for the answeres that might have been given in another time period, of another time, see "50, 100 & 150 Years Ago: The Greatest Inventions, up to 1913," at www.scientific-american. com/article.cfm?id=50-100--150-years-ago-2013-10-15.

■ What are some inventions that started out as one thing but became another, or discoveries made by accident? The most famous is probably penicillin, but others include corn flakes, potato chips, dynamite, Silly Putty, saccharin, X-rays, the microwave, pacemaker, Velcro, Teflon.

What are Maxwell's equations?

■ These principles or formulas underlying electricity and magnetism, were first stated in 1861–62 by James Clerk Maxwell, are still being studied.

■ How are they still being explored? See how recent solutions to the equations resulted in pictures of light tied in knots, at www.scientificamerican.com/slideshow.cfm?id=tying-light-in-knots-slide-show.

■ What instances have there been of art and technology meeting?

Who is Banksy?

■ What is unique about him? What has been groundbreaking about him? What tradition does he follow in? What is making him so trendy now?

■ What was the genesis of *street art* or graffitti in modern times? When did it begin to become seen as more than just the work of vandals? What is its status today? See a contemporary legal argument about public art, "Can the

Visual Artists Rights Act Save 5Pointz?" at www.wnyc.org/story/5pointz-and-visual-artists-rights-act.

■ How long a history does street or perfomance art of all kinds have, including buskers? What are the crossover points between visual street art and music?

Who are some of today's other most interesting contemporary artists?

■ Who, for example, is Do Ho Suh? (See "Do Ho Suh's Specimen Series," at www.phaidon.com/agenda/art/articles/2013/october/18/do-ho-suhs-specimen-series). Or see the artists featured at the New Museum of Contemporary Art (www.newmuseum.org).

■ What other specialized museums might be worth investigating, for contemporary or any other field of art? What about unusual museums of other kinds?

What is hypercorrection in speech?

■ Why do some people overcompensate in the way they speak, and in an attempt to be grammatically correct, instead make grammatical mistakes or mispronounce words in the process? Perhaps the most common example is the mistaken use of "you and I" when "you and me" is correct. See other examples in the blog of English and journalism professor Ben Yagoda, at www.slate.com/blogs/lexicon_valley/2013/10/22/amongst_hypercorrection_among_millennials_as_the_line_between_formal_and.html.

■ How might hypercorrection be one of the revelatory qualities of a fictional character? What does the practice of hypercorrection say about a character's social skills, or self-perception?

Do dogs have a sense of size or time? Do they feel emotions?

■ Scientists at Britain's University of Sussex studied whether and how dogs recognize the size of other dogs and concluded that they do, by using both sight and sound. Dogs use their senses together in unique ways, especially in social situations with other animals. See "How Dogs Make Sense of Size," at http://phys.org/news/2011-03-dogs-size.html.

■ Studies have also been done about dogs' ability to tell time, and how the process differs from the human perception of time. See "Do Dogs Understand the Concept of Time?" at http://animal.discovery.com/pets/do-dogs-understand-the-concept-of-time.htm.

■ Yet more recent research into dog behavior suggests that they do in fact experience emotions, and that we are not projecting or imposing our feelings on them. Gregory Berns, at Emory University, used MRIs to measure brain activity when dogs were given hand signals, when exposed to the smells of familiar humans, and when their owners came and went. The brain processes mirrored those associated with positive emotions in humans. See "Dogs Are People Too," at www.nytimes.com/2013/10/06/opinion/sunday/dogs-are-people-too.html.

Who have been some of the great literary monsters (beyond our still ongoing fascination with vampires and zombies)?

■ Consider: Gorgon. Cyclops. Beowulf's dragon, Grendel, and Grendel's dam. King Kong. Godzilla. Tolkien's Gollum and Sauron. Abominable snowman.

■ What other mythical or literary figures have become archetypes that can still work, or be transformed, in contemporary fiction? Phoenix. Nymphs. Elves. Mermaids.

Kelpies. Unicorns. Ogres and trolls. How about in African, Asian, or other cultures?

What is the 10-percent world?

■ In *The Once and Future World,* author J. P. McKinnon writes about what he says as our current world: one in which we have lost many animal and plant species that only 10 percent of the species that once co-existed with humans remain. He examines the impact and how we look at the world differently than we might if many were still extant. See "The Once and Future World: Nature As it Was, As it Is, As it Could Be," a Q&A with McKinnon at http://harpers.org/blog/2013/09/the-once-and-future-world.

■ The place of nature in the *modern* world has been lauded and argued among authors since at least the early Romantic period, with Wordsworth and Coleridge. Is nature still romanticized today? How would life be different if more species had been preserved? Imagine the fictional possibilities.

What exactly is genius?

■ How was genius originally defined, and why?

■ Can genius be taught? See "How a Radical New Teaching Method Could Unleash a Generation of Geniuses," at www.wired.com/business/2013/10/free-thinkers.

■ Create a character who is a genius, but who does not exhibit the stereotypical traits sometimes associated with geniuses in pop culture. Avoid the nerd or social misfit aspects, but create depth based on the character's perceptions of the world he or she lives in.

How near are electric vehicles (EVs) to being a widespread reality in the U.S.?

■ What part are towns, cities, states, the federal government playing as society moves toward different forms of transportation? For instance, the city council of Palo Alto, California, passed a mandate that all single-family houses now built must include EV chargers. In the future, EVs may be able to provide power, not just use it. See "Two-way Street: Electric Cars of the Future Could Give Power Back to the Grid," at www.theverge.com/2013/10/15/4838466/could-electric-cars-make-the-grid-go-p2p.

■ See business discussions of electric cars at *Electric Cars Report* (http://electriccarsreport.com).

■ What fictional modes of transportation might be at the center of a steampunk story, or a futuristic one?

Who was the famous Queen of Sheba really?

■ How much about her is fact and how much is fiction? See some of the science behind the possibilities, in "DNA Clues to Queen of Sheba Tale," at www.bbc.co.uk/news/science-environment-18526428.

■ What is the significance of the Queen of Sheba for African and Middle Eastern cultures, especially Ethiopian and Yemeni?

■ What artistic, literary, musical, and other references did she inspire in addition to appearing in the Hebrew bible and Qur'an? What were the legends and folktales? How was she depicted in the Middle Ages and Renaissance? In George Frideric Handel's *Solomon*?

How do dragonflies feed on the fly?

■ What are scientists learning about neuroscience from

dragonflies? At the Howard Hughes Medical Center, researchers are using *electronic backbacks* to study these highly efficient predators. See "Tiny Dragonfly Backpacks Reveal Mysteries of the Brain," at http://news.nationalgeo-graphic.com/news/2013/10/131008-dragonfly-backpacks-neuroscience-brain-motion, and "Nature's Drone, Pretty and Deadly," at www.nytimes.com/2013/04/02/science/dragonflies-natures-deadly-drone-but-prettier.html?_r=0.

■ Miniature transmitters have also followed the migration patterns of dragonflies (National Science Foundation, http://www.nsf.gov/news/special_reports/animals/dragonfly.jsp)

How has the human body changed over time to adapt to the world? What are the most recent adaptations?

■ *The Story of the Human Body: Evolution, Health, and Disease,* by evolutionary biologist Daniel Lieberman, explores why we walk on two feet and have a very large brain, and other developments since the Stone Age.

■ "Evolutionary mismatches" arise from a disconnect between our genes and the environment. Why do they matter for our health and longevity? Lieberman discusses myopia, diabetes, heart disease, and cancer in this context.

■ Apart from Lieberman's treatment of his subject, is the somewhat trendy paleo diet—also called the caveman diet—valid in terms of science and evolution? See "How to Really Eat Like a Hunter-Gatherer: Why the Paleo Diet Is Half-Baked," at www.scientificamerican.com/article.cfm?id=why-paleo-diet-half-baked-how-hunter-gatherer-really-eat.

What scientific evidence supports the benefits and principles of
Chinese medicine?

■ According to some, Chinese medicine was political prop-
aganda pushed in the 1950s by Mao Zedong, who allegedly
did not believe in it himself. Assistant Professor of
Chinese Philosophy and Religion Alan Levinson argues
that there is still a "staggering" amount of "misinforma-
tion about Chinese medicine." See "Chairman Mao
Invented Traditional Chinese Medicine," at www.slate.com/
articles/health_and_science/medical_examiner/2013/10/tr
aditional_chinese_medicine_origins_mao_invented_it_but
_didn_t_believe.html.

■ The U. S. government's National Institutes of Health has
a branch called the National Center for Complementary
and Alternative Medicine (http://nccam.nih.gov). What
are the alternative treatments that have been shown to be
effective for different ages and health issues—pregnant
women, back problems, aging, and so on?

Who were the Goths *and why and how do we still use the term?*

■ The Goths were a set of Germanic tribes that were present at the fall of the Roman empire, settled largely in central Europe, and included several leaders who held considerable power over the centuries, including Theoderic the
Great. They, in essence, disappeared by the end of the
Middle Ages.

■ Their name remains alive largely because of gothic architecture, which has nothing to do with the Goths. The
name was given to an architectural style that arose in
france in the twelfth century, but was not called Gothic
until the Renaissance.

■ Several Gothic Revivals, influenced by the medieval

architecture, occurred in later centuries, specifically in Britain in the 1700s and again in the 1900s. The association with *gothic* as *dark* began in the 1800s with Horace Walpole's romantic horror fiction, *The Castle of Otranto, a Gothic Story.*

■ The word goth remains in usage today in referring to someone who dresses and applies makeup in a black, somewhat morbid fashion. How might a contemporary goth teen character be shaped by some of the characteristics of Goths and gothic?

What is the story behind mustard?

■ Did you know National Mustard Day has been held in August since 1991? And that there is a National Museum of Mustard in Mount Horeb, Wisconsin?

■ While the mustard plant has been used in food since prehistoric times, its name comes from the Latin for "burning wine," *mustem ardens.* It is considered the world's oldest condiment.

■ It was first mentioned in recorded history by Hippocrates, the Greek physician, who used mustard as a medicine. Even up to modern times, mustard plasters have been used in increase blood flow because the plant has a natural ability to boost circulation.

■ The tiny mustard seed is a metaphor for growing faith in Christianity, because of Jesus's parable (Matthew 13:31-32).

■ Mustard gas has no mustard in it. The poisonous gas was given the name in World War I because they thought it smelled like mustard.

■ The French novelist Alexandre Dumas apparently loved Dijon mustard, and wrote "A Study on Mustard," for his

Grand Dictionnaire de Cuisine. Mustard is even mentioned in *The Three Musketeers.*

Are tapestries still being made as art today?

- To find modern examples of tapestry as art consult the American Tapestry Alliance (americantapestryalliance.org); see the magazine *Fiber Art Now* (fiberartnow.net); follow a tapestry board on Pinterest (www.pinterest.com/fiberart-nowmag/fiber-art-tapestry-weaving); locate private studios like Magnolia Tapestries (www.magnoliaeditions.com/about-tapestries), which uses modern computerized techniques to create contemporary tapestry art; or look to some of the major auction houses, like Christie's or Sotheby's.
- What tapestries from the past might serve as inspiration today for fine art? Or have a place in the setting or plot of a modern story? Consider these examples: the Bayeux Tapestry (actually embroidery); the Unicorn tapestries (Metropolitan Museum of Art); the tapestries that lined the Sistine Chapel when Michelangelo painted the ceiling, and actually cost more than he was paid; and after 1805, Jacquard tapestries, especially from Belgium, which were created by a new technology.
- What craft projects, for adults or children, might be based on the principles of weaving and the artistry of the tapestry?
- Tapestries in modern home design: Are they a new trend?

What are the current theories on the purpose, physiology, and psychology of dreams?

- The neurobiological theory: Dreams are nothing more

than an amalgam of arbitrary electrical brain impulses. We attach stories to them after we wake.

■ The evolutionary psychologist theory: Dreams are an inbred defense mechanism that helped people prepare for and counter possible threats or dangers.

■ A 2011 neuroscience research study found why dreams are more likely to be recalled immediately after our REM sleep, when we dream most. It has to do with *theta* waves, how well we can recall autobiographical memories while awake, and other functions of memory and emotion. Find research in the *Journal of Neuroscience,* at www.jneurosci. org/content/31/18/6674.abstract.

■ How might a character's memories be tied to a set of dreams that direct him or her to act in seemingly unpredictable ways? What physical qualities, and environmental factors, impact the dreams and the actions of your character?

What is the history of candy, and what is its standing in American culture today?

■ According to Samira Kawash, a former professor and an expert on the subject of candy (candyprofessor.com), only six percent of the added sugar we eat comes from candy, although our guilt level for eating it is so high. Her book *Candy: A Century of Panic and Pleasure,* investigates why.

■ Another interesting fact from Kawash: In the early twentieth century, candy was touted as a weight loss aid, but some people involved in the temperance movement believed candy could convert to alcohol in the stomach.

■ Candy, and trick or treating, did not become associated with Halloween until the late 1940s and 1950s in the U.S., according to Kawash. What has caused this transformation of the holiday? How would you set a children's story about Halloween in different decades?

Who are some of the active, interesting, or upcoming Native Americans leaders or cultural figures today?

■ Ray Halbritter, who represents the Oneida Indian Nation, has been pushing the NFL's Washington Redskins to change the team name, and for all teams to avoid inappropriate racial mascots. Halbritter has led the nation for more than two decades, and in that time has succeeded in gaining federal recognition of the Oneida government, built its businesses, and endowed a Harvard Law School professorship in American Indian law.

■ Diane J. Humetewa was nominated to the Arizona federal court by President Obama. Her heritage is Hopi. As of late 2013, no Native Americans serve as federal judges.

■ Mark D. Williams, a Choctaw, is an Oklahoma filmmaker who specializes in ghost hunting documentaries, and has also made two paranormal movies *The Dare* and *The Unrest*.

■ What about lesser-known Native American historical figures? One was Christine Quitasket, who used the pen name Mourning Dove to publish the first novel by a Native American woman, in 1927. It was called *Cogewea, The Half Blood: A Depiction of the Great Montana Cattle Range.*

Will all the data being gathered about each of us through technology improve or degrade our future?

■ MIT professor and author Alex Pentland's *Social Physics: How Ideas Turn into Actions* argues that humans are social animals above all, and that humans behave based on the ideas that flow through the social network. Pentland believes the data gathered and exchanged about individuals can improve society as a whole.

■ What is the state of the debate about the health care system, in relation to information shared and privacy issues? How does the right to privacy balance against widespread data uses, researchers' need for information, and the benefits of individuals being able to take advantage of digital advances like portable monitors?

■ When has a specific technology from the past changed the course of society? What writers, such as H. G. Wells or Karel Čapek (who coined the word *robot*), have explored this theme? How might you explore it in fiction today?

What makes for taste in music?

■ *Rolling Stone* has published an updated list of the greatest 500 songs of all time—within the context of rock and roll. What about the greatest music of earlier decades in the twentieth century? Or in classical music? For example, EMI lists the top 50 classical pieces of all time, ranging from Beethoven's Fifth Symphony through John Williams's theme to *Schindler's List*. How is music—like literature, art, film—measured from genre to genre, and generation to generation?

■ Our brains react to musical chords with emotions, whatever our culture. Research has also shown that our responses to music like heavy metal register as aggression in the brain, and may have a cathartic response. Certain musical chords trigger other physical reactions. Some experts also believe our musical tastes are set in adolescence. See "5 Ways Your Taste in Music is Scientifically Programmed," at www.cracked.com/article_20065_5-ways-

your-taste-in-music-scientifically-programmed.
html#ixzz2jhn4zv00www.cracked.com/article_20065_5-
ways-your-taste-in-music-scientifically-programmed.html.

■ What would be the personality and story arc be for a
contemporary protagonist who is moved by Gregorian
chant? Folk songs? Classic Chinese compositions? Cole
Porter? Broadway tunes? ABBA? The Clash? Springsteen?
Jay-Z? Adele? How can you change the mood of a story in
a *musical* way?

What are the current popular trends in other parts of the world?
■ For some of the latest trends in Japan see http://
web-japan.org. The site recently reported on the colorful
"Harajuku Kawaii" fashion, a mascot bear named
Kumamon, and the mix of traditional cakes called
Wagashi with Western cooking techniques.
■ For trends gathered from around the world, go to
Trendhunter (www.trendhunter.com). Recent items dis-
cussed included beer-infused pancakes, outdoor home
offices, taboo subjects and humor, plastic made from
beetle shells, and new bridal gifts.
■ Who are current style/fashion/culture icons who will
endure past the 15 minutes (or 15 sound bytes) of fame?
Who will be remembered as the next Madame de
Pompadour, Coco Chanel, Audrey Hepburn, Edie
Sedgwick? Why?

What makes cats love laser pointers?
■ Cats' vision is better at dawn, dusk, and the evening
because their eyes have many more *rods* than human eyes,
and a layer of tissue called the *tapetum* that brings in
light. They do not, however, see the same vibrant colors

people do in sunlight, and they have a limited range of vision—they cannot be too close or too distant because they do not have the eye muscles to adjust for distance as humans do. Cats' peripheral vision is better than ours. Compare in pictures at "Images: See the World from a Cat's Eyes, www.livescience.com/40460-images-cat-versus-human-vision.html.

■ Cats are right- or left-handed, with males primarily left-handed and females primarily right-handed.

What are some of the longest, shortest, biggest, hardest battles in military history?

■ The shortest war in history took place between Britain and Zanzibar. It lasted 45 minutes, in 1896.

■ The largest battle ever fought in northern Europe was the 1944 Battle of Tali-Ihantala, which took place between Finns armed with German weaponry and the Soviet army. Its results and significance are debated, with some seeing the Finns as defending their territory successfully and others seeing the battle as the event that eventually made Finland leave the war.

■ The largest battle in the Napoleonic Wars was the Battle of Wagram, in which the French emperor defeated Austrian and British forces. It took place in 1809.

■ Towton, in northern England, holds England's only mass grave from a medieval battle, part of the Wars of the Roses. The remains of a man who fought in the 1460 Battle of Towton have revealed to experts how different methods of fighting created wounds and killed medieval soldiers. See "The Battle of Towton: Nasty, Brutish, and Not that Short," at www.economist.com/node/17722650.

■ War literature ranges from *The Iliad* to *Beowulf* to

Shakespeare's history plays and some of the tragedies, *War and Peace, The Red Badge of Courage, All Quiet on the Western Front, For Whom the Bell Tolls, The Naked and the Dead,* and *The Quiet American.* How might war novels based on contemporary events—which have only slowly begun to appear since September 11—be shaped? What unique themes might they address?

What is the state of the African American community today?

■ According to the U.S. Census bureau, African Americans make up 13.1 percent of the population; the number does not include people of mixed race who do not identify solely as black. About 32 percent of African Americans over age 15 are married, and 47 percent have never married. Among other races, the numbers are 51 percent married and 31 percent never married.

■ According to BlackDemographics.com, and based on U.S. census figures, black-owned businesses grew dramatically between 2002 and 2007—up 60.5 percent.

■ In 2011, African American college students numbered 3.9 million, 2 million higher than in 1993; 1.6 million African Americans had an advanced degree, in comparison to 677,000 in 1995. BlackDemographics.com lists the states in which blacks have achieved the most educational success as Maryland, Colorado, Oregon, California, and Massachusetts. The states on the bottom of the list are Wisconsin, Louisiana, South Carolina, Mississippi, and Alabama.

■ In a study released in 2005, it was found that the same number of black, white, and Hispanic drivers were stopped by the police—9 percent across the board. But in comparison, only 3.5 percent of whites were searched, in comparison to 10 percent of blacks and 11 percent of Hispanics. Among whites, 2 percent were ultimately arrested, in comparison to 5.8 percent of blacks and 5.2 percent of Hispanics.

Do first-born children really succeed more in school?
■ If they do, why? New research confirms that first-borns do tend to do better in school and on IQ tests, and are less prone to adolescent problems with drugs and pregnancy. The study, conducted by V. Joseph Hotz and Juan Pantano, theorizes that the cause comes down to the difference betwen parents who are *unforgiving*—that is, monitor homework and punish poor performance—and those who are *forgiving*—or inconsistent and at some points fail to discipline for poor performance. More parents are unforgiving with first borns. The study also found that with each additional child in a family, supervision of the first born increased. See "Strategic Parenting, Birth Order and School Performance," at www.nber.org/papers/w19542. Also see the article reviewing this research, "Why First-Born Kids Do Better in School," at www.slate.com/articles/double_x/doublex/2013/10/birth_order_and_school_performance_first_borns_do_better_in_school_because.html.
■ How might these findings create a dynamic between a parent and several children in a fictional story about family tensions and sibling relationships? What kind of family diagram, for example, could be created among four siblings—eldest with second, third, and fourth child, and so on?

What are the origins of Little Red Riding Hood?

■ An anthropologist at Britain's Durham University, Jamie Tehrani studied the evolution of the story of Little Red Riding Hood and traced it to the first century. (See http://news.discovery.com/history/first-century-roots-of-red-riding-hood-found-131114.htm.) He traced the earliest stories to Africa and Asia. How would historical variations of the characters and plot change the story's theme?

■ Retellings of folktales and fairy tales remain popular today, for young readers and even adults. What story have you never heard retold? How could it be made into a contemporary story? How would you change the characters? How would you retain their universal qualities?

■ How did Tehrani use science to study literature and culture? What other applications of science in this way have been used or are possible?

CONTESTS & CONFERENCES

CONTESTS & AWARDS

For Adult & Children's Writers

Abilene Writers Guild Annual Contest
P.O. Box 2562, Abilene, TX 79604
www.abilenewritersguild.org

This annual competition is open to all writers and awards prizes in ten categories, including children's stories, novels, poetry, flash fiction, memoir/nostalgia, and general interest articles. Guidelines vary for each category. Visit the website to download the annual contest guidelines. Entry fee, $10 for short pieces; $15 for novel entries. *Deadline:* Submissions are accepted from October 1 to November 30. *Award:* First place in each category, $100; $65, second place; $35, third place.

Jane Addams Children's Book Award
Marianne I. Baker, Chair MSC 6909, 7210B Memorial Hall, James
    Madison University, 800 S. Main Street, Harrisonburg, VA 22807
www.janeaddamspeace.org

Honoring authors and illustrators of children's literature who reach standards of excellence while promoting the themes of peace, social justice, equality of the sexes, and a unified world, this award competition is held annually. Books of fiction, nonfiction, or poetry targeting children ages 2 through 12 that were published in the year preceding the contest are eligible. *Deadline:* December 31. *Award:* Honorary certificate and a cash award.

Alligator Juniper's National Writing Contest

Prescott College, 220 Grove Avenue, Prescott, AZ 86301
www.prescott.edu/experience/publications/alligatorjuniper

Alligator Juniper is published annually by Prescott College, and features the winners in national contests. This contest accepts original, unpublished entries in the categories of fiction, creative nonfiction, and poetry. Fiction and nonfiction entries should not exceed 30 pages. Poetry, limit 5 poems per entry. Entry fee, $15. *Deadline:* October 1. Contest opens August 15. *Award:* First prize in each category, $1,000 and publication in *Alligator Juniper*.

American Book Awards

Before Columbus Foundation, The Raymond House, 655–13th
    Street, Suite 302, Oakland, CA 94612
www.beforecolumbusfoundation.com/submission.html

These awards are sponsored by the Before Columbus Foundation, a nonprofit educational and service group that promotes multicultural literature and widens the audience for cultural and ethnic diversity in American writing. The awards are given for excellence and an outstanding contribution to American literature. Two copies of a book may be submitted by anyone—author, publisher, agent—for consideration in the next year. All genres are eligibile, including adult books, children's books, anthologies, and multimedia. No fees or forms are requested. *Deadline:* December 31. *Award:* Given in a ceremony at the University of California, Berkeley.

Sherwood Anderson Fiction Award

Mid-American Review, Dept. of English, Box W, Bowling Green
State University, Bowling Green, OH 43403
www.bgsu.edu/studentlife/organizations/midamericanreview

Sponsored by *Mid-American Review,* the literary journal of
Bowling Green State University, this competition is open to all
writers and accepts short story entries of high literary merit.
Entries may be in any genre of fiction, but must be original,
unpublished material. Entry fee, $10. *Deadline:* November 1.
Award: First place, $1,000 and publication in *Mid-American Review.*
Four finalists are also considered for publication.

Arizona Authors Association Literary Contest

Contest Coordinator, 6145 W. Echo Lane, Glendale, AZ 85302
www.azauthors.com

This annual contest sponsored by the Arizona Authors Association
and Five Star Publications and is open to all writers in English. It
accepts unpublished and published works in categories including
short stories, poetry, essays, articles, true stories, and novels. In
2011, two special categories included short stories from Arizona residents, set in the state or with Arizonans as characters; and an essay
with an Arizona theme, setting, or narrator. Each category is divided
into three groups: elementary school; junior high and high school;
and college and adults. Entry fee, $15-$30. *Deadline:* January 1 and
July 1. *Award:* Category winners, First prize, $100; second prize, $50;
third prize, $25 and publication in *Arizona Literary Magazine.*

Atlantic Writing Competition

Writers' Federation of Nova Scotia, 1113 Marginal Road, Halifax
NS B3H 4P7 Canada
www.writers.ns.ca

Open to writers living in Atlantic Canada, this annual competition accepts entries of adult novels, YA novels, short stories, poetry, writing for children, plays, and magazine articles or essays. Previously unpublished material only. Entry fees: novel categories, $35; all other categories, $25. WFNS members receive a $5 discount on entry fees. Published authors may not enter the competition in the genre that they have been published. Limit one entry per category. *Deadline:* November; see website for exact date. *Award:* First- through third-place winners in each category receive awards ranging from $300 to $50.

Autumn House Poetry, Fiction, and Nonfiction Contests
P.O. Box 60100, Pittsburgh, PA 15211
www.autumnhouse.org

Autumn House Press sponsors this annual contest that accepts collections of fiction, poetry, and for the first time, nonfiction. All fiction genres are welcome. Poetry collections, 50 to 80 pages. Fiction, 200–300 pages. Nonfiction, 200-300 pages on any subject; forms include personal essays, memoir, travel, historical narratives, nature or science writing. Entry fee, $30. *Deadline:* June 30. *Award:* Winning entry is published by Autumn House Press, and awarded a $1,000 and a $1,500 travel grant. All entries are considered for publication.

AWP Award Series
Association of Writers & Writing Programs, Carty House, Mail Stop 1E3, George Mason University, Fairfax, VA 22030-4444
www.awpwriter.org/contests/series.htm

The nonprofit Association of Writers & Writing Programs holds this annual award series for fiction, creative nonfiction, and poetry. The competition is open to all writers; guidelines are available at the website. *Deadline:* Entries must be postmarked between January 1 and February 28. *Award:* Poetry and short fiction winners, $5,500 and publication; novel and nonfiction winners, $2,500 and publication.

Marilyn Baillie Picture Book Award

Canadian Children's Book Centre (CCBC), 40 Orchard View
  Boulevard, Suite 101, Toronto ON M4R 1B9 Canada
www.bookcentre.ca

Fiction, nonfiction, or poetry in picture book form, for readers ages three to eight, is eligible for this award. It is given to "outstanding" books "in which the author and illustrator achieve artistic and literary unity." Titles published in the year preceding the contest are eligible for entry. Winners are chosen by a jury appointed by the CCBC. *Deadline:* February. *Award:* $20,000 and a certificate.

Doris Bakwin Award for Writing

Carolina Wren Press, 120 Morris Street, Durham, NC 27701
carolinawrenpress.org/submissions/contests

This biennial contest, held in odd-numbered years, seeks collections of shorts stories, novels, and memoirs written by women. It encourages submissions from new and established writers and accepts unpublished material only. Guidelines are posted on the website in late summer. Entry fee, $20. *Deadline:* March 31. *Award:* $1,000, and publication by Carolina Wren Press, which also runs the Carolina Wren Press Poetry Series, a contest held in even-numbered years.

Baltimore Review Competition

P.O. Box 529, Fork, MD 21051

www.baltimorereview.org

The newly relaunched online *Baltimore Review* is continuing to hold an annual competition for original, unpublished poetry, fiction, or creative nonfiction. Entry fee, $10. Submit via the website. *Deadline:* August 1 to November 30. *Award:* First place, $300 and publication in *Baltimore Review*; second place, $200; third place, $100.

Bartleby Snopes Annual Writing Contest

www.bartlebysnopes.com

In 2013, the online literary journal *Bartleby Snopes* is sponsoring its fifth writing contest. The contest focuses on dialogue, the most recent requiring a short story, to 2,000 words, composed entirely of dialogue. Stories must be original and unpublished; work posted on blogs, boards, websites is considered published and therefore ineligible. Entry fee, $10; multiple entries are allowed. Submit via the website submissions manager. Do not include your personal information on manuscript pages. *Deadline:* September 15. *Award:* Winner, $705; four honorable mentions will receive $35 each. All pieces are published in the January issue of *Bartleby Snopes*.

Pura Belpré Medal

American Library Association, 50 East Huron, Chicago, IL 60611

www.ala.org/alsc/awardsgrants/bookmedia/belpremedal

This annual award is named in honor of Pura Belpré, the first Latina librarian at the New York Public Library. Medals are presented to a Latino/Latina writer and to an illustrator in recognition of literature that best portrays and celebrates the Latino cultural experience for young readers. Authors and illustrators must be residents or citizens of U.S. or Puerto Rico; submissions must be published in the U.S. or Puerto Rico in the contest year. Fiction and nonfiction published in Spanish, English, or bilingual format are eligible. *Deadline:* December 31. *Award:* Winners are presented with medals at a June celebration.

Geoffrey Bilson Award for Historical Fiction for Young People

Canadian Children's Book Centre (CCBC), 40 Orchard View
  Boulevard, Suite 217, Toronto ON M4R 1B9 Canada
www.bookcentre.ca/award

Books of historical fiction for young people by Canadian authors are celebrated by this annual contest. Books published in the year preceding the contest are eligible for entry. Winners are chosen by a jury appointed by the CCBC. Picture books, short story collections by more than one author, and plots involving time travel are not eligible. *Deadline:* February; see website for exact date. *Award:* $5,000 and a certificate.

The *Boston Globe-Horn Book* Awards

The Horn Book, 56 Roland Street, Suite 200, Boston, MA 02129
www.hbook.com

These prestigious awards celebrate excellence in literature for children and young adults. A committee of three judges evaluates books submitted by U.S. publishers and selects a winner and up to two Honor Books in the categories of picture book, fiction and poetry, and nonfiction. No entry fee. *Deadline:* May 15. *Award:* Winners receive $500 and an engraved silver bowl. Honor recipients receive an engraved plate.

Boulevard Short Fiction Contest for Emerging Writers

6614 Clayton Road, PMB 325, Richmond Heights, MO 63117

www.boulevardmagazine.org/partners.html

Writers who have not yet published a book of fiction, creative nonfiction, or poetry with a nationally distributed press are eligible to compete in this annual contest. Entries must be original, unpublished work, to 8,000 words. Entry fee, $15. *Deadline:* December 31. *Award:* $1,500 and publication in *Boulevard*.

Briar Cliff Review Writing Competition

3303 Rebecca Street, Sioux City, IA 51104-2100

www.briarcliff.edu/bcreview

This annual contest accepts unpublished entries of fiction, creative nonfiction, and poetry. Fiction and creative nonfiction should not exceed 6,000 words. Poetry entries may include up to three poems. Entry fee, $20. *Deadline:* November 1. *Award:* First prize in each category is $1,000 and publication in *Briar Cliff Review*.

Marilyn Brown Novel Award

Jen Wahlquist, English Literature Dept., Mail Stop 153, Utah Valley
    University, 800 West University Parkway, Orem, UT 84058

www.uvu.edu/english/marilyn_brown_novel/index.html

Under the stewardship of Utah Valley University's English Department, this award is given annually for the best unpublished literary mainstream novel focusing on realistic cultural experiences of the Utah Region, or Latter-day Saints experiences. No science fiction or fantasy; mainstream literature only. Minimum of 200 pages; no maximum. No entry fee. Limit one entry per competition. *Deadline:* October 1. *Award:* $1,000.

Randolph Caldecott Medal

American Library Association (ALA), 50 E. Huron, Chicago, IL
60611

www.ala.org

Named in honor of the English illustrator, Randolph Caldecott, this award is presented to the artist of the most distinguished American picture book for children published in the preceding year. It is open to all U.S. citizens. Honor books are also recognized. *Deadline:* December 31. *Award:* The winner is announced at the ALA Midwinter Meeting and is presented with the Caldecott Medal at an awards banquet.

California Book Awards

595 Market Street, San Francisco, CA 94105

www.commonwealthclub.org/bookawards

This contest was established to find the best California writers and spotlight the high-quality literature produced in the state. The competition awards California authors with gold and silver medals in recognition of outstanding literary works. Awards are presented in the categories of fiction, nonfiction, poetry, first work of fiction, Californiana, YA literature, juvenile literature, and notable contribution to publishing. Submit six copies of entry. No entry fee. *Deadline:* December 17. *Award:* Consists of 6 to 8 gold medals and up to 6 silver medals.

Canadian Library Association's Book of the Year for Children

10 Abilene Dr., Toronto, ON M9A 2M8 Canada

www.cla.ca

Recognizing Canadian works of children's literature for ages 12 and under, this award is presented annually to works of creative writing (fiction, poetry, narrative, nonfiction, and retellings) by

Canadian citizens. All titles submitted for this award must be published in the year preceding the contest. *Deadline:* December 31. *Award:* Winner receives a leather-bound copy of their book.

Canadian Writer's Journal Short Fiction Contest
Box 1178, New Liskeard ON P0J 1P0 Canada
www.cwj.ca

This contest, sponsored by *Canadian Writer's Journal*, accepts unpublished work by Canadians in any genre, to 2,500 words. Each entry must be accompanied by a brief author biography. Entry fee, $10. *Deadline:* April 30. *Award:* First place, $150; second and third place, $100 and $50, respectively. Winning entries are published in *Canadian Writer's Journal*.

CAPA Competition
Connecticut Authors and Publishers Association, c/o Daniel Uitti,
    223 Buckingham Street, Oakville, CT 06779
aboutcapa.com/writing_contest.htm

This annual contest accepts entries of short stories (to 2,000 words), children's stories (to 2,000 words), personal essays (to 1,500 words), and poetry (to 30 lines). The competition is open to all writers and accepts multiple entries, provided each entry is accompanied by an official entry form. The new competition is announced in September of each year. Submit four copies of entry. Entry fee, $10 per story or personal essay, or up to three poems. *Deadline:* December 24. *Award:* First place, $100; second place, $50. Winning entries are published in CAPA's newsletter.

Christopher Awards
5 Hanover Square, 11th Floor, New York, NY 10004
www.christophers.org

These annual awards are sponsored by the Christophers, a Catholic organization with a ministry of communications. The awards recognize artistic work in publishing, film and television that creates a positive change in society and promotes self-worth. Profiles of courage, stories of determination, and chronicles of constructive action and empowerment are accepted. All entries must be published in the year preceding the contest. *Deadline:* November. *Award:* Winners are presented with bronze medallions at a ceremony in New York City.

Sheldon Currie Fiction Prize

The Antigonish Review, P.O. Box 5000, Street Francis Xavier
　　University, Antigonish NS B2G 2W5 Canada
antigonishreview.com

The Sheldon Currie Fiction Prize is held each year. It is open to well-written, unpublished short stories on any subject matter. Entries should not exceed 20 pages. Entry fee, $30 from the U.S. and $25 from Canada; $40 from outside North America. *Deadline:* May 30. *Award:* First place, $600; second place, $400; third place, $200. The three winning entries are published in the *Antigonish Review.*

Delacorte Press Prize for a First Young Adult Novel

Random House, 1745 Broadway, 9th Floor, New York, NY 10019
www.randomhouse.com/kids/writingcontests

This contest encourages young adult contemporary fiction. The most recent winner was *My Chemical Mountain,* by Corinna Vacco. The Delacorte Press Prize is open to writers living in the U.S. and Canada who have not yet published a YA novel. Manuscripts should be between 100 and 224 typed pages. Limit two entries per competition. All entries must feature a contemporary setting and plot suitable for readers ages 12 to 18. *Deadline:* Submissions must be postmarked between October 1 and December 31. *Award:* Book contract with Random House, advance on royalties of $7,500, and $1,500 cash.

The Amanda Davis Highwire Fiction Award

849 Valencia Street, San Francisco, CA 94110
www.mcsweeneys.net/pages/the-amanda-davis-highwire-
fiction-award

The San Francisco-based publisher McSweeney's has presented this memorial award biannually since 2004. It was created in honor of book and short story author Amanda Davis, who died in a plane crash. The award is given to a woman writer younger than 32 "who both embodies Amanda's personal strengths—warmth, generosity, a passion for community—and who needs some time to finish a book in progress." Submit a work-in-progress, 5,000–40,000 words, and a brief explanation of financial status via Submittable (www.submittable.com), to amandadavis.submittable.com. A mailed hard copy submission is also acceptable. See online guidelines for more details. Fee, $20. *Deadline:* December 15. *Award:* $2,500.

Jack Dyer Fiction Prize

Dept. of English, Faner Hall 2380, Mail Code 4503, Southern
    Illinois University–Carbondale, 1000 Faner Dr., Carbondale,
    IL 62901
craborchardreview.siuc.edu/dyer.html

Open to U.S. residents, this annual competition is sponsored by *Crab Orchard Review,* the literary journal of Southern Illinois University–Carbondale. It is open to submissions of unpublished fiction, to 6,000 words. Entry fee, $20 per entry. Limit 3 entries per competition. *Deadline:* Postmarked between March 1 and May 4. *Award:* Publication in the winter/spring *Crab Orchard Review* and a minimum payment of $500.

Margaret A. Edwards Award
50 East Huron Street, Chicago, IL 60611
www.ala.org/yalso/edwards

This award was established by the American Library Association's Young Adult Services Association and honors a living author for a body of work and special contribution to YA literature. The winner's writing will have been popular over a period of time and is generally recognized as helping teens to become better aware of who they are and their role in society. Nominations are accepted from librarians and teens. *Deadline:* November 1. *Award:* $2,000, and a citation presented during the annual ALA conference.

Arthur Ellis Awards
4C-240 Westwood Road, Guelph, ON N1H 7W9 Canada
www.crimewriterscanada.com/awards

The Arthur Ellis Awards were established to honor excellence in Canadian mystery and crime writing. The contest is open to writers living in Canada or Canadian writers living elsewhere in the world. It accepts published entries in several categories, including best short story, best nonfiction, best first novel, best juvenile novel, best novel, best crime writing in French, as well as the best unpublished crime novel. Processing fee, $35 for books, $15 for short stories. *Deadline:* December 1. *Award:* Winners receive a wooden statue at the annual awards dinner.

William Faulkner–William Wisdom Creative Writing Competition

624 Pirate's Alley, New Orleans, LA 70116-3254

www.wordsandmusic.org/competition.html

This annual competition was set up to preserve the storytelling heritage of New Orleans and the Deep South by Pirate's Alley Faulkner Society. Unpublished entries are accepted in seven categories: novel, novella, novel-in-progress, short story, essay, poetry, and short story by a high school student. Entry fees range from $40 to $75, depending on category. Visit the website for complete guidelines. *Deadline:* Entries must be received between January 1 and May 1. *Award:* Publication in the Faulkner Society's annual literary journal, *The Double Dealer.* Ranges from $750 to $7,500.

Shubert Fendrich Memorial Playwriting Contest

P.O. Box 4267, Englewood, CO 80155-4267

www.pioneerdrama.com

This competition encourages the development of quality theatrical material for educational and community theaters. It is open to playwrights who have not been published by Pioneer Drama Service. Manuscripts must have a running time between 20 and 90 minutes. *Deadline:* Ongoing. *Award:* Publishing contract and advance against royalties of $1,000.

Fineline Competition for Prose Poems, Short Shorts

Mid-American Review, Dept. of English, Bowling Green State University, Bowling Green, OH 43403

www.bgsu.edu/studentlife/organizations/midamericanreview

The literary journal of Bowling Green State University, *Mid-American Review,* sponsors this competition for literary quality prose poems and short, short stories. Entries must be original and unpublished material. Length, no longer than 500 words. Submit a set of three prose poems or stories. Verse will be automatically disqualified. Entry fee, $10. *Deadline:* June 1. *Award:* First place, $1,000 and publication in *Mid-American Review.*

H. E. Francis Award

Dept. of English, Morton Hall, Room 222, University of Alabama,
  Huntsville, AL 35899
www.uah.edu/hefranciscontest

This annual award is sponsored by the Ruth Hindman Foundation and the University of Alabama–Huntsville English Department. It accepts original, unpublished short stories that are judged by a nationally known panel of editors. Manuscripts must not exceed 5,000 words. Entry fee, $20. *Deadline:* December 31. *Award:* $2,000.

Don Freeman Memorial Grant-in-Aid

  8271 Beverly Boulevard, Los Angeles, CA 90048
www.scbwi.org

Members of the Society of Children's Book Writers and Illustrators who intend to make picture books their primary contribution to children's literature are eligible for this grant, which is underwritten by Amazon.com. The grant is presented annually to help artists further their understanding, training, and work in the picture book genre. *Deadline:* Entries must be postmarked between March 1 and March 31. *Award:* Winner, $2,000; runner-up, $500.

John Gardner Memorial Prize for Fiction

Harpur Palate, English Dept., Binghamton University, Box 6000,
  Binghamton, NY 13902-6000
harpurpalate.binghamton.edu

This contest was established to honor John Gardner's dedication to the creative writing program at Binghamton University. It is open to all writers and accepts previously unpublished short story entries. Entries should not exceed 8,000 words. Entry fee, $15 (includes a one-year subscription to *Harpur Palate*). *Deadline:* February 1 to April 15. *Award:* $500 and publication in the summer issue of *Harpur Palate*.

Glimmer Train Contests

4763 SW Maplewood, P.O. Box 80430, Portland, OR 97209
www.glimmertrain.com/writguid1.html

Glimmer Train sponsors a contest each month of the year, including Family Matters, Fiction Open, Short Story Award for New Writers, and Very Short Fiction. Lengths vary. Electronic submissions are preferred. *Deadlines:* Vary. *Award:* First place award ranges from $1,500 to $2,500 and includes publication in *Glimmer Train*, and 20 copies of the issue with the winning story.

The Golden Kite Awards

8271 Beverly Boulevard, Los Angeles, CA 90048-4515
www.scbwi.org

Presented annually by the Society of Children's Book Writers & Illustrators, the Golden Kites recognize excellence in children's fiction, nonfiction, picture book text, and picture book illustration. SCBWI members whose work has been published in the year preceding the contest are eligible. *Deadline:* July to December; see website for exact dates. *Award:* $2,500 and an expense-paid trip to the award ceremony at the Golden Kite luncheon during SCBWI's summer conference in August. Four honor book recipients also receive recognition.

The Guild Literary Complex Prose Awards

Guild Complex, P.O. Box 478880, Chicago, IL 60647-9998
guildcomplex.org

An annual contest for short fiction and nonfiction, open to Illinois residents over 21, is sponsored by Chicago's Guild Literary Complex. Submit one piece of original fiction or nonfiction, to 1,000 words. Entry fee, $5. Mail entries, or email to contest@guildcomplex.org, with "Prose Awards" in the subject line, and either a PDF or Word document attached. Do not include your name or other identifying information on the manuscript itself. *Deadline:* October 1. *Award:* $250 for the winner in each category. Winners read their fiction or nonfiction at an October event at the Chopin Theater in Wicker Park.

Gulf Coast Writer's Association Let's Write Contest

P.O. Box 10294, Gulfport, MS 39505
www.gcwriters.org

The Gulf Coast Writer's Association has held this literary contest for 25 years. It is open to all writers of fiction, nonfiction, and poetry. It accepts entries in all genres except erotica, horror, or stories with graphic violence, or exhibiting any religious, racial, or moral prejudice. Submissions must be original, unpublished work. Fiction and nonfiction, to 2,500 words; poetry, 3 poems, to 50 lines. Entry fee, $8. Mail entry with a cover letter including your information, the entry's category, and word count. Or, email via the website page. *Deadline:* January 15 to April 15. *Award:* First place, $100; second place, $60; third place; $25, and publication in the association's *Magnolia Quarterly*.

John Guyon Literary Nonfiction Prize

Dept. of English, Faner Hall 2380, Mail Code 4503, Southern Illinois

University–Carbondale, 1000 Faner Drive, Carbondale, IL 62901

craborchardreview.siuc.edu/dyer.html

Sponsored by *Crab Orchard Review*, the literary journal of Southern Illinois University–Carbondale, this competition awards excellence in original, previously unpublished literary nonfiction. The contest is open to U.S. residents. Entries should not exceed 6,500 words. Entry fee, $20 per entry (maximum 3 entries). *Deadline:* Postmarked between March and May. *Award:* $2,000 and publication in the winter/spring *Crab Orchard Review*.

Lorian Hemingway Short Story Competition

P.O. Box 993, Key West, FL 33041

www.shortstorycompetition.com

Writers of short fiction whose work has not been published in a nationally distributed publication with a circulation of 5,000 or more are eligible to enter this competition, which receives submissions from around the world. It accepts original, unpublished short stories of up to 3,500 words. There are no restrictions on theme. Entry fee, $15 for entries postmarked by May 1; $20 for those postmarked by May 15. Online submissions accepted, with the same deadlines. *Deadline:* May 15. *Award:* First place, $2,500 and publication in *Cutthroat: A Journal of the Arts*; second and third place, $500.

***Highlights for Children* Fiction Contest**

803 Church Street, Honesdale, PA 18431

www.highlights.com/highlights-fiction-contest

This annual contest sponsored by *Highlights for Children* is open to both published and unpublished writers over the age of 16. Not to exceed 500 words. Clearly mark Fiction Contest on the manuscript. No entry fee. *Deadline:* Submissions must be postmarked between January 1 and January 31. *Award:* Three prizes of $1,000 (or tuition for the Highlights Foundation Writers Workshop) and publication in *Highlights for Children.*

Monica Hughes Award for Science Fiction and Fantasy

Canadian Children's Book Centre (CCBC), 40 Orchard View
Boulevard, Suite 217, Toronto ON M4R 1B9 Canada
www.bookcentre.ca

Awarded first in 2012 by the Canadian Children's Book Centre, this award honors excellence in children's and young teen science fiction and fantasy. Books must be originally published between January 1 and December 31 of the previous year. Entries must be written by a Canadian. Acceptable subgenres or subjects include time travel, alternate or re-imagined histories, dystopian, utopian, aliens, steampunk, space operas, urban fantasies, the paranormal, domestic magic, faeries, talking animals, among others. Submit four copies of each title with a submissions form found on the website. *Deadline:* December 9. *Award:* $5,000 and a certificate.

The *Hunger Mountain* Creative Nonfiction Prize

CNF Prize, *Hunger Mountain*, Vermont College of Fine Arts, 36
College Street, Montpelier, VT 05602
www.hungermtn.org/hunger-mountain-creative-nonfiction-prize

The literary journal *Hunger Mountain* holds this annual contest for writers of creative nonfiction. Enter an original, unpublished article, to 10,000 words. Entries may be submitted by mail, or electronically via the online submissions manager. Do not include your name or address on the entry itself. For hard copy submissions, include an index card with the title, your name, address, phone number, and email address. Submit multiple entries separately. The contest is judged by the journal's editors and guest judges. Fee, $20. *Deadline:* September 10. *Award:* First place, $1,000, and publication in *Hunger Mountain;* two honorable mentions, $100 each.

Barbara Karlin Grant

Society of Children's Book Writers & Illustrators, Barbara Karlin
    Grant Committee, c/o Q. L. Pearce, 884 Atlanta Court,
    Claremont, CA 91711
www.scbwi.org

The Barbara Karlin grant was set up by SCBWI to recognize and encourage aspiring picture book writers. It is presented to a full or associate SCBWI member who has not yet published a picture book. Works of fiction, nonfiction, retellings of fairy tales, folktales, or legends are eligible for consideration. Manuscripts should not exceed eight pages. No entry fee. New applications and procedures are posted on the website yearly. *Deadline:* Submissions accepted between March 1 and March 31. *Award:* $2,000; runner-up, $500.

Iowa Short Fiction Award

Iowa Writers' Workshop, 507 North Clinton Street, 102 Dey
    House, Iowa City, IA 52242-1000
www.uiowapress.org/authors/iowa-short-fiction.htm

This annual competition of the Iowa Writers' Workshop at the University of Iowa calls for collections of short stories. It is open to writers living in the U.S. and abroad who have not previously published a volume of prose fiction. Manuscripts should be at least 150 double-spaced pages. No entry fee. *Deadline:* Entries should be postmarked between August 1 and September 30. *Award:* Award-winning manuscripts are published by the University of Iowa Press.

Coretta Scott King Book Awards
50 East Huron Street, Chicago, IL 60611-2795
www.ala.org

Honoring Martin Luther King Jr. and his wife, Coretta Scott King, for their courage and determination, this award promotes the artistic expression of the African American experience through literature and graphic arts. Sponsored by the American Library Association, the awards are given to African American authors and illustrators for inspirational and educational contributions to children's and YA literature. Submit via online submissions form. *Deadline:* December 1. *Award:* A plaque and $1,000, will be presented at the Coretta Scott King Award Breakfast at the annual ALA conference.

E. M. Koeppel Short Fiction Award
P.O. Box 140310, Gainesville, FL 32614
www.writecorner.com/award_guidelines.asp

Unpublished fiction in any genre is the focus of this annual competition open to all writers. Submissions should not exceed 3,000 words. Entry fee, $15; $10 for each additional entry. *Deadline:* October 1 through April 30. *Award:* $1,100; editors' choice awards, $100 each.

David J. Langum Sr. Prizes in American Historical Fiction and American Legal History or Biography
The Langum Charitable Trust, 2809 Berkeley Drive, Birmingham, AL 35242
www.langumtrust.org

The Langum Charitable Trust is a nonprofit that encourages high-quality historical writing addressed to the general public rather than to academics. The prize for American historical fiction is awarded annually to the book published in the preceding year that best demonstrates excellence in both fiction and history. The competition is open to works by any publisher, but not to self-published or subsidized books. The Langum Trust's prize for works of legal history or biography is awarded to an original book published in the preceding year by a university press; the winner is most accessible to the general public, and "rooted in sound scholarship." *Deadline:* December 1. *Award:* $1,000.

Literary Juice Contests
www.literaryjuice.com

The online literary journal *Literary Juice,* publishing bimonthly for three years, runs periodic contests for flash fiction and poetry. The journal specializes in risky, witty, highly creative, even "bizarre" work. Contest entries vary in length; the publication's flash fiction is 100 to 600 words and it accepts up to six poems per submission. All work must be original and unpublished. Entry fee, $5. Submit via the online submissions manager only. Multiple submissions allowed. Simultaneous submissions allowed; notify *Literary Juice* if your submission is accepted elsewhere before the contest concludes. *Deadline:* Varies. *Award:* $200 and publication in *Literary Juice.* A runner-up will receive $50 and publication.

"Looking for Love" Fiction Contest
215 Church Street, Philadelphia, PA 19106
http://quirkbooks.com

A new contest sponsored by Philadelphia-based Quirk Books, "Looking for Love" wants novel manuscripts with unconventional, original, and entertaining love stories. the 12-year-old Quirk Books is perhaps best known for it's best selling *Pride and Prejudice and Zombies. Deadline:* October 1. *Award:* $10,000 and publication.

Magazine Merit Award

Society of Children's Books Writers & Illustrators, 8271 Beverly
Boulevard, Los Angeles, CA 90048
www.scbwi.org/Pages.aspx/Magazine-Merit-Award

The Society of Children's Book Writers & Illustrators sponsors
this annual award in recognition of outstanding original magazine
work written for young people. It accepts published entries in the
categories of fiction, nonfiction, illustration, and poetry. SCBWI
members only. No entry fee. Submit four copies of each entry,
with proof of publication date. *Deadline:* December 15. *Award:*
Winners in each category receive a plaque.

Micro Award

Alan Presley, PSC 817, Box 23, FPO, AE 09622-0023
www.microaward.org

The Micro Award recognizes fiction under 1,000 words, otherwise known as flash fiction or nanofiction. Submissions must be
prose fiction published either in print or electronically in the
year preceding the award. Self-published fiction is eligible.
Authors may submit one story; editors may submit two stories
from their publications. Winners are announced on September 1
of the following year. *Deadline:* October 1 to December 31 *Award:*
$500.

Milkweed Prize for Children's Literature

Milkweed Editions, 1011 Washington Avenue South, Suite 300,
Minneapolis, MN 55415
www.milkweed.org

Fiction for readers ages 8 to 13 is the focus of this annual
competition sponsored by Milkweed Editions. The prize was
established to encourage authors to write for children. Submissions

with high literary merit that embody humane values and contribute to cultural understanding. No entry fee. *Deadline:* Ongoing. *Award:* $10,000 cash prize and publication by Milkweed Editions.

Minotaur Books/MWA Competition
175 Fifth Avenue, New York, NY 10010
www.mysterywriters.org/?q=Contests-Writers

Open to writers over 18 who have not published a novel, this competition is sponsored by Minotaur Books in conjunction with the Mystery Writers of America. It accepts original, book-length manuscripts in which murder or another serious crime is central to the plot. Submit questions to mbmwafirstcrimenovelcompetition@stmartins.com. *Deadline:* Online entry form must be completed by December 16. *Award:* Publishing contract from St. Martin's Press/Minotaur Books and $10,000 cash advance against royalties.

The Howard Frank Mosher Short Fiction Prize
HFMSFP, *Hunger Mountain,* Vermont College of Fine Arts, 36
   College Street, Montpelier, VT 05602
www.hungermtn.org/short-fiction-prize

The literary journal *Hunger Mountain* holds this annual contest for writers of short fiction. Enter an original, unpublished short story, to 10,000 words. Entries may be submitted by mail, or via the online submissions manager. Do not include your name or address on the entry itself. For hard copy submissions, include an index card with the title, your name, address, phone number, and email address. Submit multiple entries separately. The contest is judged by the journal's editors and guest judges. *Deadline:* June 30. *Award:* First-place, $1,000, and publication in *Hunger Mountain;* two honorable mentions, $100 each, and consideration for publication.

Mythopoeic Society Fantasy Awards

306 Edmon Low Library, Oklahoma State University, Stillwater,
 OK 74078

www.mythsoc.org/awards

Honoring outstanding fantasy books for young readers that
are written in the tradition of J. R. R. Tolkien and C. S. Lewis, this
award is presented to picture books through YA novels, adult fantasy, and scholarly books. Entries are nominated by members of the
Mythopoeic Society. Books and collections by a single author are
eligible for two years after publication. *Deadline:* February 28.
Award: A statuette.

National Book Awards

National Book Foundation, 90 Broad Street., Suite 604, New York,
 NY 10004

www.nationalbook.org

The National Book Award recognizes outstanding literature for
young people and adults. Awards are given for fiction, nonfiction,
poetry, and YA literture. Full-length books, collections of stories,
and collections of essays or poems are eligible. All entries must be
published in the U.S. during the year preceding the contest. This
competition is open to U.S. citizens only; books published or
scheduled to be published in the previous year only. Entry fee,
$125. Entries must be submitted by publishers. *Deadline:* Entry
forms must be postmarked by June 3; books, bound galleys, or
bound manuscripts due by August 1. *Award:* Category winners,
$10,000; Four finalists, $1,000.

National Children's Theatre Medal

280 Miracle Mile, Coral Gables, FL 33134

www.actorsplayhouse.org

Held yearly, this competition is sponsored by the Actors Playhouse at the Miracle Theatre. It welcomes submission of unpublished musicals that are appropriate for children ages 5 to 12. Submissions should feature a cast with no more than 8 adults, who may play multiple roles. Works that received limited production exposure, workshops, or staged readings are encouraged, as are musicals with simple settings that appeal to both children and adults. Running time, 45 to 60 minutes. Entry fee, $10. Include sheet music and the submission form found at the website. *Deadline:* Entries must be postmarked by April 1. *Award:* $500 and a full production of the play at the National Children's Theatre Festival in May.

Horatio Nelson Fiction Prize
http://blackballoonpublishing.com/contest.html

Black Balloon Publishing inaugurated this award in 2013, with the first prize going to *Fat Man and Little Boy,* by Mike Meginnis. The annual award is open to original, unpublished, complete manuscripts, 50,000 words and up. Black Baloon named the prize after the British admiral, "who defied convention at every turn," and looks for similar qualities, including "relentless creativity and perseverence, in manuscripts. No entry fee. Using Submittable at blackballoonpublishing.submittable.com, enter with a summary and an excerpt to 4.000 words, after April 1. *Deadline:* E *Award:* $5,000 and a book deal with the small press.

The John Newbery Medal
American Library Association, 50 East Huron Street, Chicago, IL
   60611
www.ala.org/alsc/awardsgrants/bookmedia

This prestigious medal is presented by the Association for

Library Service to Children to honor the year's most distinguished contribution to American literature for children up to the age of 14. Titles eligible for consideration must have been written by a U.S. author and published in the year preceding the contest. Books are judged on literary quality and overall presentation for children. Nominations are accepted from ALSC members only. *Deadline:* December 31. *Award:* The Newbery Medal is presented to the winning author at the ALA midwinter banquet.

New Millennium Writings Award

P.O. Box 2463, Room M2, Knoxville, TN 37901
www.newmillenniumwritings.com/awards.php

This annual contest is sponsored by *New Millennium Writings,* a literary journal. It accepts entries in the categories of short-short fiction, fiction, nonfiction, and poetry. It accepts previously unpublished material, and material that has been published online or in a print publication with a circulation under 5,000. Short-short fiction, to 1,000 words. Fiction and nonfiction, to 6,000 words. Poetry, to three poems, five pages total. Entry fee, $20 per submission. Submit online or via mail. *Deadline:* February 28. *Award:* $1,000.

New Voices Award

Lee & Low Books, 95 Madison Avenue, New York, NY 10016
www.leeandlow.com/p/new_voices_award.mhtml

Encouraging writers of color who have not published a children's picture book, this annual award is sponsored by Lee & Low Books. It welcomes original material that addresses the needs of children of color, ages 5 to 12. Works of fiction, nonfiction, and poetry are accepted, but folklore and stories about animals are not. Entries should not exceed 1,500 words and must be accompanied by a cover letter with the author's contact information and relevant cultural/ethnic information. Limit two submissions per entrant. No entry fee. *Deadline:* Submissions will be accepted between May 1 and September 30. *Award:* $1,000 and publishing contract with Lee & Low Books; Honor Award winner, $500.

Ohio State University Prize in Short Fiction

Ohio State University Press, 180 Pressey Hall, 1070 Carmack
   Road, Columbus, OH 43210-1002
www.ohiostatepress.org

This prize, awarded annually since 1997, recognizes excellence in a collection of short stories, novellas, or a combination of both, whether published or unpublished. Manuscripts must be between 150 and 300 typed pages; individual stories or novellas in the collection may not exceed 125 pages. Entry fee: $20. *Deadline:* Submissions must be postmarked in January. *Award:* Winning author receives publication, with a $1,500 advance against royalties.

On-the-Verge Emerging Voices Award

Society of Children's Book Writers and Illustrators, 8271 Beverly
   Boulevard., Los Angeles, CA 90048
www.scbwi.org

In 2012, SCBWI created this award "to foster the emergence of diverse voices in children's books" and honor writers and illustrators from traditionally under-represented cultures in children's literature. The award will be given annually to two writers or illustrators. Manuscripts must be original, unpublished, unagented, not under contract, and written in English; authors must be over 18. Entries and applications should be emailed to voices@scbwi.org. Include an autiobiography, to 250 words; a description of why the work represents an under-represented culture, to 250 words; a synopsis, to 250 words; and a PDF of the complete manuscript. *Deadline:* November 15. *Award:* All-expenses paid trip to the SCBWI winter conference, a year's membership to SCBWI, an SCBWI mentor for a year.

Orbis Pictus Award for Outstanding Nonfiction for Children
National Council of Teachers of English, Orbis Pictus Committee Chair, 1111 West Kenyon Road, Urbana, IL 61801-1096
www.ncte.org/awards/orbispictus

This award for excellence in children's nonfiction recognizes books used in kindergarten to eighth-grade classrooms character-ized by outstanding accuracy, organization, design, and style. Eligible titles must be published in the year preceding the contest. Nominations may come from National Council of Teachers of English (NCTE) members, or the education community. Text-books, historical fiction, folklore, and poetry are not eligible. To nominate a book, write to the committee chair with the author's name, title of book, publisher, copyright date, and a brief expla-nation of why you liked the book. *Deadline:* December 31. *Award:* A plaque at the NCTE Convention.

OWFI Annual Writing Contest
Oklahoma Writers' Federation, Inc., 832 NW 16th St., Moore, OK 73160
www.owfi.org

The annual contest of the Oklahoma Writers' Federation opens on December 31 of each year. It is open to members, and to full-time students. This large contest gives awards in 29 categories of unpublished manuscripts, as well as four awards for published books. The categories include mainstream fiction, romance fiction, historical fiction, mystery/suspense, westerns, science fiction and fantasy, nonfiction, picture books, middle-grade books, and YA books, among others. Unpublished manuscripts should be sent as DOCs and book entries must be sent as PDFs. Include the official cover sheet, available online, with each submission. Entries may be submitted electronically or by regular mail. For details, see the website. Entry fee, $20. *Deadline:* February 1. *Award:* For unpublished entries, first place, $50; second place, $35; and third place, $20. For published books, a trophy.

Pacific Northwest Writers Association Literary Contest

PMB 2717, 1420 NW Gilman Boulevard, Suite 2, Issaquah, WA
   98027

www.pnwa.org

Sponsored by the Pacific Northwest Writers Association, this annual contest accepts unpublished entries in 12 categories that include: young adult novel, screen writing, mainstream, adult short topics, poetry, children's picture book/chapter book, historical, and romance. Each entrant receives two critiques of their work. Entry fee, $35 for members; $50 for nonmembers. Limit one entry per category. *Deadline:* February 22. *Award:* First place, $700 and the Zola Award; second place, $300.

The Katherine Paterson Prize for Young Adult and Children's Writing

KPP, *Hunger Mountain,* Vermont College of Fine Arts, 36 College
   Street, Montpelier, VT 05602

www.hungermtn.org/katherine-paterson-prize-for-young-adult-
   and-childrens-writing

The literary journal *Hunger Mountain* holds this annual contest for writers of picture books, and middle-grade and young adult literature. Enter an original, unpublished short story, to 10,000 words; it may be a picture book, short story, or novel excerpt. Entries may be submitted by mail, or electronically via the submissions manager. Do not include your name or address on the entry itself. For hard copy submissions, include an index card with the title, your name, address, phone number, and email address. Submit multiple entries separately. The contest is judged by the journal's editors and guest judges. *Deadline:* June 30. *Award:* First-place, $1,000, and publication in *Hunger Mountain;* two honorable mentions, $100 each, and consideration for publication.

PEN Center USA Literary Awards
269 South Beverly Drive, #1163, Beverly Hills, CA 90212
penusa.org/awards

Writers living west of the Mississippi River are honored for their literary achievements through this annual awards program. Entries that have been published in the year preceding the contest are accepted for nomination in the categories of children's literature, graphic literature, fiction, creative nonfiction, journalism, drama, teleplay, research nonfiction, poetry, translation, and screenplay. Entry fee, $35 per entry. *Deadline:* Book category submissions, December 31; non-book category submissions, January 31. *Award:* Category winners, $1,000 and a free PEN membership.

PEN/Phyllis Naylor Working Writer Fellowship
588 Broadway, Suite 303, New York, NY 10012
www.pen.org/page.php/prmID/281

This fellowship provides support for promising authors in the field of children's or YA fiction. Eligible authors must have published at least two novels. Books must be published by a U.S.

publisher. Likely candidates are those whose books have been well-reviewed but have not achieved high sales volume. Nominations are accepted from editors and fellow writers and should include a detailed letter of support; a list of the nominated author's published work and reviews; and a description of the nominee's financial resources. Three copies of the outline of a work in progress and 50 to 75 pages of the text must also be submitted. *Deadline:* Letters of nomination must be postmarked between October 1 and December 16. *Award:* $5,000 fellowship.

Phoebe Winter Fiction Contest

Phoebe 2C5, George Mason University, 4400 University Drive,
   Fairfax, VA 22030
www.phoebejournal.com

This annual contest is sponsored by *Phoebe,* the literary journal of George Mason University. It accepts unpublished short fiction. Entries, to 7,500 words. Entry fee, $12 per submission. *Deadline:* December 15. *Award:* $1,000 and publication in *Phoebe.*

Edgar Allan Poe Awards

Mystery Writers of America, 1140 Broadway, Suite 1507, New
   York, NY 10001
www.mysterywriters.org/?q=AwardsPrograms

The Mystery Writers of America sponsors these annual awards, which are considered among the most prestigious for writers. They are presented for work published in the year preceding the contest in several categories that include best fact crime, best YA mystery, best juvenile mystery, best first novel by an American author, and best play. Books must be submitted by publisher. No entry fee. *Deadline:* Varies. *Award:* An Edgar Award is presented to each winner at a banquet; cash award.

Prairie Fire Press Contests

423-100 Arthur Street, Winnipeg MB R3B 1H3 Canada

www.prairiefire.ca/contests/

Two annual competitions honor works of creative nonfiction and short fiction. Creative fiction entries should not exceed 5,000 words and must be unpublished. Short fiction, to 10,000 words. Entry fee, $32. *Deadline:* November 30. *Award:* First prize, $1,250; second prize, $500; third prize, $250. Winning entries are published in *Prairie Fire* magazine.

Michael L. Printz Award for Excellence in Young Adult Literature

50 East Huron Street, Chicago, IL 60611

www.ala.org/yalsa/printz

This award, from the Young Adult Library Services Association and *Booklist*, recognizes excellence in YA literature. Anthologies and works of fiction, nonfiction, and poetry that target ages 12 to 18 and were published in the preceding year are eligible. ALA committee members may nominate titles. Entries are judged on overall literary merit, taking into consideration theme, voice, setting, style, and design. Controversial topics are not discouraged. *Deadline:* December 1. *Award:* An award seal, presented at the ALA midwinter conference.

Prism International Literary Nonfiction Contest

Creative Writing Program, University of British Columbia, Buchanan E462, 1866 Main Mall, Vancouver BC V6T 1Z1 Canada

prismmagazine.ca/contests

This annual contest honors excellence in literary nonfiction. Entries of creative nonfiction may be on any subject, and should not exceed 6,000 words. Entry fee, $35 for Canadian; $40 for U.S.; $5 for each additional story (includes a one-year subscription to *Prism international*). *Deadline:* November 28. *Award:* Grand prize, $1,500 and publication in *Prism international*.

Prism international Short Fiction Contest

Creative Writing Program, University of British Columbia, Buchanan E462, 1866 Main Mall, Vancouver BC V6T 1Z1 Canada

prismmagazine.ca/contests

This competition is open to all writers, with the exception of those currently enrolled in the creative arts program at the University of British Columbia. It looks for original, unpublished short stories up to 6,000 words. Entry fee, $35 for Canadian; $40 for U.S.; $5 for each additional story (includes a one-year subscription to *Prism international*). *Deadline:* January 23. *Award:* Grand prize, $2,000 and publication in *Prism international*. Three runner-up prizes of $300 and $200 are also awarded.

Roanoke Review Fiction Contest

221 College Lane, Salem, VA 24153

roanokereview.wordpress.com

This annual contest is sponsored by the literary journal of Roanoke College and looks to encourage the writing of short fiction. It is open to all writers. Entries should not exceed 5,000 words. Entry fee, $15. All entrants receive a copy of the journal. Enter online or via mail. *Deadline:* November 1. *Award:* First place, $1,000; second place, $500. Winning entries are published in the *Roanoke Review*.

William Saroyan International Prize for Writing

Administrator of The Saroyan Prize Committee, Stanford
   University Libraries, 557 Escondido Mall, Stanford, CA 94305
   http://library.stanford.edu/projects/william-saroyan-international-
   prize-writing

Stanford University Libraries joins with the William Saroyan Foundation to present a biennial award for new titles that reflect the life and legacy of the author and Pulitzer Prize-winning dramatist. Among Saroyan's best-known works are *The Time of Your Life* and *The Human Comedy*. Eligible for the prize are, for fiction, novels, short story anthologies, and drama; for nonfiction, biography, history, and memoirs. The literary legacy of the Saroyan prize is described as "characterized by originality, stylistic innovation" and "exuberant humanism" that can "move art in new directions." Books should have been published in the preceding two years. All entries must be in English. Entry fee, $50. *Deadline:* January 31, alternate years. *Award:* Announced in the summer of the award year.

San Antonio Writers Guild Writing Contest

P.O. Box 100717, San Antonio, TX 78201
www.sawritersguild.org

This competition accepts entries in the categories of novel, short story, flash fiction, essay/memoir, and poetry. It accepts previously unpublished submissions only. Word limits vary. Visit the website for complete information. Entry fee, $10 for members; $20 for nonmembers. *Deadline:* First Thursday in October. *Award:* First place, $150; second place, $75; third place $50.

The A. David Schwartz Fiction Prize

Cream City Review, Dept. of English, University of Wisconsin-
   Milwaukee, P.O. Box 413, Milwaukee, WI 53201

www.creamcityreview.org/submit/#contests

Cream City Review is a nonprofit literary magazine run by volunteers that pushes boundaries of writing. It publishes fiction, poetry, creative nonfiction, interviews, reviews, criticism, comics, and art. Its annual contest looks for well-crafted short fiction, creative nonfiction, and poetry as long as it is in English, original, and previously unpublished. *Cream City Review* especially wants to support new voices. Entries should not exceed 20 pages. Entry fee, $15. *Deadline:* December 31. *Award:* $1,000 and publication in *Cream City Review*.

Seven Hills Literary Contest
2910 Kerry Forest Parkway D-4-357, Tallahassee, FL 32309
www.tallahasseewriters.net

Sponsored by the Tallahassee Writers' Association, this annual contest offers prizes in the categories of best short story, creative nonfiction, flash fiction, and children's chapter books/stories (for children 4–8). The competition is open to all writers and accepts unpublished, original entries only. Entries should not exceed 2,500 words (500 words for flash fiction). Entry fee, $12 for members; $17 for nonmembers. *Deadline:* August 31. *Award:* First place, $100; second place, $75; third place, $50. Winners are published in *Seven Hills* literary journal.

Mary Shelley Award for Imaginative Fiction
Rosebud Magazine, N3310 Asje Road, Cambridge, WI 53523
www.rsbd.net/NEW/

Established to promote speculative and imaginative fiction in a literary context, this contest accepts original, unpublished works of fantasy, fiction, horror, and mystery, as well as entries that stretch beyond the boundaries of these genres. Entries should be between 1,000 and 3,500 words. Entry fee, $10. *Deadline:* October. *Award:* First place winner receives $1,000 and publication in *Rosebud.* Four runners-up receive $100 and publication.

Kay Snow Writing Contest
2108 Buck Street, West Linn, OR 97068
www.willamettewriters.com

This annual competition, sponsored by the Willamette Writers, encourages writers to reach their personal goals. It accepts original, unpublished entries in the categories of adult fiction, adult nonfiction, juvenile short story or article, poetry, screenwriting, and student writing. Entry fee, $10 for members; $15 for non-members. Word lengths vary for each category. Visit the website for complete guidelines. *Deadline:* April 23. *Award:* Ranges from $10 to $300 in each catagory. The Liam Callen award, $500, is presented to the best overall entry.

Society of Midland Authors Awards
P.O. Box 10419, Chicago, IL 60610
www.midlandauthors.com/contest_about.html

Authors and poets who reside in, were born in, or have strong ties to any of the 12 Midwestern states are eligible to enter this annual contest. Awards are presented for adult fiction and non-fiction, biography, poetry, and children's fiction and nonfiction. Entries must have been published in the year preceding the contest. No entry fee. Complete the awards entry form at www.midland-authors.com/contest_form.html. *Deadline:* February 1. *Award:* $500 and a recognition plaque, to be given at a banquet in May.

So to Speak Contests

George Mason University, MSN 2C5, 4400 University Drive,
   Fairfax, VA 22030

sotospeakjournal.org/contests/

So to Speak, a feminist literary journal, sponsors this contest for fiction, nonfiction, and poetry. Entries may also be personal essays, memoirs, and profiles. Fiction and nonfiction, to 4,500 words. Poetry, to five poems per submission, not to exceed 4,500 words. Entry fee, $15. *Deadline:* Nonfiction and poetry deadline, October 15. Fiction deadline, March 15. *Award:* First prize in each category is $500 and publication in *So to Speak.*

John Spray Mystery Award

Canadian Children's Book Centre (CCBC), 40 Orchard View
   Boulevard, Suite 217, Toronto ON M4R 1B9 Canada

www.bookcentre.ca

This award, established in 2011 by the Canadian Children's Book Centre, honors outstanding mysteries for readers 8 to 16. Entries may be thrillers, crime novels, or whodunits, and must be written by a Canadian. Titles published in the year preceding the contest are eligible for entry. No fantasy, science fiction, or graphic novels. *Deadline:* December 9. *Award:* $5,000 and a certificate.

SouthWest Writers Annual Contest

3200 Carlisle Blvd NE, Suite 114, Albuquerque, NM 87110

www.southwestwriters.com/contestAnnual.php

This annual contest is sponsored by SouthWest Writers and honors distinguished unpublished work in a variety of categories including novel, short story, short nonfiction, personal essay, book-length nonfiction, children's book, screenplay, and poetry. Entry fees, word lengths, and other requirements vary for each category; check website for specific information. Manuscript critiques are available for an additional fee. *Deadline:* May 1. *Award:* First-place winners in each category receive $200; second-place, $150; third-place, $100. First-place winners compete for a $1,500 Storyteller Award.

Stanley Drama Award
Wagner College, One Campus Road, Staten Island, NY 10301
www.wagner.edu/theatre/stanley-drama/

The Stanley Drama Award was set up to encourage and reward aspiring playwrights. The competition is open to original, full-length plays or musicals, or a series of two or three related one-act plays that have not been professionally produced or published as trade books. Musical entries must be accompanied by an audiocassette or CD. Entry fee, $30. *Deadline:* October 31. *Award:* $2,000.

The Ruth Stone Poetry Prize
RSPP, *Hunger Mountain,* Vermont College of Fine Arts, 36 College Street, Montpelier, VT 05602
www.hungermtn.org/ruth-stone-poetry-prize

The literary journal *Hunger Mountain* holds this annual poetry contest. Submit three original, unpublished poems. Entries may be submitted by mail, or electronically via the submission manager. Do not include your name or address on the entry. For hard copy, include an index card with the title, your name, address, phone number, and email address. Submit multiple entries separately. The contest is judged by the journal's editors and guest judges. Fee, $20. *Deadline:* December 10. *Award:* First-place, $1,000, and publication in *Hunger Mountain* online; two honorable mentions, $100 each, and publication in *Hunger Mountain* online.

Sydney Taylor Manuscript Competition
Aileen Grossberg, 204 Park Street, Montclair, NJ 07042-2903
www.jewishlibraries.org/ajlweb/awards/st_ms.htm

This annual competition is open to original fiction containing Jewish content targeting children ages 8 to 13. Entries should deepen a child's understanding of Judaism. Manuscripts should be between 64 and 200 pages. Short stories, plays, and poetry are not eligible. No entry fee. Limit one entry per competition. *Deadline:* September 30. *Award:* $1,000.

Utah Original Writing Competition
617 East South Temple, Salt Lake City, UT 84102
arts.utah.gov/funding/competitions/writing.html

Since 1958, this annual competition has honored Utah's finest writers in several categories, including YA book, novel, personal essay, short story, poetry, and general nonfiction. The competition accepts unpublished entries from Utah residents only. Writers entering in the categories of novel, general nonfiction, book-length collection of poems, and juvenile book may not have a book published or accepted for publication in the category. Word lengths vary for each category. Check the website for complete information. No entry fee. *Deadline:* Entries are accepted beginning April 4 and must be postmarked by June 28. *Award:* To $1,000.

Laura Ingalls Wilder Medal
American Library Association, 50 East Huron Street, Chicago, IL
  60611
www.ala.org

Every other year this award is presented to honor an author or illustrator whose body of work has contributed substantially to children's literature. It is open to books that were published in the U.S. during the year preceding the contest. Nominations are made by Association for Library Services to Children members. The winner is chosen by a team of children's librarians. *Deadline:* December 31. *Award:* A bronze medal is presented to the winner.

Tennessee Williams Fiction Contest
938 Lafayette Street, Suite 514, New Orleans, LA 70113
www.tennesseewilliams.net/index.php?topic=contests

This competition is open to writers who have not yet published a book of fiction. It accepts entries up to 7,000 words by hard copy or through the website. Entries are subject to blind judging. Author's name should not appear on manuscript itself. Include a cover letter with story title, name, and full contact information. Entry fee, $25. *Deadline:* Submissions are accepted between June 1 and November 15. *Award:* $1,500, airfare and accommodations at the Tennessee Williams Literary Festival, a reading at the festival, and publication in *Louisiana Literature.*

Tennessee Williams One-Act Play Competition
938 Lafayette St., Suite 514, New Orleans, LA 70113
www.tennesseewilliams.net/index.php?topic=contests

This annual contest recognizes and rewards excellence in one-act plays from writers around the world. The winning script should require minimal technical support and a small cast of characters. Multiple entries are accepted. Entry fee, $25 per entry. Plays should run no longer than one hour and must not have been previously produced or published. *Deadline:* November 1. *Award:* $1,500 and a full production of the play at the Tennessee Williams New Orleans Festival.

Paul A. Witty Short Story Award

Steven L. Layne, Chairing, Poetry and Prose Awards Subcommittee,
    Judson University, 1151 North State Street, Elgin, IL 60123-1404
www.reading.org

The International Reading Association presents this annual award to a short story that was published in a magazine for children during the year of the contest. Submissions should be of the highest literary merit. No entry fee. *Deadline:* May 1 to November 15. *Award:* $1,000.

Work-in-Progress Grants

8271 Beverly Boulevard, Los Angeles, CA 90048
www.scbwi.org/Pages.aspx/WIP-Grant(1)

Each year, the Society of Children's Book Writers & Illustrators offers several grants to children's writers to complete projects that are not currently under contract. Grants are available to full and associate members of SCBWI in the categories of general work-in-progress; contemporary novel for young people; nonfiction research; and previously unpublished author. All applications should include a 750-word synopsis and a writing sample of no more than 2,500 words. *Deadline:* Submissions must be postmarked no earlier than March 1 and received no later than March 15. *Award:* Seven winners receive $2,000; seven runners-up receive $500.

WOW! Women on Writing Flash Fiction Contests

www.wow-womenonwriting.com/contest.php

This ezine presents quarterly flash fiction contests to inspire creativity and communication and provide recognition to its winners. All styles of writing are welcome. Entries should be from 250 to 750 words. Accepts entries through the website only. Entry fee, $10, entry with critique, $20. *Deadline:* February 28;

May 31; August 31; and November 30. *Award:* First place, $350; second place, $250; third place, $150; seven runners up; 10 honorable mentions. Winners also receive publication on the *WOW!* website.

The Write Now New Plays Competition and Workshop
900 S. Mitchell Drive, Tempe, AZ 85281
www.writenow.co/competition

Write Now is an organization that advocates for plays for children, and for new and established playwrights. Its biennial competition and workshop aims to strengthen the national drama community, and is a collaboration of the Indiana Repertory Theatre and Arizona's Childsplay at the Sybil B. Harrington Campus for Imagination and Wonder. The competition's history originates in the former Waldo M. and Grace C. Bonderman Youth Theatre Playwriting Competition. Submissions are accepted from playwrights 18 and over, one per competition. Four or more scripts become finalists and move on to the workshop for rehearsal and revision at Childsplay in Tempe, Arizona. Plays must be unpublished, although previous production in an educational or other nonprofessional setting is allowed. The audience may be any targeted group between kindergarten and high school. Musicals are not eligible for the 2013 competition. Submit electronically with the online entry form. *Deadline:* July 31. *Award:* The top four winners receive $1,000 and a staged reading of their plays.

Writers at Work Fellowship Competition
P.O. Box 540370, North Salt Lake, UT 84054-0370
www.writersatwork.org

Writers at Work, a nonprofit literary arts organization, sponsors this annual contest that recognizes emerging writers of fiction. Writers not yet published in the category of their entry are eligible to submit original work. Manuscripts must not exceed 7,500 words. Only online submissions are accepted. Entry fee, $20. *Deadline:* November 15, 2013 to March 1, 2014. *Award:* First prize, $1,000 and publication in *Quarterly West;* two honorable mentions in each category awarded $250.

Writer's Digest Annual Writing Competition

8469 Blue Ash Road, Suite 100, Cincinnati, OH 45236
www.writersdigest.com/competitions

This annual competition calls for entries in 10 different categories including children's/YA fiction, short stories, screenplays, magazine article, and plays. It accepts previously unpublished work only. Multiple entries are accepted. Word counts vary. Entry fee, $15 for the first poem and $10 for each additional poem; all other entries, $25 for the first manuscript and $15 for each additional manuscript submitted in the same online session. *Deadline:* See website. *Award:* Prizes vary by category.

Writers-Editors Network Annual International Writing Competition

P.O. Box A, North Stratford, NH 03590
www.writers-editors.com

Open to all writers, this contest honors authors of fiction, nonfiction, children's literature, and poetry. Entries of children's literature must be previously unpublished or self-published only. Poetry may be traditional or verse. Specific category guidelines are available at the website. Entry fees vary for each category. *Deadline:* March 15. *Award:* First- through third-place awards are $100, $75, and $50.

Writing for Children Competition
Writers' Union of Canada, 90 Richmond Street East, Suite 200,
Toronto ON M5C 1P1 Canada
www.writersunion.ca

Canadian writers who have not yet published a book are eligible to enter this competition from the Writers' Union of Canada. It was established to encourage new Canadian talent in the field of children's literature. Entries should not exceed 1,500 words. Entry fee, $15. Multiple entries are accepted. *Deadline:* April 24. *Award:* $1,500.

The Zebulon
Pikes Peak Writers, P.O. Box 64273, Colorado Springs, CO 80962
www.ppwc.net

The Zebulon, formerly known as Pikes Peak Writers Fiction Writing Contest, is open to writers who have not yet published book-length fiction or short stories. This contest accepts entries in the categories of children's books, YA, romance, mainstream, historical fiction, mystery/suspense, and science fiction/fantasy. Entry fee, $20. Critiques are available for $20. For book submissions, include a synopsis (to 1,250 words) and sample pages of the manuscript (beginning with chapter one or the prologue, to 4,000 words); short stories to 5,000 words. Describe the target market. Submissions must be sent electronically. *Deadline:* September 16 to November 1. *Award:* The Paul Gillete Award, First place, $100 or a refund of the Pikes Peak Conference fee; second place, $40; third place, $20.

***Zoetrope: All-Story* Short Fiction Contest**
916 Kearny Street, San Francisco, CA 94133
www.all-story.com/contests.cgi

Sponsored by *Zoetrope: All-Story*, a magazine founded by Francis Ford Coppola, this annual contest seeks to encourage talented writers and to introduce those writers to leading literary agencies. Unpublished literary fiction of all genres are accepted. Submissions should be 5,000 words or less. Entries from outside the U.S. are welcome. Entry fee, $15 per story. *Deadline:* Entries are accepted between July 1 and October 1. *Award:* First prize, $1,000; second prize, $500; third prize, $250. The three prize winners and seven honorable mentions are considered for representation by several prominent literary agencies.

CONFERENCES & WORKSHOPS

For Adult & Children's Writers

American Society of Journalists and Authors
Annual Writers Conference
1501 Broadway, Suite 302, New York, NY 10036
www.asja.org/wc

Held each spring since 1971, this conference offers concurrent morning and afternoon panels, which are ranked to help beginning to advanced writers choose appropriately. More than 100 editors, authors, agents, and publicists take part in this weekend event, which allows time for keynote speeches and networking. *Date:* April 25–27. *Location:* New York, New York. *Cost:* See website for member and nonmember pricing. One-day rates are also available.

Ann Arbor Book Festival Writer's Conference
1118 Granger Avenue, Ann Arbor, MI 4810
www.aabookfestival.org

Coinciding with the Ann Arbor Book Festival, this annual conference is a full Saturday event. Attendees can sign up for three small-group sessions focused on writing skills and one large-group session on publishing, all of which are led by a noted group of authors and instructors. *Date:* June. *Location:* Ann Arbor, Michigan. *Cost:* $100.

Annual Writers Conference at Penn

University of Pennsylvania, College of General Studies,
    3440 Market Street, #100, Philadelphia, PA 19104
www.pennwriters.org

Sponsored by Pennwriters, a multi-genre writer's organization, this annual event joins writers of all levels and genres with agents, editors, and fellow authors for three days of workshops, critiques, pitch sessions, and networking. The option of a one-day conference is available. *Date:* May. *Location:* Eden Resort, Lancaster, Pennsylvania. *Cost:* $275 for three-day conference, including meals; $194 for one day.

Antioch Writers' Workshop

c/o Antioch University Midwest 900 Dayton Street,
    Yellow Springs, OH 45387
www.antiochwritersworkshop.com

This weeklong conference features morning lectures and afternoon intensives, with evenings reserved for readings, panel discussions, and workshops. Programs focus on fiction, nonfiction, screenwriting, playwriting, poetry, and the business of publishing. *Date:* July. *Location:* Yellow Springs, Ohio. *Cost:* $610 ($550 for past registrants and local residents), plus $125 non-refundable registration fee. *A la carte* tuition, $250–$325. Manuscript critique, $75.

Appalachian Heritage Writers Symposium

Southwest Virginia Community College
P.O. Box SVCC, Richlands, VA 24641
appheritagewritersym.wordpress.com

Fiction, memoir, poetry, and children's writing workshops, ands panel discussions, are offered during this two-day symposium.

Date: June. *Location:* Richlands, Virginia. *Cost:* $50; includes continental breakfast and awards luncheon. College credit, optional.

Arizona State University Writers Conference

P.O. Box 875002, Tempe, AZ 85287

www.piper.asu.edu/conference/2014-conference/

Intimate master classes, panel discussions on publishing and the writing life, readings, and conversations with faculty are the main components of this four-day conference. Its emphasis is on developing fiction, nonfiction, and poetry in a true community of writers. *Date:* February. *Location:* Tempe, Arizona. *Cost:* $375. Master class tuition (registration required), $125. Discounts are available.

Aspen Summer Words

110 E. Hallam, Suite 116, Aspen, CO 81611

www.aspenwritersfoundation.org

Aspen Summer Words is a six-day festival and retreat for writers in all their guises, from novelists and poets to filmmakers, songwriters, and comedians. The writing retreat includes workshops in fiction, memoir, poetry, young writers, and digital storytelling. Online applications are accepted through April 15. *Date:* June. *Location:* Aspen, Colorado. *Cost:* Fees vary. Some scholarships are available.

Bay to Ocean Writer's Conference

P.O. Box 1773, Easton, MD 21601

www.baytoocean.com

The Eastern Shore Writers' Association sponsors this one-day conference of workshops, speeches, and panels on topics pertaining to the craft of writing and the business of publishing. Presenters include authors, editors, publishers, journalists, freelance writers,

and literary agents. Manuscript reviews are offered. *Date:*
February. *Location:* Chesapeake College, Wye Mills, Maryland.
Cost: Contact for cost information.

Erma Bombeck Writers' Workshop
University of Dayton, 300 College Park, Dayton, OH 45469
www.humorwriters.org

"The workshop for humor writing, human interest writing,
networking, and getting published," this event is held every
other year. The next conference is scheduled for 2014. Past
sessions covered such topics as writing a humor column for a
national new-paper and creating humorous children's books. The
faculty is made up of experienced and entertaining writers and
publishing professionals. *Date:* April. *Location:* Dayton, Ohio.
Cost: $375.

Canadian Authors Association CanWrite! Conference
74 Mississaga Street East, Suite 104, Orillia ON L3V 1V5 Canada
www.canwriteconference.com

Attendees will learn computer tips for making their writing life
easier, and how to create PowerPoint presentations to enhance
book launches. Other workshops will explore the world of ebooks
and explain electronic rights for writers. Fiction, nonfiction,
poetry, public speaking, and writing for young adults are some of
the other sessions planned. *Date:* June. *Location:* Location of the
next conference is yet to be confirmed. *Cost:* Full conference,
$399 for members and $495 for nonmembers. Two-day rates
available at website.

Cape Cod Writers' Conference
Cape Cod Writers' Center, P.O. Box 408, Osterville, MA 02655

www.capecodwriterscenter.org

Over the course of five days, attendees take part in morning and afternoon courses and master classes on the craft of writing romance, mystery, poetry, screenwriting, journalism, memoir, and children's fiction, among others. Panels, faculty readings, and speeches are also scheduled during this annual conference. *Date:* August. *Location:* Hyannis, Massachusetts. *Cost:* $200 per course; $150 for mentoring; $150 for manuscript evaluation. Registration fee, $35 (waived for members). Shorter courses are offered at lower rates.

Carolinas Writers Conference
South Piedmont Community College
P.O. Box 126, Polkton, NC 28135
ansoncountywritersclub.org

About 250 to 400 people attend this annual event, which focuses on the craft of writing and the promotion of reading. The program covers children's and YA writing; fiction, including the genres of romance, science fiction, fantasy, horror, and mystery; screenwriting; poetry; marketing; and publishing. *Date:* April. *Location:* Wadesboro, North Carolina. *Cost:* $30.

Cat Writers' Association Writers Conference
22841 Orchid Creek Lane, Lake Forest, CA 92630
www.catwriters.org

The business and technical aspects of a career that centers on writing about cats are explored at this three-day annual conference, which also offers panels and lecture sessions on various fiction genres, nonfiction, and writing for children and young adults. Private 15-minute appointments with editors/agents are available. *Date:* November. *Location:* Visit the website for location.

Cost: $150 for members; $200 for nonmembers (early registration, $100 for members and $125 for nonmembers).

Chautauqua Institution Conferences
P.O. Box 28, Chautauqua, NY 14722
writers.ciweb.org

The Writers' Center at Chautauqua Institution sponsors weekly workshops during the summer months. Topics include business and technical writing, playwriting, autobiography/memoir, journalism, poetry, romance, mystery, and humor writing, among others. A four-day Writer's Festival is held as well, which features workshops, panel discussions, readings, and lectures. *Date:* Summer workshops, June, July, and August. Writers' Festival, June. *Location:* Chautauqua, New York. *Cost:* Summer workshops, $110 a week. Writers' Festival, $400 (10 percent discount for returnees.)

Colgate Writers' Conference
13 Oak Drive, Hamilton, NY 13346-1398
cwc.colgate.edu/home.aspx

Veteran and novice writers alike are welcome at this annual weeklong conference. Mornings are devoted to craft talks and workshops, while afternoons are set aside for individual consultations with instructors. Panel discussions, readings, and informal conversations round out the program. *Date:* June. *Location:* Hamilton, New York. *Cost:* $995 for residential attendees; $745 for day students; $1,245 for novel and memoir tutorial students. Discounts and fellowships are available.

DFW Writers' Conference
dfwwritersconference.org

Sponsored by the DFW (Dallas-Fort Worth) Writers' Workshop, this annual two-day conference offers writers at different levels of experience the opportunity to network with fellow writers and meet agents, published authors, and editors. Registration gives participants access to more than 40 classes on the art and business of writing, and includes agent appointments on a first-come, first-served basis. *Date:* May. *Location:* Hurst, Texas. *Cost:* $345.

East Texas Christian Writers Conference
East Texas Baptist University
One Tiger, Marshall, TX 75670
www.etbu.edu/news/cwc/workshops.htm

In addition to one-hour writing workshops scheduled for Saturday, this conference also holds pre-conference workshops on Friday afternoon. Workshops offer intense, personal, and practical application for those willing to get directly involved in the writing process. The conference gives aspiring writers the opportunity to have contact, conversation, and exchange of ideas with each other. *Date:* October. *Location:* Marshall, Texas. *Cost:* Individual, $90; student, $60. Fee covers the Friday evening banquet and attendance at five to six writing workshops on Saturday. Preconference workshops, additional $45.

Green Mountain Writer's Conference
47 Hazel Street, Rutland, VT 05701
www.vermontwriters.com

At this annual weeklong conference, developing writers attend workshops run by professional authors who teach the craft of writing fiction, creative nonfiction, poetry, journalistic pieces, nature articles, essays, memoir, and biography. Working sessions and writing assignments are scheduled around readings and panel discussions. *Date:* August. *Location:* Tinmouth, Vermont. *Cost:* $650 (early registration, $600); includes snacks, lunches and readings.

Highlights Foundation Workshops
814 Court Street, Honesdale, PA 18431
www.highlightsfoundation.org

Long known for its annual summer conference for children's authors at New York's Chautauqua Institution, a dozen years ago the Highlights Foundation started moving toward smaller, specialized workshops, held year-round. It now offers nearly 40 workshops yearly. Each includes 10 to 30 participants and several faculty members, including editors, agents, publishers, academics, and art directors. The workshops take place at The Barn at Boyds Mills, a conference center and 21 cabins built on the original Poconos property of the founders of *Highlights for Children*. They generally take place either from Thursday to Sunday or Friday to Monday. In 2014, workshop topics include: religious and inspirational writing on the theme of "sharing our hope"; rhyming picture books; narrative-driven interactive media; fantasy and speculative fiction; nature writing; and more. Applications available online. Tuition includes the workshop, lodging, food, and an airport shuttle, if required. See the website for details. *Dates:* Vary; check the online calendar. *Location:* Honesdale, Pennsylvania. *Cost:* Tuition varies. Payment plans are available. Scholarships are available.

Idaho Writers' League Annual Writers Conference
IWL Conference, 519 14th Avenue, Caldwell, ID 83605
www.idahowritersleague.com

This two-day conference offers morning and afternoon workshops, luncheons, and a banquet. The theme for this year's conference is Writing Up A Storm. Check website for list of workshop topics and presenters. *Date:* September. *Location:* Boise, Idaho. *Cost:* $150 for members; $140 for nonmembers.

Iowa Summer Writing Festival

C215 Seashore Hall, University of Iowa, Iowa City, IA 52242
www.continuetolearn.uiowa.edu/iswfest

Weeklong and weekend workshops are held over the course of six weeks and four weekends at this well-known annual event for serious writers. Some workshops are devoted to critiquing manuscripts that participants bring with them, others to generating new work through exercises and assignments. Writing for children and young adults, screenwriting, playwriting, poetry, travel writing, and nature writing are some of the many workshops offered. *Date:* June and July. *Location:* Iowa City, Iowa. *Cost:* $590 to $610 per week; includes special events, dinner on the Sunday evening of registration, and the Friday banquet. Weekend only, $305; includes Saturday breakfast.

Jackson Hole Writers Conference

P.O. Box 1974, Jackson, WY 83001
www.jacksonholewritersconference.com

In addition to workshops led by novelists, creative nonfiction writers, poets, agents, editors, and publishers, this conference offers three manuscript critiques. The 2010 conference offered classes on fiction, creative nonfiction, poetry, YA fiction, memoir, and magazine writing. This four-day event is held annually. *Date:* June. *Location:* Jackson Hole, Wyoming. *Cost:* $365; includes all conference events, the welcome cocktail party, and the barbecue. Manuscript critique, $30, or $110 for longer manuscripts.

James River Writers Conference
320 Hull Street, #136, Richmond, VA 23224
www.jamesriverwriters.org

In addition to workshops, panel discussions, and speeches, this conference offers the opportunity for one-on-one meetings with literary agents or editors and first-page critique sessions. Last year's two-day conference featured workshops on pitching articles, stories, and books; using Facebook to maximize exposure; and one-on-one meetings with agents. *Date:* October. *Location:* Richmond, Vi. *Cost:* $240; one-day only, $170. Preconference workshop, $40.

Jewish Authors Conference: Writing for Adult Readers
520 8th Avenue, 4th Floor, New York, NY 10018
jewishbookcouncil.org

The Jewish Book Council holds an annual day-long conference attented by authors, editors, agents, and publicists. The overall focus is publishing books on Jewish themes, Jewish publishing, and networking with others in the field. *Date:* December. *Location:* New York, New York. *Cost:* $139 ($119, early registration).

Jewish Children's Book Writers & Illustrators Conference
520 8th Avenue, 4th Floor, New York, NY 10018
jewishbookcouncil.org

Sponsored by the Jewish Book Council, which promotes public awareness of books that "reflect the rich variety of the Jewish experience," this day-long conference is held annually. It offers presentations from authors, literary agents, publishers, and editors designed to help new as well as published authors advance their careers. *Date:* November. *Location:* New York City, New York. *Cost:* $122.

Kentucky Women Writers Conference
232 East Maxwell Street, Lexington, KY 40506
www.womenswriter.as.uky.edu

This two-day conference, held annually since its inception in 1979, attracts women at all stages of their writing careers. Workshops are limited to 12 members each. Pre-registration is required, and enrollment is done on a first-come, first-served basis. Fiction, nonfiction, poetry, and writing for young adults are among the workshops offered. *Date:* September. *Location:* Lexington, Kentucky. *Cost:* $195 for two days; $30 for students.

Kenyon Review Writers Workshop
Kenyon College, Gambier, OH 43022
www.kenyonreview.org/workshops/writers

Generating and revising new writing are the focus of the *Kenyon Review* workshops in poetry, fiction, and literary nonfiction. The retreat is scheduled around morning workshops, private time for writing in the afternoon, and public readings in the evening by instructors, visiting writers, and participants. Applications are accepted January 1 to May 1. *Date:* June 15–22. *Location:* Kenyon College, *Cost:* $1,195; $200 discount for returning participants.

Manhattanville Summer Writers' Week
2900 Purchase Street, Purchase, NY 10577
http://mvillemfa.com/summer-writers-week/the-30th-annual-summer-writers-week/

Three-hour workshops are held each morning of this five-day conference. Participants choose from workshops offered in the categories of fiction, poetry, nonfiction, children's/YA, and alternative media. Afternoons are devoted to special workshops, readings, sessions with editors and agents, and individual manuscript consultations. A major presenter is scheduled each year. *Date:* June. *Location:* Purchase, New York. *Cost:* $725; two graduate credits available for an additional fee.

Mendocino Coast Writers Conference
College of the Redwoods
P.O. Box 2087, Fort Bragg, CA 95437
www.mcwc.org

This three-day conference, which is limited to 100 participants, features all-day genre intensives. Those who wish to attend one of these novel, short fiction, memoir, or poetry intensives are required to pre-submit a sample of their work, which will be critiqued in the small group sessions. Those attending only the afternoon lectures and discussions are not required to send work in advance; however, those who wish to take advantage of a 30-minute consultation with an author, editor, or agent must pre-submit 10 pages of a manuscript. *Date:* July. *Location:* Mendocino Campus of College of the Redwoods, California. *Cost:* $575; early registration, $525. $60 fee for private consultation with conference faculty.

Northern Colorado Writers Conference
108 East Monroe Drive, Fort Collins, CO 80525
northerncoloradowriters.com

Writers of all genres and levels attend this annual two-day conference for inspiration and information. Sponsored by Northern Colorado Writers, the event offers over 20 workshops on a variety of topics for both fiction and nonfiction. Last year's program included an editor's panel, editor pitch sessions, and read and critique sessions with authors and editors. *Date:* March. *Location:* Fort Collins, Colorado. *Cost:* Visit the website for cost information.

North Wildwood Beach Writers' Conference

City of North Wildwood Financial Officer, City Hall, 901 Atlantic
   Avenue, North Wildwood, NJ 08260

www.nwbwc.com

Speakers, workshops, manuscript evaluations, contests, and a
book bazaar are the components of this day-and-a-half event.
Workshops cover writing for children and young adults; fiction
writing, including romance; nonfiction writing, including journalism and memoir; screenwriting; and poetry. Other workshops
cover marketing and the business of publishing. The Beach
Writers also hold retreats in the spring and fall. *Date:* June.
Location: North Wildwood, New Jersey. *Cost:* See website for
information.

Oklahoma Writers' Federation Writers Conference

Barbara Shepard, OWFI, P.O. Box 54302, Oklahoma City, OK
   73154

www.owfi.org

This annual three-day conference has been held for more than
45 years. Workshops generally cover writing and marketing fiction
(including science fiction and thrillers) and nonfiction for children,
young adults, and adults. The most recent theme of the conference
is "Create, Compose, Commit." *Date:* May. *Location:* Oklahoma
City, Oklahoma. *Cost:* $175 (includes 2 days of seminars, two
banquets); early registration, $150. Single-day seminars, $70 each.
Extra workshops, $15–$25.

Outdoor Writers Association of America
Annual Conference

615 Oak Street, Suite 201, Missoula, MT 59801

owaa.org

First held in 1927, this gathering attracts writers who specialize in informing the public about outdoor recreational activities and the responsible use of natural resources. Workshops and seminars focus on craft improvement as well as on issues of specific interest to those who write about the outdoors. Topics include the business and technical sides of writing, marketing, and publishing, photography, technology, and nature journalism. The three-day conference also devotes sessions to national and local news related to outdoor activities and conservation. *Date:* September. *Location:* Varies yearly; most recently, Fairbanks, Alaska. *Cost:* Visit the website for cost information.

Pikes Peak Writers Conference
P.O. Box 64273, Colorado Springs, CO 809662
www.pikespeakwriters.com

This annual conference offers more than 30 workshops that focus on fiction writing for children and teens as well as for adults. In addition, agents and editors are available to attendees seeking to pitch their work. Manuscript evaluations and critique sessions round out the three-day program. *Date:* April. *Location:* Colorado Springs, Colorado. *Cost:* Visit the website for cost information.

St. David's Christian Writers' Conference
87 Pines Road East, Hadley, PA 16130
www.stdavidswriters.com

Three days of workshops led by nationally known authors and editors are the centerpiece of this Christian writing conference, which also offers one-on-one tutorials and professional critiques for additional fees. Keynote addresses and literary readings, evening meditations, and after-hours social events are other features of the conference. The theme for this year's conference is

Loaves and Fishes. *Date:* June 17–21. *Location:* Grove City, Pennsylvania. *Cost:* Rates vary depending on whether participants are commuting or staying on campus. Visit website for this year's tuition costs.

San Diego State University Writers' Conference
College of Extended Studies, 5250 Campanile Drive, San Diego,
   CA 92182-1920
www.ces.sdsu.edu/Pages/Engine.aspx?id=735

Held for 30 years, the SDSU writer's conference offers new and published authors sessions on writing skills and marketing, including specific sessions on queries, fiction genres, children's books, nonfiction markets, and career paths. Consultations with editors and agents are available. *Date:* January. *Location:* San Diego, California. *Cost:* $300 for early birds; $435, regular registration; $500, at the door. Consultations, $50 for early birds; $60 otherwise.

San Francisco Writers Conference
1029 Jones Street, San Francisco, CA 94109
www.sfwriters.org

San Francisco Writers sponsors this President's Day Weekend conference, which features more than 50 workshops, panels, social events, and one-on-one networking with presenters. In addition, editors from major publishing houses participate in Ask-A-Pro sessions. Speed Dating for Agents is an optional add-on event. *Date:* February. *Location:* San Francisco, California. *Cost:* $725 (early registration, $650). Additional $50 to participate in Speed Dating for Agents.

Sewanee Writers' Conference

University of the South, 119 Gailor Hall, Stamler Center, 735
    University Avenue, Sewanee, TN 37383-1000
sewaneewriters.org

With a focus on fiction, playwriting, and poetry, the Sewanee
Writers' Conference offers workshops that meet for five two-hour
sessions on alternating days. Over the course of the 12-day program, participants attend daily readings, lectures on craft, panel
discussions, and Q&A sessions with distinguished faculty members. *Date:* July/August. *Location:* Sewanee, Tennessee. *Cost:* Visit
the website for cost information.

Society of Children's Book Writers & Illustrators (SCBWI) Annual International Conferences

Society of Children's Books Writers & Illustrators, 8271 Beverly
    Boulevard, Los Angeles, CA 90048
www.scbwi.org

The annual summer conference, held for 42 years, was joined
14 years ago by a winter conference. Both offer workshops, master
classes, manuscript and portfolio consultations, panel discussions,
and a variety of keynote speeches over the course of their three-
day programs. The faculty consists of more than 50 authors,
illustrators, editors, and agents. *Date:* January and August. *Location:*
Winter conference, New York, New York. Summer conference, Los
Angeles, California. *Cost:* Visit the website for cost information.

SCBWI Big Sky Fall Conference

www.scbwi.org/Regional-Chapters.aspx?R=4&sec=Conf

The Montana chapter of SCBWI hosts this weekend gathering
for attendees to "learn, write, and share" with fellow children's
authors and illustrators. Opportunities for both critiques and

intensives followed by roundtable discussions are offered. The conference features writing and illustrating workshops led by authors, editors, and agents centering around story, craft, and character. *Date:* September. *Location:* The 320 Ranch, near Yellowstone National Park. *Cost:* Visit the website for cost information.

SCBWI Carolinas Fall Conference
P.O. Box 1216, Conover, NC 28613
www.scbwicarolinas.org

The fall conference of the Carolinas SCBWI has been held for 20 years. Sessions and workshops cover writing for the middle-grade reader, picture book creation, and making an impression on the first page. Manuscript critiques are available for an additional fee. *Date:* September. *Location:* North Carolina. *Cost:* Visit website for registration information.

SCBWI Florida Regional Conference
scbwiflorida.com

The Barnyard is the theme for this year's three-day midwinter conference for SCBWI members. Scheduled throughout the weekend are workshops, first-page critiques, and writing and illustrating intensives. Time is also reserved for informal critique groups and keynote speeches on a variety of topics related to children's writing. For information, the current Regional Advisor, Linda Rodriguez Bernfeld, can be reached at lrbjsb@bellsouth.net. *Date:* January 17–19. *Location:* Miami, Florida. *Cost:* $175.

SCBWI Kansas Fall Conference
P.O. Box 3987, Olathe, KS 66063
www.kansas-scbwi.org

Writers at all stages of their careers gather at this two-day conference to attend workshops led by editors, agents, authors, illustrators, and other prominent professionals from the world of children's and young adult publishing. Panel discussions, keynote speeches, and manuscript critiques round out the event. *Date:* October. *Location:* Overland Park, Kansas. *Cost:* Costs vary depending on days attending, and sessions or critiques desired.

SCBWI MD/DE/WV Conferences
mddewvscbwi.org, aseraserburns.wordpress.com

This regional branch of the Society of Children's Book Writers and Illustrators holds conferences in Maryland, where most of its members live, twice a year. It offers writers and illustrators of books for children and young adults a hands-on, craft-centered literary weekends in fiction and nonfiction. Individually focused break-out sessions are also available. *Date:* March and September. *Location:* Frederick, Maryland. *Cost:* Visit website for registration information.

SCBWI Michigan Spring & Fall Conferences
www.kidsbooklink.org

The workshops at this weekend conference are led by award-winning authors and illustrators, literary agents, and art directors and editors from major publishing houses. Although the conference is open to members and nonmembers, only SCBWI members are eligible to enter the lottery for a paid manuscript or portfolio critique. The current Regional Advisor is Leslie Helakosi and may be reached for information at lelhel@hotmail.com. *Date:* May, October. *Location:* Visit website for location information. *Cost:* Varies.

SCBWI Mid-Hudson Valley Conference

scbwi-easternny.org

The Mid-Hudson Valley SCBWI holds two conferences a year, in June and November. The spring conference is a single day, and the Falling Leaves Master Class takes place over a weekend. Breakout sessions, hands-on workshops, panel discussions round out the day, and manuscript critiques are available. *Date:* November. *Location:* Silver Bay, New York. *Cost:* Members, $225; nonmembers, $275.

SCBWI Midsouth Fall Conference

P.O. Box 396, Cordova, TN 38088

www.scbwi-midsouth.org

Editors and art directors from prominent publishing houses and bestselling authors are among the presenters at this weekend conference. Attendees may enter a fiction manuscript contest or illustrator contest. The most recent conference covered picture books for writers and illustrators, co-authoring, agent secrets, finding your voice, pacing, and how the Common Core will affect children's publishing. Individual paid manuscript and portfolio critiques are available. *Date:* September. *Location:* Nashville, Tennessee. *Cost:* Visit the website for cost information.

SCBWI Nevada Tahoe Writers' Retreat

P.O. Box 19084, Reno, NV 89511

www.nevadascbwi.org

The Nevada chapter of the Society of Children's Book Writers and Illustrators offers this hands-on, intensive weekend of group and one-on-one critiques with guest authors and literary agents, as well as workshops. *Date:* October or November. *Location:* Lake Tahoe, Nevada. *Cost:* $600 for members; $550 for nonmembers.

SCBWI New England Annual Conference
www.nescbwi.org

The 2014 conference embraces the theme "Create Bravely: Make Your Mark," and will explore whta drives writers forward in their work. Paid editor critiques, peer critiques, a query session with agents, keynote speeches, book signings, and book sales are scheduled around the workshops and writing intensives present-ed at this weekend conference. *Date:* May. *Location:* Springfield, MA. *Cost:* Visit the website for cost information.

SCBWI Oregon Spring Conference
P.O. Box 336, Noti, OR 97461
http://oregon.scbwi.org

The Oregon regional SCBWI group has expanded its confer-ence and added a fall retreat. The annual conference brings together an esteemed team of professional authors, illustrators, editors, art directors, and agents. Features of the two-day event include first page sessions, intensives for illustrators, keynote presentations, master craft workshops, and individual manuscript and portfolio consultations. Continuing education credits are available. *Date:* May. *Location:* Portland, Oregon. *Cost:* Visit website for registration information.

SCBWI Rocky Mountain Conference
www.rmcscbwi.org

The Rocky Mountain chapter of SCBWI holds a fall conference each year. In addition to workshops presented by editors from some of the best-known New York City-based publishing houses, this conference offers manuscript critiques with editors, agents, and published authors; one-on-one portfolio reviews; and first-page critiques. A weekend conference, it attracts writers and illustrators from Colorado and Wyoming. *Dates:* September. *Location:* Lakewood, CO. *Cost:* Visit website for registration information.

SCBWI San Francisco North/East Bay Fall Conference
www.scbwi.org

This one-day conference for children's writers and illustrators at all stages of their careers offers a program full of inspiration, craft development and mastery, marketing tips, and more. One of the two all-day sessions focuses on picture books. *Date:* October. *Location:* Oakland, California. *Cost:* Visit the website for cost information.

SCBWI Southern Breeze Fall Conference
P.O. Box 26282, Birmingham, AL 35260
www.southern-breeze.net

Four sessions comprised of approximately 30 workshops are offered at this two-day event where attendees can tailor the day to fit their specific interests. The faculty includes authors, illustrators, agents, art directors, editors, and other publishing professionals. Both private and group critiques are also available. *Date:* October. *Location:* Birmingham, Alabama. *Cost:* Visit website for registration information.

SCBWI Spring Spirit Conference
P.O. Box 487, Placerville, CA 95667
www.scbwi.org/Regional-Chapters.aspx?R=5

The California North/Central regional chapter of SCBWI hosts this one-day conference, which offers a diversity of workshop options for attending writers and illustrators. The event closes with a question- and-answer panel. Written manuscript and art sample critiques are available for an additional fee. Date: April 5. Location: Citrus Heights, California. Cost: Members, $135; nonmembers, $155.

SCBWI Texas: Austin Regional Conference
201 University Oaks Boulevard, Suite 1285 #170, Round Rock, TX 78665. http://austin.scbwi.org/

The Austin SCBWI chapter is changing the format of its conference, and moving to a new venue. It continues to be of interest to members and nonmembers fwho write, illustrate, or share the passions for children's literature. Hour-long general assembly sessions are held throughout the course of this three-day gathering. In addition to small-group intensives, consultations with literary agents, editors, and accomplished authors and illustrators are available for an additional fee. Personal social media evaluations and portfolio reviews are also offered. *Date:* February. *Location:* Austin, Texas. *Cost:* See website for various registration costs, ranging from the early bird member fee of $230 for the full weekend to one-day and other costs.

SCBWI Texas: Houston Annual Conference
2013 Registration, c/o Mary E. Riser, 19 Spotted Fawn Court, The Woodlands, TX 77381-3895 www.scbwi-houston.org

This conference offers a full-day of networking with other writers and learning about the world of publishing through talks by impressive guest presenters. Author/editor critiques are available for an additional fee. *Date:* April 13. *Location:* Katy, Texas. *Cost:* $135, members; $160, nonmembers. Early registration, $120, members; $145, nonmembers.

SCBWI Tri-Region Workshops, Writer's Days, Retreats
www.scbwisocal.org/days/index.html

SCBWI Los Angeles, SCBWI San Bernardino/Riverside, and SCBWI Cen Cal hold a variety of events, including Writer's Days, retreats, each year. Spotlight presentations by authors and illustrators, an editors' panel, and speeches by representatives from major publishing houses are featured activities. Check the calendar on the website for dates, topics, and locations. *Dates:* Vary. *Location:* Vary. *Cost:* Visit website for registration information.

South Carolina Writers Workshop Conference
P.O. Box 7104, Columbia, SC 29202
www.myscww.org

This weekend conference begins on Friday morning with optional intensive workshops. Saturday and Sunday are filled with sessions on various career topics. In previous years, conferences have featured interactive *slush fest* sessions with agents and editors. One-on-one pitch sessions and critique appointments with conference faculty members are available for an additional fee. *Date:* October. *Location:* Myrtle Beach, South Carolina. *Cost:* Visit website for this year's registration information.

Southern California Writers' Conference
1010 University Avenue, #54, San Diego, CA 92103
www.writersconference.com

Interactive workshops, panels, special events, and one-on-one consultations are scheduled during this three-day conference. Planned workshops cover fiction, nonfiction, "read and critique," and business and marketing. Screenwriters, authors representing a variety of genres, agents, and editors are among the faculty members. *Date:* February. *Location:* San Diego, California. *Cost:*

$425. Early registration discounts. Additional fees for critique sessions and one-on-one consultations.

Space Coast Writers' Guild Annual Conference
P.O. Box 262, Melbourne, FL 32902-0262
www.scwg.org

The goal of this two-day conference is to provide inspiration, entertainment, and encouragement for writers of all genres. The Guild brings together area authors with publishers, agents, and editors from around the country, and occasionally from around the world. A self-publishing workshop is among the presentations and workshops scheduled for this year's event. Others cover plays, YA novels, first chapters, breaking into publishing, memoirs, settings, and more. *Date:* January 24–26. *Location:* Cocoa Beach, Florida. *Cost:* $200, members; $240, nonmembers. Half-day and single-day rates are available.

Tin House Summer Writers Workshop
P.O. Box 10500, Portland, OR 97296
www.tinhouse.com/writers-workshop/

Held on the campus of Reed College, this weeklong program consists of morning workshops limited to 12 participants. Craft seminars and career panels are scheduled in the afternoons, with author readings held in the evenings. Workshops are led by the editors of *Tin House* and Tin House Books. For an additional fee, mentorships are available to participants who have completed a collection of stories or poems, a memoir, or a novel. *Date:* July. Applications are accepted beginning January 1 through March 15. *Location:* Portland, Oregon. *Cost:* Visit the website for cost information. Scholarships are available.

Wesleyan Writers Conference
294 High Street, Room 207, Middletown, CT 06459
www.wesleyan.edu/writing/conference

This conference, held for 57 years, welcomes all writers, from beginners to veterans. The five-day program consists of seminars, readings, panels, lectures, and optional manuscript consultations. Each seminar typically includes a lecture, a discussion, and optional writing exercises. Seminar topics include novel, short story, fiction techniques, narrative in fiction and nonfiction, poetry, literary journalism, short and long-form nonfiction, memoir, and multimedia and online work. Private manuscript consultations are available with faculty members or teaching fellows. Attendees also have the opportunity to meet with editors and agents who are looking for new writers. *Date:* June 13–16; one-day program available June 15. *Location:* Middletown, Connecticut. *Cost:* Day students, tuition, $975; with meals, $1,250. Boarding rate, $1,425. One-day, $225. Scholarships and fellowships are available.

Western Writers of America Convention
www.westernwriters.org

Workshops, panels, discussions with editors and authors, and book signings are all part of this five-day convention. Workshops focus on writing fiction and nonfiction—including writing for children and young adults—and all are geared toward preserving the rich history of the American West. The business side of publishing is also examined, as is marketing. *Date:* June 24–28. *Location:* Las Vegas, Nevada. *Cost:* Visit the website for updates.

Willamette Writers Conference

9045 SW Barbur Boulevard, Suite 5A, Portland, OR 97219-4027

www.willamettewriters.com

Participants have almost 100 workshops to choose from at this weekend conference. Topics include historical fiction, self-help books, children's books, screenplays, mysteries, romance, and science fiction, among many others. Literary agents, Hollywood agents and producers, and editors are among the workshop leaders. Only those attending the conference for the full three days may submit up to two manuscripts for advanced critiques for an additional fee. *Date:* August 1–3. *Location:* Portland, Oregon. *Cost:* Visit the website for cost information.

Winnipeg International Writers Festival

624-100 Arthur Street, Winnipeg MB R3B 1H3 Canada

www.thinairwinnipeg.ca

Workshops, lectures, interviews, keynote speeches, and readings fill the days of this weeklong festival, which has been held annually since 1997. More than 50 representatives from the publishing world offer presentations on playwriting, poetry, children's and young adult writing, journalism, mystery, horror, and other topics. Programs target children as well as adults, and are presented in both English and French. *Date:* September. *Location:* Winnipeg, Manitoba. *Cost:* Visit the website for updates.

Write on the Sound Writers' Conference

700 Main Street, Edmonds, WA 98020

www.ci.edmonds.wa.us/artscommission/wots.stm

Sponsored by the City of Edmonds Art Commission, this conference is a highly anticipated regional event that fills up early. With more than 30 workshops to choose from, it draws noted authors and other publishing professionals as faculty. The program begins on Friday afternoon with pre-conference workshops, and continues with two full days of workshops and other events on Saturday and Sunday. Manuscript critique appointments are available for an additional fee. *Date:* October. *Location:* Edmonds, Washington. *Cost:* Visit the website for cost information. The conference brochure will be available in July.

Writers in Paradise
4200 54th Avenue South, Street Petersburg, FL 33711
www.writersinparadise.com

This eight-day program from Eckerd College offers workshops on short story, novel, nonfiction, and YA writing. Lectures, panels, roundtable discussions, readings, and book signings fill out the rest of the schedule at this annual convention. Individual manuscript consultations are offered for an additional fee. *Date:* January 18–25. *Location:* St. Petersburg, Florida. *Cost:* $700; optional manuscript consultation, $200. Scholarships available.

The Write Stuff
Greater Lehigh Valley Writers Group
3650 Nazareth Pike, PMB #136, Bethlehem, PA 18020-1115
www.glvwg.org

This weekend conference has been held annually since 1993. In addition to writers' workshops, it offers sessions on the business of writing, panel discussions, manuscript critiques, opportunities to meet with agents and editors, and a book fair. *Date:* March 16–17. *Location:* Allentown, Pennsylvania. *Cost:* Visit the website for cost information.

INDEX

A